ANCIENT INDIAN TRADITION AND MYTHOLOGY

Translated by
A BOARD OF SCHOLARS

Edited by
PROF. J.L. SHASTRI

VOLUME 29

ANCIENT INDIAN TRADITION AND MYTHOLOGY SERIES

[PURĀṆAS IN TRANSLATION]

Volumes Released

ŚIVA 1-4
LIṄGA 5-6
BHĀGAVATA 7-11
GARUḌA 12-14
NĀRADA 15-19
KŪRMA 20-21
BRAHMĀṆḌA 22-26
AGNI 27-30
VARĀHA 31-32
BRAHMA 33-36
VĀYU 37-38
PADMA 39-48
SKANDA, PARTS I-XX, 49-68
VĀMANA 72

Volumes Under Preparation

SKANDA, PARTS XXI-XXIV
BHAVIṢYA
BRAHMAVAIVARTA
DEVĪBHĀGAVATA
KĀLIKĀ
MĀRKAṆḌEYA
MATSYA
VIṢṆU
VIṢṆUDHARMOTTARA

THE AGNI-PURĀṆA

Translated and Annotated by

N. GANGADHARAN

PART III

MOTILAL BANARSIDASS PUBLISHERS
PRIVATE LIMITED • DELHI

Reprint : Delhi, 2000, 2006
First Edition : Delhi, 1986

ISBN: 81-208-0174-1

MOTILAL BANARSIDASS
41 U.A. Bungalow Road, Jawahar Nagar, Delhi 110 007
8 Mahalaxmi Chamber, 22 Bhulabhai Desai Road, Mumbai 400 026
236, 9th Main III Block, Jayanagar, Bangalore 560 011
203 Royapettah High Road, Mylapore, Chennai 600 004
Sanas Plaza, 1302 Baji Rao Road, Pune 411 002
8 Camac Street, Kolkata 700 017
Ashok Rajpath, Patna 800 004
Chowk, Varanasi 221 001

UNESCO COLLECTION OF REPRESENTATIVE WORKS—Indian Series.
This book has been accepted in the Indian Translation Series of the UNESCO Collection of Representative Works, jointly sponsored by the United Nations Educational, Scientific and Cultural Organization (UNESCO) and the Government of India.

Printed in India
BY JAINENDRA PRAKASH JAIN AT SHRI JAINENDRA PRESS,
A-45 NARAINA, PHASE-I, NEW DELHI 110 028
AND PUBLISHED BY NARENDRA PRAKASH JAIN FOR
MOTILAL BANARSIDASS PUBLISHERS PRIVATE LIMITED,
BUNGALOW ROAD, DELHI 110 007

PUBLISHER'S NOTE

The purest gems lie hidden in the bottom of the ocean or in the depth of rocks. One has to dive into the ocean or delve into the rocks to find them out. Similarly, truth lies concealed in the language which with the passage of time has become obsolete. Man has to learn that language before he discovers that truth.

But he has neither the means nor the leisure to embark on that course. We have, therefore, planned to help him acquire knowledge by an easier course. We have started the series of Ancient Indian Tradition and Mythology in English Translation. Our goal is to universalize knowledge through the most popular international medium of expression. The publication of the Purāṇas in English Translation is a step towards that goal.

PREFACE

This volume contains the *Agni Purāṇa* Part III (chapters 252-311) in *English Translation.* This is the twenty-ninth volume in the series of *Ancient Indian Tradition and Mythology.*

The project of the Series was envisaged and planned in 1970 by Lala Sundar Lal Jain of Messrs Motilal Banarsidass. Thirty-two volumes of the series (comprising English translation of *Śiva*, *Liṅga*, *Bhāgavata*, *Garuḍa*, *Nārada*, *Kūrma*, *Brahmāṇḍa*, *Varāha*, *Agni* Parts I & II, and *Brahma* Parts I & II) have already been published and released for sale.

The Agni Purāṇa, like most of the other Purāṇas, is of an encyclopaedic character. Like the first two parts this part also contains topics of diverse nature, as a glance through the contents will show. They include the art of wielding common weapons like sword, mace etc., judicature, settlement of civil disputes and criminal proceedings against offenders, the use of Vedic hymns for accomplishing specific secular and religious purposes, observances for averting bad effects of portents and planets, modes of worshipping various deities, description of the recensions of the Vedas, merits accruing from making gifts of Purāṇas etc. Several chapters are devoted to the description of Solar, Lunar and other royal dynasties. There is a lot of material of medical interest. In addition to human diseases and their treatment by herbs and sacred formulas those of horses and elephants are also discussed and remedies prescribed for their cure. Different kinds of snakes, medical treatment for their bites, the use of herbs and incantations to remove their poison are taken up at length. In brief, the reader will find a wide range of interesting and useful material therein.

It is our pleasant duty to put on record our sincere thanks to Dr. R.N. Dandekar and the UNESCO authorities for their kind encouragement and valuable help which render this work more useful than it would otherwise have been. We are extremely grateful to Dr. Gangadharan of the Sanskrit Department, University of Madras, for his lucid translation of the text. We also thank all those who have been helpful in our project.

—Editor

CONTENTS

PART III

ABBREVIATIONS

Common and self-evident abbreviations such as Ch(s)—Chapter(s), p—page, pp—pages, V—Verse, VV—Verses, Ftn—footnote, Hist. Ind. Philo.—History of Indian Philosophy are not included in this list.

ABORI	*Annals of the Bhandarkar Oriental Research Institute*, Poona
AGP	S. M. Ali's *The Geography of Purāṇas*, PPH, New Delhi, 1973
AIHT	*Ancient Indian Historical Tradition*, F. E. Pargiter, Motilal Banarsidass (MLBD), Delhi
AITM	*Ancient Indian Tradition and Mythology* Series, MLBD, Delhi
AP	*Agni Purāṇa*, Guru Mandal Edition (GM), Calcutta, 1957
Arch.S.Rep.	Archaeological Survey Report
AV	*Atharva Veda*, Svādhyāya Mandal, Aundh
Bd. P.	*Brahmāṇḍa Purāṇa*, MLBD, Delhi 1973
BG	*Bhagavadgitā*
Bh. P.	*Bhāgavata Purāṇa*, Bhagavat Vidyapeeth, Ahmedabad
Br.	*Brāhmaṇa* (preceded by name such as Śatapatha)
BS. P.	*Bhaviṣya Purāṇa*, Vishnu Shastri Bapat, Wai
BV. P.	*Brahma Vaivarta Purāṇa*, GM, 1955-57
CC	*Caturvarga Cintāmaṇi* by Hemādri
CVS	*Caraṇa Vyūha Sūtra* by Śaunaka; Com. by Mahidāsa
DB	*Devī Bhāgavata*, GM, 1960-61
De or GDAMI	*The Geographical Dictionary of Ancient and Mediaeval India*, N. L. De, Oriental Reprint, Delhi, 1971
Dh. S.	*Dharma Sūtra* (preceded by the author's name such as Gautama)
ERE	*Encyclopaedia of Religion and Ethics* by Hastings
GP	*Garuḍa Purāṇa* Ed. R. S. Bhattacharya Chowkhamba, Varanasi, 1964

GS	*Gṛhya Sūtra* (preceded by the name of the author such as Āpastamba)
HD	*History of Dharma Śāstra*, P. V. Kane, G. O. S.
IA	*The Indian Antiquary*
IHQ	*The Indian Historical Quarterly*
JP	*Purāṇa* (Journal of the Kashiraj Trust), Varanasi
KA	*Kauṭilya Arthaśāstra*
KP	*Kūrma Purāṇa*, Veṅkaṭeśvara Press Edt. Bombay, also Kashiraj Trust Ed., Varanasi, 1971
LP	*Liṅga Purāṇa*, GM, 1960; also MLBD, Delhi, 1981
Manu.	*Manusmṛti*
Mbh.	*Mahābhārata*, Gītā Press, Gorakhpur, VS 2014
MkP	*Mārkaṇḍeya Purāṇa*
MN	*Mahābhārata Nāmānukramaṇi*, Gītā Press, Gorakhpur, VS 2016
MtP	*Matsya Purāṇa*, GM, 1954
MW	Monier Williams' *Sanskrit-English Dictionary*, MLBD, Delhi, 1976
NP	*Nāradiya* or *Nārada Purāṇa*, Veṅkaṭeśvar Press, Bombay
PCK	*Bhāratavarṣiya Prācina Caritrakośa*, Siddheshwar Shastri, Poona, 1968
Pd. P.	*Padma Purāṇa*, GM, 1957-59
PE	*Purāṇic Encyclopaedia*, V. Mani, English version, MLBD, Delhi, 1975
PR or PRHRC	*Puranic Records on Hindu Rites and Customs*, R. C. Hazra, Calcutta, 1948
ṚV	*Ṛg-Veda*, Svādhyāya Mandal, Aundh
Śat. Br.	*Śatapatha Brāhmaṇa*
SC or SMC	*Smṛti Candrikā* by Devanna Bhaṭṭa
SEP	*Studies in Epics and Purāṇas*, A.D. Pusalkar, Bharatiya Vidya Bhavan (BVB), Bombay

CHAPTER TWO HUNDRED AND FIFTY-TWO

The mode of wielding the swords, maces etc.

Fire-god said :

1-4. *Bhrāntaṁ, udbhrāntaṁ, āviddhaṁ, āplutaṁ, viplutaṁ, sṛta, saṁpātaṁ, samudīrṇaṁ, śyenapātaṁ, ākulaṁ, uddhūtaṁ, avadhūtaṁ, savyaṁ, dakṣiṇaṁ, anālakṣita, visphoṭa, karāla, indramahāsakha, vikarāla, nipāta, vibhīṣaṇa, bhayānaka, samagra* (the entire), *ardha* (half), *tṛtiyāṁśa* (one-third), *pāda, pādārdha, vārija, pratyālīḍhaṁ, ālīḍhaṁ, varāhaṁ* and *lulitaṁ* are known to be the thirty-two kinds of employment of the sword and armour in a battle.

5-6. *Parāvṛttaṁ, apāvṛttaṁ, gṛhītaṁ,* that known as *laghu, ūrdhvakṣiptaṁ, adhaḥkṣiptaṁ, sandhāritaṁ, vidhāritaṁ, śyenapātaṁ, gajāpātaṁ* and *grāhagrāhyaṁ* are the eleven ways of manipulating a noose.

7. Great men hold that the five ways of casting a noose are : extending in a straight line, long, broad, horizontal and whirling.

8. The uses of a disc (are) : cutting, piercing, felling, whirling and severing.

9. May you know that the uses of a spear are : slapping, thrashing, cleaving, frightening, incarcerating and, the sixth, striking down.

10. O Excellent Brahmin ! It has been declared that an iron club (TOMARA) (is used) in striking the eyes, the arms (and) sides (of the enemy) and should be countered with an arrow of the defendent.

11-12. O Brahmin ! It has been declared that a mace (GADĀ) is used for the acts (such as) *āhata, gomūtra, prabhūta, kamalāsana, ūrdhvagātra, vāmanamita, dakṣiṇanamita, āvṛtta, parāvṛtta, pādodbhūta, avapluta, haṁsamardda* and *vimarda*.

13. The use of a battle-axe is said to be *karāla* (dreadful), *avaghāta* (sharp blow), *daṁśa* (cutting), *upapluta* (leaping),

kṣiptahasta (that has been released from the hand), *sthita* (remaining in the original position) and *śūnya* (void).

14. O Brahmin! The use of a *mudgara* (mace) is for striking, cutting, pounding, causing deluge and killing

15. The uses of a *bhindipāla* (sling) are for *saṁśrānta*, *viśrānta* and *govisarga* and *sudurdhara* (that is extremely unbearable). The same are the uses of a *laguḍa* (club).

16. O Excellent Brahmin! The uses of a mace (VAJRA) are for (striking) with the end, with the middle, turning back and commanding. The same (are the uses) of a *paṭṭiśa* (a kind of spear with sharp edge).

17. Taking away, cutting, killing, piercing, anointing, felling and snapping are indicated as the uses of a sword.

18. The functions of a sling are indicated to be frightening, protecting, killing and helping a big fighting column. The same are the functions of a machine also.

19-30. The methods of using the mace (GADĀ) should be known as total discharge, stimulating, throwing upwards in the posture of a boar, using the hand and the back of the hand, standing with the right knee being advanced and the left leg retracted, (holding) with one hand, (holding) by the back of the hand, (holding) with two hands, with the arms thrown round as in embracing, discharging from the hip, raising upwards, striking on the chest, striking on the forehead, *bhujāvidhamana* (?), raising with the hand, lifting skywards, striking at the feet, injuring the feet, pressing the body together, putting an end, total destruction of the body, striking after raising up, blowing, intermittently (striking), wielding in the left or right (hand), enabling to cross, enabling to protect, (like a) stick, fettered like the braid of hair, agitating, transversely locked up, removal, frightening speed, good looking, attacking like lion or elephant or an ass. The modes of wrestling are drawing (the enemy), drawing apart the base of the hands, the turning about of the neck, the breaking of the back, the terrible one, revolution, reversion, the manner of slaughtering animals, *ajāvika* (?), hitting the feet, slapping (as done with the arms), discharging from the hip, resting on the shoulder, (using) the earth as a contrivance, striking at the chest and forehead, open conquest, raised one, as a wave, moving transverse, riding an elephant, casting down, not having the face turned aside, the path of the celestials, downward path, moving haphazardly, consistent, striking with a club, casting down, tearing the earth, locking up in the knees, locking up by the arms, embracing by the body, the terrific one, backwards, together with water, shining one and enclosed with the arms. At the time of the battle, (the warriors) should be ready with the weapons, elephants and other (divisions).

31-33. Two soldiers (should be) bearing excellent goads, one of them on the neck (of the elephant) and the other on the shoulder and two archers and two (soldiers) carrying the sword on the elephant. Three cavalry men should be there (to defend) a chariot or the battle-front or the elephant man. It is said (that there should be) three archers to guard the cavalry. Armoured men should be employed for the protection of the archers. Whoever goes for a war after having worshipped the weapon with the respective sacred formula or (the sacred formula known as) the one captivating the three worlds, would conquer the enemies and would govern the earth well.

CHAPTER TWO HUNDRED AND FIFTY-THREE

The description of the administration of justice

Fire-god said :

1-4. I shall describe the administration of justice that gives the discriminative knowledge of justice and injustice. It is said (to comprise) four feet, four places and four means. That which is beneficial to four (classes of men), extends to four (different parties) and benefits fourfold. In the same way (it is said to comprise) eight parts and hundred divisions. (It has) three sources, two sorts of statements, two parties and two kinds of issues. The codes of law, justice, conduct and the command of the king are the four feet in the administration of the justice. (Among these) each subsequent one is the means for the previous one. Therein righteousness rests on truth. A law suit (rests) on the witnesses.

5. The conduct of a person (rests) on the opinion of the people. The decree (depends) on the command of the king. Since (a legal case) could be decided by the means such as the conciliation (and the like), they are said to be the four means.

6-12. Since it is protecting the four institutions (such as the student life), it is said to be beneficial in four ways. Because (the suit) encompasses the plaintiff, witness, assessors and the king, one-fourth each, it is said to be encompassing four-fold. It is said to be the instruments of four kinds, because it accomplishes the four—righteousness, material prosperity, fame and esteem of man-kind. The king with the attendant, courtiers, scripture, astrologer, scribe, gold, fire and water are stated to be the eight accessories (in a law-suit). It is said to be having three sources because it results from the three such as lust, anger and greed. Hence these three are the cause of a law-suit. The cause of the law-suit are two such as apprehension and firm disquisition. Among these, apprehension is known from association with six things and the genuine (fault) from the preceding events of six kinds. Because the suit has two sides it is said to be having two openings. Among these (two), the first one is the plaintiff and the other one is the defendant. The two courses are said to be that which has happened and the guise.

13. (The term) debt (denotes that admitted) by a person as payable or that denied by him as not payable or that which is given as gift (to another).

14. One's own property placed out of trust (with another) without any doubt is said by wise men to be a trust that is a matter of dispute.

15. The place where the merchants and others collectively transact business (called) the active occupation is known to be a matter of dispute.

16. If one wants to take back that he has paid (to another), that is called the withdrawer of a gift and is known to be the matter of dispute.

17. Having agreed to do service (to another), if one refuses

to do so, it (is known as) refusal to do service and is said to be a matter for dispute.

18. The wage of a servant is said to be coming under the head of debts and the non-payment (of the same) is deemed to be a matter of dispute.

19. If one sells the entrusted property of another or the lost (property of another) after having got it or having stolen it without the knowledge (of the owner), it is known to be selling of another's property.

20. After having sold the goods for money if (the goods) are not made over to the buyer, it is non-delivery of sold (articles) and is a matter for dispute.

21-22. If a purchaser opines that the articles bought are not good after having bought (it is also a disputable thing). That condition of a wicked (assuring) good conduct is said to be conventional practice. The transgression of the conventional practice is said to be a matter for dispute.

23. The dispute that arises in respect of the right over the land that has been determined by a bridge or a field or drawn boundaries is said to be that (dispute) arising from the land.

24. Where the marriage rite of men and women is declared that is named as the union of women and men and is a matter for dispute.

25. That which is termed the division of the ancestral (property) by the sons is said to be the partition of the property and a matter of dispute by the wise men.

26. A rash act done by those haughty of their strength is said to be a crime and is declared as a matter for dispute.

27. It is said to be an abusive language that (is spoken) out of hostility with reference to the country, caste and family and the like with gestures.

28. It is said to be an assault if injury (is inflicted) on other's bodies with hands, feet, weapons and destructive materials such as the fire.

29. It is said to be divine gambling (when it is played) with dice, *vajra* (diamond) and rod etc. It is termed as animal gambling (if it is played) with animals, and birds kept for pleasure.

30. That dispute is again known to be a miscellaneous one if it does not rest on anything. The violation of the command of the king as well as not carrying out that command (also constitute an offence).

31. Thus disputes are of eighteen kinds and there are one hundred divisions of these. These hundred divisions (of disputes) are stated to be due to difference in the acts of men.

32-37. A king should examine the disputes with the help of learned brahmins without becoming angry. The courtiers (jurists) should be disposed equally towards the enemies and friends. They should not be greedy and they should be proficient in the scriptures. When such men cannot be found, a brahmin should be engaged with (the help of) the courtiers. Judges swerving from the codes of law and the like out of attachment, greed or fear should be punished separately. The fine is double as that for a quarrel. If a person that has been annoyed by others by following a method that is contrary to the codes of law and practice, informs the king, that is (known to be) a matter for dispute. The year, month, fortnight, day, name, caste and the marks (on the body) should be recorded by the complainant as known to him in the presence of the defendant. The reply of the defendant after having heard (that of the complainant) should be recorded in the presence of the complainant. Then the complainant should record (the arguments) that would accomplish his statement. He would get success if it is established or the contrary if otherwise.

38-46. These are the four steps indicated (by experts) in disputes. Without having settled a plaint, (the court) should not accept a cross-suit. One should not take up a case rejected by another (tribunal). A counter-suit could be made only in the case of a quarrel or violence. An appropriate bail should be collected from both (the parties) in deciding optional cases. One should pay (a fine of) equal amount to the king for the denial of an established matter. Double the fine has to be collected for a false plaint from the plaintiff. Cases of rash acts, theft, abusive language, pronouncing a curse and disappearance of women should be examined at once. It has been said that in other cases, they may be (put off to a different) time optionally. One that wanders from one place to another, one that licks the corners of the mouth, one whose fore-head perspires, one whose face gets discoloured and one who by his nature gets changed in his thought, speech and physical actions is said to be a defamer for a plaint and witness. (A witness) (uttering) words of ambiguous import, uttering voluntarily something (not being summoned), falling down (when questioned), not telling something when summoned is known to be punishable if he is rich. Among the witnesses of both the sides, the witness of the plaintiff (should be heard first).. When the examination of the plaintiff is completed, (the examination) of the defendant would be done. If the dispute is between members of the same clan, the younger should be punished.

47-49. The king should conduct the proceedings with respect to money paid or property or riches of a rich man after removing the fraud by (employing) the messenger. The king should confiscate all treasures, if it is concealed wholly or partly. All such properties should not pass over to the sovereign unless voluntarily offered (by the parties). In the case of conflict between two law codes in deciding a suit, equity relevant to the suit (should be considered as) stronger.

50-51. The codes of law are deemed to be stronger than the science of wealth. The documents, actual enjoyment and the witnesses are said to be evidences (in a law suit). An oath is prescribed in the absence of one of these. The later incidents are stronger in all the law suits.

52-59. The preliminary (events) are stronger in the case of a mortgage, gift or purchase. (The ownership) of a ground taken possession of forcibly by another with the knowledge of the rightful owner could be disputed only within twenty years. The wealth enjoyed by another (could be disputed by the legitimate owner) only within ten years, except in the case of a mortage, an encroachment, a property held in trust, wealth belonging to an idiot or an infant, or treasures or wealth belonging to the sovereign, to a woman or a brahmin. One who sells away a mortgaged property should pay the value to the owner of the property and pay an equal amount of fine or that befitting his ability to the king. Possession is title, even in the absence of (proof of) continuous enjoyment. But possession without (proof of) even a little enjoyment has no strength (for the title). An enjoyment with good possession (of a property) becomes valid. An enjoyment without proper possession could not be valid. The possession made by the trespasser should be recovered by a suit. It would be of no avail that the present possessor had got it from the son or the son's son of the original trespasser. In the case of the death of the possessor, the value of the property should be recovered from the property left by him. An enjoyment without a sound possession could not be a valid reason (against that). (The king) should prevent the encroachment by force or deceit.

60-62. A transaction done by a woman or in the night or inside a room or outside or made by an enemy (as well as that done) by a drunkard, lunatic or one addicted to evil, an infant or a frightened one or one that is defective is not valid. The king should cause (the mortgager) to return to the mortgagee the property mortgaged. If not possible, an amount equal to the property should be paid. The king should pay to the village headman the property stolen by a thief.

63-66. The interest relating to (a loan for which interest accrues) every month is one eightieth (of the amount lent). Otherwise the interest should be two, three, four or five (per cent) in the order of the castes (to which they belonged). It is seventieth part in the case of animals and women, eight times in the case of food, four or three or two times in the case of dress, food grains, gold and other things. If (the money is lent) to a person of a different village, (it should be) ten (per cent) and if beyond the ocean, (it should be) twenty (per cent). (Members of) all castes may pay (rates of) interest of their choice. A king would not be censurable by paying money to those in need. One that would go to the king after having obtained (a loan) would be liable for punishment and that money should be confiscated.

CHAPTER TWO HUNDRED AND FIFTY-FOUR

Debts and their repayments

Fire-god said :

1-4. A debtor may pay the borrowed money to a creditor in instalments. One has (to pay) to the king after paying to a brahmin first. It is said that the debtor should be made to pay ten per cent of the loan by the king (as fine). In case the debtor had realised his money back, five per cent (of the amount) should be made payable (to the king). (A debtor belonging to) the low caste and impoverished should be made to work in lieu of the debt. A brahmin (debtor) who is impoverished should be made to pay leisurely after the betterment. The money that the creditor does not accept when offered, should be deposited with an arbitrator and it would cease to bear any interest.

5. One that inherits a property, as well as the wife of a deceased person that inherits the property should be made to pay the (incurred) debt. The debt of a sonless owner of a property (should be paid) by the person that inherits the property.

6-7. The debt that is incurred on an undivided family for the sake of the family should also be paid similarly (by the person that inherited that property). When the head of a family is dead or had gone abroad, (it should be done similarly). The wife (is) not (bound to repay) (the loan incurred by the husband or the sons and the father (is not bound to repay) the loan incurred by the son. The husband need not repay the loan incurred by the wife unless it has been (taken) for the sake of the family.

8. The husbands of the women of the *gopa* (a guard), *śauṇḍika* (a distiller and seller of spirituous liquors), *śailūṣa* (an actor or dancer), *rajaka* (a washerman) or *vyādha* (a hunter) (castes) should repay the loan incurred by them because their livelihood is dependent on them (those women).

9. The wife need not repay any other loan except that (incurred by her husband) with her consent, or that incurred jointly with her husband or that incurred by herself.

10. When the father has gone abroad, is dead, overpowered by misfortune, the loan (incurred by him) should be paid by

the sons and grandsons. If (the loan incurred by the father) is not known (to the son), (it should be paid) on being established by the witness.

11. The son need not repay the debt incurred by the father by drinking or wenching or by way of the balance of fine inflicted by the court or by making improper gifts.

12. A loan should be got by a member of the undivided family against the surety of the brothers, the husband and wife, the father or the son.

13. A surety consists in being a witness, or in giving a guarantee (for the repayment of a debt). When a property is pledged by a person that has no right of possession, the sons of that mortgager should be liable to repay (the incurred loan).

14-16. The sons of the deceased persons who had been sureties as witnesses or as guarantors, need not pay that money. But those who had induced to make the payment should pay (in similar cases). In case if there were many guarantors to an advance made, the guarantors should be made to pay their respective shares. A creditor will have the choice (of realising his dues) from any one of the sureties of the joint bond. A debtor should pay double the amount to his surety, in case if the latter pays the loan with the knowledge of the debtor.

17. If the hypothecated thing is one's own progeny or the wife or cattle or grains, double the amount (has to be paid to redeem). It is said that four times that in the case of dressing material and eight times that in the case of condiments (has to be paid to redeem).

18. A mortgage shall be forfeited if that is not redeemed by paying double the amount. (The right for redemption) would cease at the lapse of the period agreed upon at the time of the mortgage. But it would not cease if enjoyments of the proceeds have been ageed upon.

19-20. Interest need not be paid on a thing left as a deposit or in a deposit that has been left for enjoyment. (If the mortgaged property) is lost on account of any reason other than fate or the king, it should be restored (to its original state). On the acceptance of the hypothecated property (by the mortgagee), it becomes valid. If (the mortgaged property) being governed, gets deteriorated, a different property should be mortgaged. Otherwise the creditor should be paid money (in lieu of it).

21. Money borrowed by pledging one's character, should be repaid together with interest. Money borrowed on a solemn affirmation should be returned double (that).

22-24. (A mortgaged property) should be released (by the mortgagee), when it is sought for. Otherwise he would be liable for punishment. If the money-lender belongs to one's own family (and advances money on the security) of one of his co-parceners, he should be looked upon as a mortgagee. The value (of that property) should be determined according to the market at that time and it should remain without any interest. The property may be sold without (the consent) of the debtor in his very presence, if the debt on the mortgage gets doubled. The mortgaged property should be released if double the amount is produced (by the debtor).

25-27. A packet that has been entrusted with another without disclosing its contents is (said to be) a deposit and it should be returned in the same condition. If it (the contents of that packet) has been destroyed by (the acts of) the king, fate or the robbers, it need not be restored. If that is found after search and the custodian returns it after being urged (to do so), (the custodian) should be punished to pay an amount equal to that. If the custodian wilfully derives benefit (from that), he is punishable and should pay together with the benefit. The same rule (holds good) in the case of deposits such as *yācita*, *āhita* and *nyāsa*.

CHAPTER TWO HUNDRED AND FIFTY-FIVE

Description of rules relating to disputes and different kinds of ordeals

Fire-god said :

1-2. There should be five or three witnesses such as those who are ascetics, munificent, born in noble families, truthful, virtuous, honest, having progeny, wealthy and regular in performing the *pañcayajña*[1]. They may all belong to the same *jāti* or *varṇa*[2] or from all (the castes).

3-7a. Those who are not suitable to be witnesses are women, old men, children, cheats, intoxicated, lunatics, injured, actors, heretics, men of the writer caste, those having defective sense organs, those that take food from degraded persons, relatives or friends or enemies (of the persons contesting the dispute) and thieves. All people are deemed to be witnesses in cases of thefts, violence and rashness. A virtuous man accepted by both the parties may be a witness. A person that refuses to answer the questions relating to a loan in which (interest) at the rate of ten per cent (has been allowed) should be made by the king to pay the full amount (together with interest) within fortysix days. The vilest person that does not depose the facts even though he is aware of them, is (considered) as equivalent to the sins of false witnesses and is also liable for similar punishment.

7b-10a. The witnesses (of the plaintiff as well as the defendant) should be questioned in the presence (of the parties) (as follows): "A person making a false statement would incur all (the sins) that would accrue to the sinners, deadly sinners, incendiaries and the murderers of women and children. You also know that the few good deeds that you had done in hundreds of your previous births, would befall that person whom you defeat by fraud."

10b-13. In the case of conflict of evidences (among the witnesses), (one should accept) the statements of the numerous. (If the statements of the witnesses of both the sides) are equal, then that of the virtuous (should be accepted). In the case of conflict (among the views) of the virtuous, the statement of more virtuous should be accepted. That person whose witnesses make the truthful declaration, would become the winner. That plaintiff whose (witnesses) are different (from the above), his

1. These are the five obligations that a person has to discharge daily—the act of the religious instruction, offering water to the manes, oblations for the gods, oblations to the goblins and entertaining the guests.

2. The word *jāti* denotes the castes in general and the word *varṇa* denotes the four principal castes.

defeat is certain. When a set of witnesses have deposed, if more virtuous men or double (the previous number) make statements against that, the previous witnesses become false witnesses. Then the forgers and (false) witnesses should be punished separately.

14-15. The punishment would be double that of the (fee for) litigation. A brahmin (witness in similar circumstances) should be banished (from the country). A person that conceals, on account of his ignorance, the statements of evidences heard from others, should be fined eight times. A brahmin (in similar circumstances) should be banished (from the country). A false statement may be made only when a brahmin (stands) to be capitally punished.

16-19. If a property has been accepted after mutual consent of two parties, the loan-bond should be endorsed by the witness in the presence of the creditor. That bond should bear (the details such as) the year, month, fortnight, date, name, caste, one's own clan, and the name of one's fellow-student, one's own name and that of the father etc. When the bond has been completed, the debtor should enter his name in his own handwriting (and also write), "I, so and so, son of so and so, fully agree to the statements made above." Then the witnesses also should write their names after (having written) the names of their fathers (and write) "I, so and so, son of so and so, put my name as a witness".

20-21. An unlettered debtor should cause (the writer of the deed) to write his assent. A witness (that does not know how to read and write) (should cause his assent to be written) by another witness in the presence of the other witnesses. Then the scribe of the deed should write "I so and so, son of so and so, being requested by both the parties have written this deed" and then write the deed.

22. A deed that has been written in the handwriting of the mortgager is valid even without the attestation by the witnesses, except in (cases) where undue compulsion had been made.

23. The debt mentioned in a deed has to be discharged by the three men (the debtor, the son or grandson). A mortgage remains in force until the pledge is not redeemed.

24. A new deed has to be written when the old one has been taken abroad or the original writing has been forged or lost or erased or seized or torn or mutilated or burnt.

25-27. One should record in his own hand, things that are explanatory of ambiguous terms, on the back of the deed, such as total, receipt, investigation, indication, relation, addition and means. The creditor should endorse all that he has received from the debtor with his own mark. A deed should be destroyed after paying the debts and another deed of release should be executed. It should duly be attested by the witnesses, if the original one was also made in the presence of witnesses.

28-31. The balance, fire, water, poison and holy water are the divine ordeals (to test) one's innocence. These ordeals (should be instituted) in cases of great offences when the accuser agrees to undergo punishment. Or one may be made to undergo the ordeal, and the other to undertake the agreement to undergo punishment. They may be made to undergo an ordeal even without the agreement in cases of treason and sin. One should not carry the ploughshare, the balance, or the poison for matters of less than a thousand (coins). In the case of treasons one should always agree to carry (these ordeals to show their) innocence. The balance and other (ordeals) are instituted in the case of (matters) exceeding one thousand and the holy water (is instituted) even for minor (offences). If it is lesser than that and the innocence has been established in the ordeal, one should pay fifty (coins). If the offence has been proved, one has to be punished.

32. (The accused) that has bathed together with the dress and observed fast should be called up and made to carry all the ordeals in the presence of the king and brahmins.

33. The balance is for women, boys, the aged, the blind, the lame, brahmins and the sick. The (ordeals of) fire, water and seven *yava*[1] (weights) of poison are for the *Śūdra*.

34. (The accused) that is resorting to the balance is weighed by those conversant with balances. After the balance comes to rest, line is drawn and (the accused) is taken off.

1. a kind of grain.

35-37. (The accused should begin the ordeal thus) : "The Sun, the Moon, the Wind, the Fire, the Sky, the Earth, the Waters, the Heart, the god of Death, the Day, the Night, the two Twilights[1], as well as the god of Virtue know the acts of man! O Balance! You are the abode of truth. You were created by the gods in olden days. Speak the truth. O Auspicious one ! Deliver me from suspicion. If I am a sinner, O mother ! Then lead me downwards. If I am pure then take me upwards." Thus one should address the balance.

38-42. One should mark the hands of a person that has rubbed rice, and then place seven leaves of the holy fig tree (on those hands) and (fix them) with a string wrapped as many times. (Then he should be made to utter as follows) : "(O Agni !) O Purifier ! You reside in all beings. O Truthful one ! speak the truth like a witness about my good deeds and sins." After he has said this, (the judge) should place a red-hot, round ball of iron weighing fifty *palas* on both his hands. After he has taken that, he should walk slowly through the seven circles. The inner space of the circle is known as sixteen *aṅgulas* (four finger breadth). After he has released the fire and rubbed rice (between his hand), the one that is not burnt gets (freed) as innocent. If the ball falls in between or if there is doubt, he should carry it again.

43-45a. (One should say as below in the water ordeal) : "You are the most holy among the holy. O Purifier ! You purify the accused. O Varuṇa ! (You) protect me with the truth." Having addressed (the water) thus, one should enter the water holding onto the thighs of a man standing in water upto his navel. His innocence would be established, if one bringing back an arrow simultaneously discharged, finds him fully dived (into the water).

(In the case of the ordeal of poison one should address the poison as follows) :

45b-47a. "O Poison ! the son of Brahmā : One established in truth and Virtue ! Deliver me with your truth from this curse. You become ambrosia for me." After having said

1. In the morning and in the evening.

thus, he should take the *śārṅga*[1] poison that is got from the Himālaya mountain. His purity should be declared if he could assimilate (the poison) without vomitting.

47b-50. (Alternatively), one should collect the waters for bathing dreadful gods after having worshipped them. (He) should proclaim (that he has not done the crime) and drink three handfuls of that water. He should be deemed undoubtedly pure if no dreadful malady afflicts him within fourteen days. Truth, vehicles, weapons, cattle, grain and gold, the feet of the gods and preceptors and the consecrated tanks are the easy oaths proclaimed for minor matters.

CHAPTER TWO HUNDRED AND FIFTY-SIX

Description of the procedure for the division of properties

Fire-god said :

1-2. A father that desires to partition (his properties), should divide (them) either equally among his sons, or (set apart) a greater portion for the eldest son. The wives that had not been given private property by their husbands or fathers-in-law, should be given a share in the division, if equal divisions are made (for the sons).

3. After having given a little (of the share) to the wealthy that does not wish to have (the share then), the division (should be made afterwards). Unequal divisions made by the father (should be held as) legal.

4. The sons should equally divide (among themselves) the liabilities of their father afterwards. The outstanding debts of the mother (should be borne by) the daughters, if they had no progeny.

5. That which one has earned (by his effort) without the destruction of the paternal property, (that acquired) from friends (as a gift) and through marriage, cannot be claimed by the co-parteners (for a share).

1. The poison got from the *śṛṅga* plant.

6. The benefits of a common property should be divided equally. The sons of different fathers (forming an undivided family) should take their shares according to (the shares of) their fathers.

7. Both the father and the son would be entitled to equal shares in the property or wealth of the land acquired by the grand-father.

8. If a son is born to a man through his wife of his own caste after the division of the property, a share should be set apart, even after the settlement of the accounts after it is seen.

9. One should not give to the co-parceners an ancestral property that was lost and recovered by him, as well as that acquired by (his own) skill.

10. The property that has been given to one by his parents would be his own. But the mother also would have an equal share in the property that has been divided by the grand-father.

11. Marriage of the unmarried sisters should be done by the brothers already married (in the event of the death of the father) by giving a fourth part of their share.

12. The sons of a brahmin father would be eligible for four, three, two or one share respectively according to the caste (of their mothers). (Similarly) the sons of a warrior caste (would be eligible) for three, two or one shares and that of a tradesman for two or one shares.

13. The property that has been wrongly taken possession of by somebody and divided should again be equally divided. That is the practice.

14. A son got by one not having a son by *niyoga*[1] through another's wife inherits the properties of both the parents. He (is allowed) by the codes of law to do the obsequies (of his father).

15. A son born to one through his lawful wife (is called) *aurasa* (legitimate). A daughter's son (is deemed) to be ranking

---

1. A practice prevalent in ancient times which permitted a childless widow to cohabit the brother or any near kinsman of her deceased husband to raise up issue to him.

equally with him. A son begotten through the wife of a man by one belonging to his own *gotra* (clan), or by anyone else, is known as *kṣetraja*[1] (a legitimate son).

16. A son clandestinely begotten in the (paternal) house (of a woman) is known to be born in secret. A son born to a virgin (is known as) *kānina* and is held to be the son of the maternal grandfather (girl's father).

17. A son born (of a married woman by another), whether she had menstruated or not, (is known as) *paunarbhava*. A son given as adoption by his mother or father would be a *dattaka* (an adopted son).

18. A son sold by them (his original parents) is known as *krita* (bought). A son adopted without the consent of his parents would be (known as) artificial. A son offering himself (as a son) to another is (known as) *dattātman* (one that offers himself). A son in the womb (at the time of his mother's marriage) is known as *sahoḍaja* (son of a woman pregnant at marriage).

19. A son deserted (by his father) and becoming a filial (of another) is known as *apaviddha* (abandoned). (All these) are eligible to offer cakes (at the obsequies) and to inherit their shares. Among these, the subsequent ones (are eligible) if the preceding ones do not exist.

20-21. I have described to you the injunctions in the case of sons (born of the parents) of the same castes. A son got by a *śūdra* out of lust through a slave girl would be entitled to have a share (in the property of his deceased father). On the decease of (his father), his brothers should give him half a share. Such a person should take the entire property (after the death of the father) in the absence of any brothers or son of sisters.

22-23. The wife, daughters, parents, brothers, their sons, one born in the same *gotra*, a relative, a disciple and co-students (are deemed as heirs to a sonless man), each one of the latter being eligible in the absence of the former. This rule (holds good) in the case of those diea without progeny belonging to all the castes.

---

1. One of the twelve kinds of sons allowed by the law for inheritance; the others being, *aurasa*, *paunarbhava*, *dattaka*, *krīta*, *kṛtrima*, *sahoḍaja*, *apaviddha*, *gūḍhotpanna*, *kānīna*, *svayaṁdatta and śaudra*. (See *Manu* IX. 158-60. 166-80)

24. The preceptor, the good disciple, the fellow religious student of the same religious order are duly the heirs to the properties of a *vānaprastha* (forester), ascetic and a religious student.

25. A coparcener and a brother may give to a coparcener or a brother that is born or may take away from a coparcener or a brother that is dead.

26. The coparcener not born of the same womb should not inherit the property of one not born of the same womb. A coparcener not born of the same womb should not inherit the property of one born of different mother.

27-28. A degraded person, his son, a eunuch, a lame person, a mad man, a dull person, one suffering from incurable diseases should be entitled for maintenance but not a share (in the ancestral property). The sons of these (persons), those born of the same womb and those born to a different mother not having any of the above defects (are permitted) to get their share. The daughters of such persons are to be maintained until they are got married.

29. The wives of men not having sons should be maintained if they follow pious paths. But those (wives) that are unchaste and infidels should be banished.

30. The wealth of women is said to be that given by the father, mother, husband, brother and that presented to her near the fire and the *ādhivedanika*.[1]

31. The presents made to a woman by her relatives at the time of her marriage would be inherited by her relatives in the event of her death without progeny.

32. The wealth of a woman not having progeny (would belong) to the husband after her death (applicable to) all the four castes such as the brahmins etc. The daughters (would be the legal heirs) if they had delivered a child. Otherwise it would go to the father.

33. One who takes away the property given to his daughter is liable to punishment. (He) is bound to defray the expenses incidental to her marriage and aintenance. In the event of her

1. Property, gifts etc. made to a first wife upon marrying a second.

death, he may take away that given to her after checking the two expenses (mentioned above).

34. A husband need not return the wealth of his wife in the event of (it being spent to meet) a famine, religious observance, illness or on account of imprisonment.

35. One should pay an amount of wealth to his second wife equal with what he has done to his first wife. If he has not given to the first wife already, he should pay a half now.

36. In case that share has been kept as a secret, the division has to be made on being attested by his own people and relatives as witnesses. This should be known as the method by which the division of the house and property and that relating to the dowry (is made).

CHAPTER TWO HUNDRED AND FIFTY SEVEN

Settlement of disputes relating to the boundaries of fields

Fire-god said :

1-2. In the event of a dispute relating to the boundary of a field, the guards, the assembly of elders, cowherds, the tillers of the bordering lands and all the foresters should lay down (the boundaries) demarcated by coal, husks, trees, mounds, ant-hills, slopes, bones, and pile of stones.

3. Four or eight or ten guards wearing (garland of) red flowers and red dress should be there in each village for laying the boundaries.

4. (Those that make a) false statement (relating to the boundaries of a field) should be punished with the *madhyamasāhasa.*[1] In the absence of men familiar with the fields or the marks of identification, the king himself should demarcate.

5. The same procedure is known (to be applicable) in the case of groves, temples, villages, reservoirs, gardens, houses and channels of rain water.

1. One of three kinds of penalties or modes of punishment.

6. If one transgresses the boundary or encroaches into (another's) field or removes the boundary, that person is to be punished with the *adhama* or *uttama* or *madhyama* (*sāhasa*).[1]

7. A minor encroachment should not be obstructed if it is for the sake of a bridge that benefits (all). (Similarly) one that encroaches another's field for a well occupying a little space and providing copious water (should not be obstructed).

8. If a bridge is built in a field without informing its owner, the owner will have the right to its use after it is completed. The king (would have the right to its use) in the absence of an owner.

9. One who does not cultivate or employ (someone) to cultivate in a field that has been tilled should not be given the fruits of the cultivation and the field should be made over to another (for cultivation).

10-11. The owner of a she-buffalo that (trespasses on another's field and) causes destruction of the grains, should be fined eight *māṣas* (a particular weight of gold). (The owner) of a cow (should be fined) four (*māṣas*), of a shegoat two (*māṣas*) (for the same offence). (They should be levied) twice that told above, if they sit (and watch) them grazing in the pasture land. The same amount (of fine) has to be levied as that for the she-buffalo, if an ass or camel (trespasses into another's field).

12. The owner of the field would get the same quantity of grains that has been destroyed (as above). The keeper (of the animal) should be beaten and the owner of the cow should get the punishment already described.

13. But it is not objectionable (if the grazing is done) on a field laying along the roadside, or at the end of the grazing grounds of a village if done unintentionally. But if it is done wantonly, (the concerned person) deserves to be finished like a thief.

14. The cows let loose by strong bulls, (the cow) that has delivered (a calf), the cow that has strayed and those that have the keeper should be freed (i.e. not to be punished). (So also cows) injured accidentally or by the king (should also not be punished).

---

1. Three kinds of fines of varying proportions.

15. The cowherd should return the cows in the evening as entrusted to him (in the morning). A paid servant is bound to pay (the price of the animals) that were killed or lost (in his custody) by his negligence.

16. A cowherd is to be punished in the event of a cow being killed on account of his negligence. In such cases, he has to pay a fine of half of thirteen *paṇas* (*paṇa* is a particular coin) to the master and also (restore a similar) animal.

17. The pasture land should be set apart (at a place) according to the wish of (the people of) the village or being beneficial to the land and the king. A brahmin may collect grass, fuel and flowers from any land as if it were his own.

18. The extent of the interspace between the village and the field should be one hundred *dhanus*,[1] while that between the market-town (and the field) should be two hundred (*dhanus*) and that between the city (and the field should be) four hundred (*dhanus*).

19. If a property is sold to another without disclosing its defects, then (the purchaser) has the right to take it at a lower price. If it is sold at a higher price than its real value (the excess amount has to be returned). If it is sold without defining the boundaries, (the disposer is considered) as a thief.

20. (A man) who has found out a lost and stolen (article) should cause the thief to be apprehended. But if there was a lapse of time and (was found), at a distant place, (the owner) should himself apprehend (the thief) and hand him over (to the authorities).

21. (The purchaser) gets free after showing the seller (of a stolen property). The owner (would get) the property. The king (would get) the fine. The purchaser would get his money back from the seller.

22. Allowance should be made for wear and tear by way of addition or enjoyment (for an article). If it exceeds the limit, a five-fold fine (should be paid) to the king.

23. A man who recovers or takes back a stolen or lost article from another, without intimating the king should be fined (to pay) ninetysix *paṇas*.

---

1. One *dhanus* is equal to four times the length of the fore-arm.

24. A lost or stolen article recovered by the customs officers or sentinels (should be given) to the owner if it is less than a year (after its loss) and thereafter (it should be) with the king.

25. One should pay (as interest) four *paṇas* for a single hoofed animal, five for a slave, two for a buffalo, camel and cow and one fourth of that for a goat and sheep.

26. One may give away (his possessions), except his wife and son, for interest, without causing hardship to his own family members, if not objected to by any of them. If he does not have the progeny, he may give all his possessions.

27. The acceptance (of a property) should be made public, especially of an immovable property. After having given the promised thing that is payable to one, one should not take it back.

28. A person who gives the seed, iron, vehicle, gem, woman, milch animal and a man should wait for ten, one, five, seven days, a month, three days and a fortnight respectively (for interest).

29-31. In the case of gold (that does not get) reduced in fire as well as silver, (interest would be) two *palas* for (every) hundred *palas*, eight *palas* in the case of tin and lead, five in the case of copper and ten for iron. Interest (would be) ten (*palas*) for hundred for wool and cotton. For mediocre quality it is known to be five *palas* and in extremely thin varieties it is three *palas*. The wastage is known to be a thirtieth part (of the original weight) in the case of embroidered and woollen mixed material. No allowance for decay or interest in the case of silk and bark (garments).

32. The experts should declare with certainty the allowance to be made (on things) after knowing the place (of origin) of the things, the season, the wear and tear and the strength of the materials.

33-34. One who has saved the life of his master and has been forcibly made a slave by thieves and sold should be made free (by the king) even by paying a ransom. A religious mendicant who has renounced his order is a slave of the king until his death. For the (four castes), men of the next natural order of castes alone could be a slave, but not of the reverse order.

35. A pupil who has completed his studies should stay for the stipulated period at the house of his preceptor and has to serve him for the food got from him.

36. The king should allot a frontal place to the brahmins (in his city), provide for their livelihood by means of the three *Vedas* and tell them, "May you adhere to your own duty".

37-38. One who adheres to the work agreed upon without conflicting with one's own duties should also be protected by the king with care. One who transgresses the discipline laid down by the king, who swindles the property of the society and who breaks an agreement should be deprived of all his possessions and banished from the country.

39. Everyone should follow the words of those who preach for the welfare of the society. One who does the contrary should be made to pay the first (*sāhasa*) fine.

40. One who is entrusted with a task relating to the society should offer (to the king) all that he gets. If he himself does not offer, he should be made to pay a fine eleven times (that collected by him).

41. Those who think of public service should be learned in the scriptures and not greedy. (All) should follow the words of those who speak for the welfare of the society.

42. The same rule (holds good) in the case of guild of traders, assembly of interpreters of the scriptures and those professing other religions. The king has to maintain the separate entities of these and govern the former profession.

43. One who does not do a work after having received the wages (for the same) should pay double the amount (as fine). (If the amount) has not been taken, one has to pay an equal amount (as fine). The supplementary grants (given to the servants) should be retained by them.

44. One who gains by trade, cattle or grains without obtaining the previous permission should be made to pay one tenth (of the gain as fine) by the king.

45. It is the discretion of the employer to pay (an employee) if one does work for more than the stipulated period and does work beyond the country that was stipulated. More (money) should be paid if more work has been done.

46. One's wages would be commensurate with the work done by him. If both the parties find it untenable, it should be done as laid down in the scriptures.

47. A carrier should restore to the owner, the article that he was carrying but was lost due to causes other than the government or accident. One who causes obstruction to a public carrier should pay double the amount of the wages.

48. If the carrier abandons the goods at the start, or on the way or on half the way, (he) would be required to pay one seventh or one fourth or the entire wages respectively.

49-53. If the stake at gambling is in the multiples of hundreds, then the king's share would be five hundred (*paṇas*). If they are cheats and swindlers, then the king should take one thousand *paṇas*. The manager at the gambling house should run it properly and pay the king's share as laid down. The defeated person should be made to deposit the amount that is payable to the victor. One should hear the true words (of the gamblers) patiently. When the king has obtained his share in the reputed society of the gamblers, he should put the defeated in the midst of the gamblers to pay the fine. If not, he should not. They are who see and the witnesses in such transactions. Those who indulge in false die and fraudulent ways should be banished by the king along with the marks (on their person). There should be only one leader of the gambling house in order to know the cheats (in gambling). The same is the procedure ir gambling with fighting animals and betting after setting animals to fight.

CHAPTER TWO HUNDRED AND FIFTY-EIGHT

Punishments for making defamatory speeches and committing other offences

Fire-god said :

1. If a person abuses the sick and men having defective organs, by means of lampoons, whether true or untrue or otherwise, he should be fined thirteen and a half *paṇas*.

2. The king should levy a fine of twentyfive (*paṇas*) on one that abuses another (with the words) "I copulate with your sister or (I copulate with your) mother".

3. A punishment should be awarded after due consideration of the higher or lower caste. (A man of the higher caste committing adultery (on women) of the lower caste (should be levied) half (the fine) and (a man of the lower caste committing adultery) on (women) of the higher caste (should be levied) double (the fine).

4. The men of lower orders of castes censuring the men of the next higher order should be levied double or three times the fine. But in the case of censures made by men of the higher orders on those of lower orders, half the fine should be levied.

5. The fine (that should be levied) on a capable person uttering words threatening the injury of the hands, neck, eyes and thighs (of another) should be levied (the *sāhasa*) fine. It is half the fine, if it relates to the foot, nose, ear and arms.

6. An incapable person who says as above should be levied a fine of ten *paṇas*. So also a capable person should give surety for the safety of that person.

7. The middle *sāhasa* fine should be levied on that person who abuses one ascribing degrading sin (to him). The first kind of *sāhasa* should be levied on one who ascribes (another) with minor sin of second degree.

8. The highest *sāhasa* (should be levied) for offences villifying the brahmins, kings and gods. Middle (*sāhasa*) (should be levided for offences villifying) one's own relatives and the members of the village assembly and the first (*sāhasa*) (for speaking ill of one's own) village or country.

9. In the case of charge of murder without witness, (the judge) should pronounce (the judgement) after considering the marks, reasoning and written testimony, in order to safeguard (himself) from being misled by false marks.

10. The fine for touching (another) with ashes, mud or dust is said to be ten *paṇas* and for touching with filth or the heels or spitting, double (that).

11. (For offences against women) of one's own (caste) single (fine should be levied) and twice that in the case of other women as well as of higher castes. The fine is half in the

case of (offences against those) belonging to lower castes. (For offences done) under delusion or the influence of liquor, (there is) no punishment.

12. The organ of a non-brahmin that inflicts pain on a brahmin should be cut off. First (*sāhasa*) punishment (should be preseribed) for one who raises (one's arms and strikes a brahmin) and half that (fine) if one touches.

13. If the hand and the leg are held and pulled, the fine is ten and twenty (*paṇas*) respectively. If (several men) one by one (hold and pull), the scriptures (prescribe) the middle *sāhasa* for all of them.

14. The fine for pulling the feet or hair or the garment or hand is ten *paṇas*. The fine for causing affliction or pulling or dragging after putting cloth around or placing foot (on a person) is one hundered (*paṇas*).

15. One who causes misery by means of a log of wood etc. and (if there be) no blood (injury), should be fined thirtytwo *paṇas*. Double that (is the fine), if blood is seen.

16-17. The middle (*sāhasa*) fine is levied for breaking hand, foot and teeth and cutting ear and nose. Similarly one causing injurious wounds, (one who) strikes fatally, (one who) impairs (organs of) movement, eating and speaking, (one who) pierces eyes etc., and (one who) breaks neck, arm and thigh (should be punished with) middle *sāhasa*.

18. If many persons (jointly) assault a man, each one of them (should be levied) double the (amount of) fine laid down before. Articles (forcibly) taken away after a quarrel should be returned and the fine is said to be double.

19. A person who causes grief should pay the cost of recovery (of the article) and the fine is said to be the same as laid down in the case of a quarrel.

20. A ferry-man collecting a land-toll should be punished (to pay) ten *paṇas*. A brahmin (going to dine) at the neighbour's house uninvited, (shall be liable) for the same punishment).

21. One has to be fined five, ten, twenty and sixty *paṇas* respectively for assaulting, piercing, cutting and breaking the house (of another person).

22. One should be fined sixteen *paṇas* for having thrown into another's house, an object, that would cause misery or death to another. The abettor should be fined the middle *sāhasa*.

23. One should duly be fined two *paṇas* onwards for having caused misery or bleeding injury or breaking the limbs of the body of a small animal.

24. (One should be fined) the middle (*sāhasa*) and should pay the price for having cut off the genital organ (of an animal) or having killed it. In the case of bigger animals, in these instances, the fine would be double (the above).

25. The fine is forty (*paṇas*) for lopping the branches, trunk of the tree or the whole tree that is growing and providing sustenance.

26. One who causes another to indulge in a violent act shall have to pay double the fine and one who says that he would pay (if fine is imposed) and causes another to do (a violent act) (shall be required to pay) four times (that fine).

27-28. It has been fixed that, a person who reviles or shows disrespect to a respectable person, one who beats the wife of his brother, one who does not give the promised gift, one who breaks the summer-house built in the midst of water and one who injures the neighbours, shall be fined fifty *paṇas*.

29-32. One who copulates with a licentious widow, one who assaults (another) uttering abuses, one who abuses (another) without any reason, a man of the low caste touching the men of higher castes, a *śūdra* (a man of the fourth caste) eating the meal at the time of the ceremony of a mendicant and in the divine and ancestral ceremonies, one who makes an improper oath, an incompetent person who does the act of a competent person, one who castrates the bulls or small animals, one who hides a well-known matter, one who destroys the foetus of a servant woman, one who disregards any one of the following—father, son, sister, brother, husband or wife, preceptor and pupil, that has not been degraded, shall be fined a hundred (*paṇas*).

33. A washerman who wears the dress of others (given to him for washing) should be fined three *paṇas*. It is ten *paṇas* if

he sells them or requests others to take (them) without any charges.

34. One who deals with those who make false (marks) on weights and measures and make counterfeit coins should be fined the highest (*sāhasa*).

35. The coin-tester who declares the genuine as counterfeit and the counterfeit as genuine should be fined the first (*sāhasa*).

36. A physician who gives wrong medical treatment to birds and animals, men (in general) and men of royal (household), should be punished with the first, middle and the highest fine respectively.

37. (An officer) who keeps in custody a man that should not be kept incarcerated and allows an untried (criminal) to escape, should be fined the highest (*sāhasa*).

38. One who steals an eighth part (of the real weight) of an article, by means of (false) scale or (fraudulent) measurement, should be fined twentytwo *paṇas*, no matter, whether (the real weight) has been increased or decreased by that fraction.

39. One who mixes low-standard (material) in medicines, oils, salts, perfumes, grains and molasses etc. should be fined sixteen *paṇas*.

40. A thousand (*paṇas*) is said to be the fine (to be imposed) on the artisans who collectively (indulge) in affecting the value (of the goods) (or cause) the decrease or the increase of the wealth.

41. It is considered to be profitable for the traders to sell or purchase everyday, goods that are dependent on the king.

42. A trader should take five per cent profit on indigenous goods and ten percent (profit) on foreign goods that are bought and sold immediately.

43. (A trader), after having added the incidental expenses relating to the goods, to (the price) of the goods, should settle its price with the seller or purchaser.

44. A trader not delivering the goods to the purchaser from whom the cost has been collected, should be made to pay (the amount) along with the profit or the profit (allowed) on the foreign (goods) if (the goods) have come from the foreign (country).

45. Goods that are sold (already) could (again) be sold, if the previous purchaser has not taken delivery (of the goods). The defects in the goods due to the purchaser's fault should be borne only by the purchaser.

46. In the case of any damage to the goods caused by political disturbances or natural calamities, or due to non-delivery at the desired time, the consequences have to be borne only by the seller.

47. The fine payable by a seller for the damage or the apparent damage to goods sold through his agent would be double the value of the cost (of the goods).

48. A trader who has purchased the goods without the knowledge of the decrease or increase (in their prices) should not reopen the negotiation. In case he does so, he should be punished (to pay) one sixth (of the value of the whole stock).

49-50. The profits and losses of traders trading as partners for the sake of profit, (should be divided) proportionately to their shares in the capital, or according to agreement made (at the commencement of the business). (A partner) should make good the loss sustained by him on account of doing the prohibited thing or doing a thing that he has not been asked to do or on account of folly. A partner who has saved (the goods) from destruction is eligible to get one tenth (of the value of the goods).

51. The king shall take a twentieth part (of the value) of the abandoned goods as tax. The contraband (goods) fit for royal use and sold (to someone) should go to the king.

52. A deceitful purchaser or seller giving out false measures and going away from the toll office should be fined eight times (the value of the goods).

53. Relatives and rightful heirs who have come should get the properties of a person on his death or his settlement abroad and the king (should get) in the absence of them (the legal heirs).

54. The (following) injunctions have been laid down for the officiating priest and ploughman : They should eschew dishonesty. They should not be greedy. They should get the task done by (employing) another in the case of (personal) incapacity.

55. A thief is apprehended by constables on finding the stolen property in his possession, by (his) foot-print, his past crime and dirty clothes.

56-57. Others that hide their caste, name etc. should also be held on account of suspicion. Persons addicted to gambling, wenching and drinking and those who turn pale and speak in a dry and broken voice (should also be held). Those who enquire about the properties and houses of others, those who wander in disguise, those who spend (much) without income, those who sell lost goods (should also be held).

58. If one who is held on suspicion for theft cannot expiate (himself), he should restore the stolen property. He should be punished as a thief.

59. Stolen (articles) should be recovered from the thief and he should be put to death by different (methods). A brahmin (convicted of theft) should be branded and banished from his country.

60-61a. The headman of a village should be held responsible for murder and theft, if (the criminal) has not left his jurisdiction. He should be brought to account in the village where he sets his foot. Similarly five or ten villages within a radius of two miles (of the place) (are held responsible).

61b-62a. Those men who abduct the captives, horses and elephants and those who murder violently should be put on the (iron) stake.

62b-64. A stealer of clothes and a pick-pocket should be deprived of both the hands (ie., hands should be cut off). (Or) for the latter offence, one hand and leg should be cut off. (Putting) a thief or a murderer to death by means of giving food or stimulant, (or by means of) fire, water, *mantra* or weapon is known as excellent punishment. The highest (*sāhasa*) (should be) the punishment for causing abortion/miscarriage by means of a weapon.

65. The highest or the lowest (fine) (should be imposed) on those who kill a man or a woman. A woman who kills a man by giving poison should be fastened to a stone and thrown into water.

66. A woman who kills by giving poison or setting fire to

her preceptor or offspring should be deprived of her ears, hands, nose and lips and killed by (employing) cows.

67. Incendiaries of fields, dwelling houses, forests, villages, pasture lands and threshing floors and a person who has had intercourse with the king's wife should be burnt by fire fed on straw placed around.

68. A man should be caught by the hair when he is having adultery with other women. The highest (*sāhasa*) is the fine if (the woman belonged) to his own caste and middle fine (is prescribed) if (the woman belonged) to the lower caste.

69a. (But) if (the woman) belonged to the higher caste (than the adulterer), the man should be killed and the ears of the woman should be cut off.

69b-71a. One who forcibly removes the garments covering the waist, breast, navel and braids (of a woman), and one who engages in conversation (with a woman) at an inappropriate place and time and who stays with her (similarly) (is liable to be fined). If it is prohibited for a woman, she has to pay (a fine) of one hundred (*paṇas*) and (if for a man), he (has to pay) two hundred (*paṇas*). (In spite of the prohibition if they indulge in the above crimes), they have to be fined as in the case of adultery.

71b. A person mating with an animal shall be fined one hundred (*paṇas*), and (one mating) with a woman of low caste or with a cow (shall be fined) the middle (*sāhasa*).

72. A person (who mates) with a slave girl or a maid-servant held in captivity, though otherwise fit for cohabitation, should be fined fifty *paṇas*.

73. The fine is said to be ten *paṇas* if one forcibly copulates with a slave girl. One who mates with a woman of the last caste and a woman mendicant should be fettered and banished (from the country).

74. A person who adds or omits in copying the royal edict or one who releases a seducer should be fined the highest (*sāhas*).

75a. One who pollutes a brahmin (by mixing) forbidden food, should be fined the highest (*sāhasa*).

75b-76a. One who deals in counterfeit gold and one who

sells unclean meat should be maimed and fined the highest (*sāhasa*).

76b-77. An owner who releases the wild boars and horned cattle, though he is capable (of keeping them penned), should pay the first *sāhasa* (as fine). (If it is accompanied) by shouting, (the owner should pay) double (the fine). (A man) who calls an innocent man a thief should be made to pay a fine of five hundred (*paṇas*).

78-79. One who utters undesirable words against the king, one who abuses the same, one who sells things connected with a dead body, one who beats his preceptor, one who divulges his (preceptor's) *mantra*, should be banished (from the country) with his tongue cut off. The fine for a person who rides the carriage or sits on the seat of the king, is the middle *sāhasa*.

80. The two eyes should be plucked out in the case of a person who acts hostile to the king or the nation. A *śūdra* living like a brahmin (should be) fined eight hundred (*paṇas*).

81. If one has been defeated in the proper way, thinks that he is unconquered, he should be defeated (again) when he comes and should be punished (to pay) double the (amount of) fine.

82. A king who has fined a person unjustly should offer the amount to (lord) Varuṇa[1] and pay thirty times (the amount) to the brahmins.

83. Piety, wealth, fame, esteem of mankind, favour, love of the subjects and permanent residence in heaven, dispensing justice even as (people) watch are the seven qualities of a king.

CHAPTER TWO HUNDRED AND FIFTY-NINE

The application of the mantras of the Ṛgveda

Fire-god said :

1. I shall (now) describe to you the application (of the *mantras*) of the *Ṛg* (*veda*), *Yajur* (*veda*), *Sāma* (*veda*) and

1. Lord of ocean and righteousness.

Atharva (*veda*) that yield enjoyment and emancipation when repeated and (are used for making) oblations (as) described by Puṣkara to Rāma.

Puṣkara said :

2. I shall (now) describe the (religious) rites (relating) to each one of the *Vedas*. You listen first to the application of the *Ṛg* (*veda*) that would yield enjoyment and emancipation.

3. The repetition of the *Gāyatrī* (*mantra*)[1] especially with (the practice) of *prāṇāyāma* (regulated breathing), (while remaining) in the water as well as at (the time of making) oblations confers the fulfilment of heart's desires.

4. O Brahmin ! The repetition of the *Gāyatrī* ten thousand times by a man eating only in the night and bathing many times (during the day), destroys all the sins then and there.

5. One who repeats (the *mantra*) a lakh times while eating the oblations, becomes fit for emancipation. The *praṇava* (the syllable *Oṁ*) is identical with the Supreme Braman and its repetition destroys all the sins.

6. One who repeats the syllable *Oṁ* while remaining in waist-deep water and drinks the water becomes free from all sins.

7. (The *praṇava* consists of) three *mātrās* (syllabic instants), three *Vedas*, three gods (Brahmā, Viṣṇu and Śiva) and three fires.[2] The *mahāvyāhṛtis*[3] are the seven worlds[4]. An oblation made with these destroys all the sins.

8. *Gāyatrī* is the most excellent (among the *mantras* fit) for repetition. The *mahāvyāhṛtis* are also of similar nature. O Rāma ! The *aghamarṣaṇa* (*sūkta*)[5] (destroyer of sins) should be repeated (while remaining) in the water.

9-11a. The hymn *agnimīle purohitaṁ*[6] (is sacred) for the Fire-god. One should repeat (this hymn) over a year holding

1. RV. 3. 62.10.
2. The three sacrificial fires—*gārhapatya*, *āhavanīya* and *dakṣiṇa*.
3. The syllables *bhūḥ*, *bhuaḥ*, *svaḥ*, *mahaḥ*, *janaḥ tapaḥ* and *satyam*.
4. The same as in footnote 2 above.
5. RV. 10.190.
6. RV. 1.1.1.

the fire on the head, (performing) oblation three times (a day) with *soma* (juice), living on alms and without lighting the fire (for cooking). Then the seven *ṛks* (hymns) known as Vāyu etc. should be daily repeated devoutly. Thus one will realise all his desires.

11b. One who desires to improve his memory should repeat the hymn known as *sadasaspatim*[1].

12-13a. These nine hymns (beginning with) *anvayò yan*[2] are said to be destroyers of death. One who is a captive or being obstructed should repeat (the hymn) *śunaḥśepaṁ ṛṣiṁ*[3]. One becomes free from all sins (by this). One who is sick becomes free from sickness.

13b-14. One who is desirous of (gaining) permanent pleasures and the friendship of the wise Purandara (Indra) should repeat daily the sixteen hymns (beginning with) *indrasya.*[4] One who repeats (the hymn) *hiraṇyastūpaṁ*[5] will cause affliction to the enemies.

15-16a. One who repeats (the hymn) *ye te panthāḥ*[6] will be safe on his journey. One who praises lord *Īśāna* with six Rudra hymns everyday or one who offers oblation to Rudra will have greatest peace.

16b-17a. One who extolls the rising Sun with (the hymn) '*ud*'[7] and offers water with folded palms seven times will be able to dispel his mental grief.

17b-18. One who repeats the half hymn *dviṣantaṁ*[8] ending with *yadvipra* will get his sin destroyed within seven nights. One who desires health or one who is sick should repeat (the hymn) *praskannasyottamaṁ*[9].

1. RV. 1.18.6.
2. Not tracable.
3. Not traceable.
4. RV. 1.32.1.
5. Probably RV. 10.149. 5a.
6. RV. 1.35.11a.
7. See Bloomfield, *Vedic Concordance* p. 261.
8. RV. 1.50.13.
9. Not traceable.

19-20. One who repeats the half hymn *uttamastasya*[1] in various postures will get long life; if it is repeated at midday one will get radiance; if (repeated) at sunset one will afflict his enemies. One who repeats the hymns *na vadhaḥ*[2] will destroy his enemies.

21. One who repeats the eleven *suparṇa*[3] hymns will accomplish all the wishes. One who repeats (the hymn) *ādhyātmikiḥ ka*[4] will get emancipation.

22-23. (One who repeats the hymn) *ā no bhadrā*[5] will get long life. One should look at the rising moon with (the repetition of) the hymn *tvam soma* and worship with the twig in the hand. He will certainly get garments. One who desires (long) life should always repeat the hymn of Kautsa (beginning with) *imaṁ*.[6]

24. By glorifying the Sun at midday with (the hymn) *apanaḥ śośucad*[7], one gets freed from sin like (a bow) when the arrow is discharged.

25-26. One's pathway becomes safe by the repetition of (the hymn) *jātavedasa*[8]. One gets free from all fears. That person enjoying auspicious things will get houses. This (hymn) destroys the bad dream of the previous night. One should repeat (the hymn) *pramandina*[9] and (a woman) who is delivering a child will do so with ease.

27. A man will get free from all sins after bathing with (the repetition of the hymn) *upannindraṁ*[10] and offering clarified butter as oblation (while repeating) the seven *Vaiśvadeva* (hymns).

28-29. One who repeats (the hymn) *imām*[11] always will get all his desires fulfilled. One who fasts for three nights and

1. Not traceable.
2. Not traceable.
3. Cf. RV. 105.Ia.
4. Not traceable.
5. RV.1.89.1a.
6. Not traceable.
7. RV. 1.97.1a.
8. RV. 1.99.1a.
9. RV.101.1a.
10. Could not be traced.
11. Cf. Bloomfield, *Vedic Concordance* p. 233.

offers the twigs of *udumbara* (tree) dipped in clarified butter with (the repetition of) the two (hymns) *mā nastoka*[1] etc. after becoming pure will cut all the fetters of death and live free from disease.

30-31a. One who having glorified Lord Śambhu with (the repetition of) this hymn with arms raised, binds the tuft into a knot while repeating the hymn *mānastoka*, no doubt, becomes invincible by all beings.

31b-32a. One should worship the Sun daily at the three twilights with (the repetition of the hymn) *citraṁ*[2] holding the twig. Thus he will get the desired wealth.

32b-33. One will destroy the entire bad dreaṁ and get good food by the repetition of (the hymn) *atha svapna*[3] in the morning and noon everyday. (The hymn) *ubhe pumān* is said to destroy the demons.

34. One who repeats the hymn *ubhe vāsā*[4] will get all the pleasures. A person repeating (the hymn) *na sāgan*[5] will escape from the murderer.

35. One who repeats (the hymn) *kayā śubha*[6] will attain caste-excellence, and (the hymn) *imaṁ nṛsomaṁ*[7] will give all the pleasures.

36. Conveying obeisance with (the hymn) *pitaḥ*[8] one will always acquire riches. Oblation made with ghee with (the repetition of the hymn) *agne naya*[9] also shows the path.

37. One who repeats *suśloka*[10] will always get a progeny of heroes. One is able to destroy all poisons by (the repetition of) the hymn *kaṅkato na.*[11]

---

1. RV. 1.114. 8a.
2. Same as above.
3. RV. 1.115.1a.
4. Cf. RV. 1.33.1.
5. Could not be traced.
6. RV. 1.165.1a.
7. Could not be traced.
8. Could not be traced.
9. RV. 1.189.1a.
10. Cf. Tait. Sam. 1.8.16.2.
11. RV. 1.191.1a.

38. One will get all the pleasures by (the repetition of) the hymn *yo jāta*[1]. One will get an excellent friend by (the repetition of) the hymn *gaṇānām*[2].

39-41a. (One should repeat) the hymn *yo me rājan*[3] that destroys bad dream. One who commences a journey and faces an unpraiseworthy or praiseworthy enemy should repeat the (hymn) *kuvidaṅga*[4]. One will enjoy all the desired pleasures by repeating the excellent hymn *ādhyātmika*[5] consisting of twenty-two verses on the full and new moon days.

41b-43. One should offer an oblation of clarified butter with concentrated (mind) repeating the hymn *kṛṇuṣva*[6]. One will take away the lives of enemies and destroy even the demons (by this). One should worship daily the Fire (god) with the hymn *pari*[7]. The Fire (god) having a face on every side Himself protects that person on all sides. One should look at the Sun, (remaining) pure and (repeating) the (hymn) *haṁsaḥ śuciṣad.*[8]

44-47. A man about to cultivate a field should offer oblations of pot-boiled porridge at the centre of the field as laid down with the five (hymns) *svanī svāhā*[9]. A farmer should derive his plough in the approriate manner (and offer oblations) to (the gods) Indra, Maruts, Parjanya and Bhaga. One should then worship Indra and these deities with perfumes, garlands and prostrations (after having worshipped) the ploughshare (saying) (the yoke) has been fastened for the sake of grains. Agriculture will thus always thrive and the work relating to sowing (the seeds), cutting, threshing and ploughing will yield profuse results.

48-49. One will get the desired things from the Fire (god)

1. RV. 2.12.1a.
2. RV. 2.23.1a.
3. RV. 2.28.10.a
4. RV. 10.131.2a.
5. Could not be traced.
6. RV. 4.4.1a.
7. RV. 10.10.13d, 14b.
8. RV. 4.40.5a.
9. Could not be traced.

by (the recitation of) the hymn *samudrāt*[1]. One who worships the Fire (god) with the two hymns (called) *viśvānara*[2], surmounts all difficulties, gets undiminishing fame, abundant wealth and unsurpassed victory.

50. One gets the desired riches by propitiating (the Fire god) with (the hymn) *agne tvam*[3]. A person desirous of having progeny should repeat the three hymns of Varuṇa daily.

51-52. (Each) morning, one should recite the three *svasti*[4] hymns, whereby one (will) always secure great prosperity. By the recitation of (the hymn) *svasti panthām*[5] one will have safe journey. One who desires to conquer (should repeat the hymn) *vanaspate*[6], (by which) enemies will be laid down with disease. (By the recitation of the same hymn) a woman having a dead foetus will have a good delivery.

53. One who is desirous to get rain should employ the hymn *acchāvada*[7] after fasting and wearing wet clothes. It will rain in no time.

54. A person who desires to have a cow should repeat (the hymn) *manasaḥ kāma.*[8] One who desires to have progeny should bathe (reciting the hymn) *kardamena*[9], after becoming pure and practising vow.

55-56. A man who wants to acquire kingdom should bathe with (the repetition of the hymn) *aśvapūrvāṁ*[10]. A brahmin should bathe (standing) on a deer-skin as laid down. A king (should bathe standing) on a tiger-skin and a man of the merchant class on a goat (skin) in the same way. It has been declared that ten thousand oblations (should be done) in each case.

---

1. RV. 4.58.1a.
2. Cf. RV. 186.1b and 7.76.1b.
3. RV. 5.24.1a.
4. Cf. Bloomfield, *Vedic Concordance* pp. 1053-4.
5. RV. 5.51.15a.
6. RV. 6.47.26a.
7. RV. 5.83.1a.
8. RV. khila 5.87.10a.
9. RV. khila 5.87.11a.
10. RV. khila 5.87.3a.

57. If a person desires to have (the herds of cattle) always undiminshing (in his cowpen), he should worship the cow, the mother of the worlds, in the cowpen with (the recitation of) the hymn *āgāvo*[1].

58. A king should consecrate the (royal) drum with the three (hymns beginning with) *upa*[2]. (By this) he will get radiance and strength and rout the enemy.

59. One who is surrounded by the demons should repeat the hymn *rakṣoghnam*[3] holding grass in the hand. By repeating the hymn *ye ke ca jama*[4] one will gain long life.

60. One should consecrate the constituents of his army by the hymn *jimūta*[5] first like a liṅga. Then the king will destroy the enemies in the battle.

61-62. One will gain undiminishing wealth by (the recitation of) the three hymns (beginning with) *āgneya*[6]. One may fix goblins by (the repetition of) the hymn *amivaha*[7] in the night. One should repeat this hymn in danger, difficulty, when caught in a fort, taken as a prisoner, while setting out some time, while running away, or when held as a captive.

63-64a One should fast for three nights with self-control, boil sweat gruel and cast one hundred oblations with that with (the repetition of) the hymn *tryambaka*[8] in honour of (Lord) Śiva. One will thus live happily for hunderd years.

64b-65. One should worship the rising Sun and the Sun at the middle (of the day) after bathing and with the hymn *taccakṣuḥ*[9] if one desires to have long life. The hymn (called) *indrā soma*,[10] (when repeated), is said to destroy the enemy.

66. A person who has lost his vow by mistake or on account

---

1. RV. 6.28.1a.
2. Cf. Bloomfied, *Vedic Concordance* pp. 2 64-68.
3. RV. 10.82.1.a
4. Could not be traced.
5. RV. 6.75.1a.
6. Cf. *Vedic Concordance* p. 155.
7. RV. 7.55.1a.
8. RV. 7.59.12a
9. RV. 7.66.16a.
10. Cf. Bloomfield, *Vedic Concordance* p. 225.

of association with the *vrātyas*[1], should fast and offer oblation with clarified butter with (the recitation of the hymn) *tvamagne vratapā*[2].

67. A person who repeats the hymn *āditya*[3] and *samrāja*[4] will get victory in debate. One will become free from great fear by (the repetition of) the four (hymns beginning with) *mahi*[5].

68. One will get all the pleasures by the repetition of the hymn *yadi hyctat*[6]. One will destroy his enemies by the repetition of the fortytwo *aindra*[7] hymns.

69-70. One gets good health by repeating (the hymn) *vācāmahi*[8]. A person who eats food repeating the two (hymns) *śanno bhava*[9] after becoming clean and controlling the senses and touches the heart with the hand will not be attacked by diseases. One will destroy the enemy by offering oblations with (the hymns) *uttamedaṁ*[10] after bathing.

71. One will get food by making oblation with the hymn *śanno' gnir*[11]. One will get free from the defects of the quarters (on journey) by (repeating) the hymn *kanyāvārarṣi*[12].

72. One is able to subjugate the whole universe by the repetition (of the hymn) *yadetya kavya*[13] at (sun) rise. One's speech gets refined by the repetition of (the hymn) *yadvāk*[14].

73. One gill get good speech by repeating (the hymn) *vāco vidaṁ*[15]. The *pāvamānya*[16] hymns are considered to be most sacred.

---

1. A man of the first three classes who has lost caste owing to the non-performance of the principal purificatory rites enjoined.
2. RV. 8.11.1a.
3. Cf. Bloomfield, op. cit. pp. 162-63.
4. Cf. RV Khila 10.128.5a.
5. RV. 1.22.13a.
6. Could not be traced.
7. Could not be traced.
8. RV Khila 5.6.7.
9. RV Khila 10.37.10.
10. Could not be traced.
11. Cf. RV. 7.35.4.
12. RV. 8.91.1.
13. Could not be traced.
14. RV 8.100.10.
15. Could not be traced.
16. Cf. MS. 3.11.10a.

74. The thirty *vaikhānasa*[1] hymns are considered to be extremely sacred. O Foremost among the sages ! the *parasva*[2] hymns are said to be sixtytwo.

75. The sixty-seven hymns—*svādiṣṭayā*[3]—are declared as destroyers of all sins, purifiers and conferrers of welfare.

76. The six hundred and ten hymns of *pāvamānya*[4] when repeated and used for making oblations will enable one to conquer the dread of death.

77. One should repeat (the hymns) *āpo hiṣṭha* while standing in the water to destroy the fear of sin. A man passing through a desert should repeat (the hymn) *pradevanna*[5] after the control (of senses).

78. When one is haunted by the fear of death, one will get (the end of) his life quickly. One should repeat the single hymn *prāveyābhi*[6] mentally in the night.

79. (If it is repeated) at dawn or at sunrise one will get victory in gambling. One who has lost his way will find his way by (repeating the hymn) *mā pragāma*[7].

80-81a. If one thinks that the life of a friend of himself is running out, he should bathe and touch the head of the friend (reciting the hymn) *yatteyam*[8] thousand times for five days. He will thus find him long-lived.

81b-82. A wise man should offer a thousand oblations with ghee with (the repetition of the hymn) *idam medhya*[9]. One who desires to have cattle (should do it) at the cowpen and one who desires riches, at the crossroads. One who repeats (the hymn) *vayaḥ suparṇā*[10] will acquire wealth.

---

1. Could not be traced.
2. Cf. *parasyā* RV. 8.75.15.
3. RV. 9.1.1a.
4. See 73.2.
5. RV. 10.9.10a.
6. Could not be traced.
7. Could not be traced.
8. RV. 10. 75.1.
9. RV. 4.5.6.
10. Kaṭha Sam. 9. 19a; TB. 2.5.8.3a.

83. One will become free from all sins by the repetition of (the hymn) *haviṣyantiyam*[1]. His diseases will get cured and the digestive power increased.

84. (The hymn) *yā oṣadhayaḥ*[2] (when repeated) is a means of securing prosperity and curing all the diseases. One who wishes to have rain should employ (the hymn) *bṛhaspate ati*[3].

85. (The hymns) *sarvatra*[4] and *pratiratha*[5] are known (to confer) supreme peace. (The recitation of the hymn) *sūta saṅkāśyapaṁ*[6] daily is commended for a person desirous to have progeny.

86. A person who (recites the hymn) *ahaṁ rudra*[7] becomes an eloquent speaker. The learned person who recites (the hymn) *rāti*[8] in the nights is not born again.

87. The person who recites the *rātrisūkta*[9] in the night spends the night safely. By doing the recitation of (the hymn) *kalpayanti*[10] daily (one will be able to) destroy the enemies.

88. (The recitation of) the great *Dākṣāyaṇa*[11] hymn confers longevity and radiance. A person who has undertaken a vow should recite (the hymn) *uta devā*[12], that will destroy the diseases.

89. When there is fear from fire, one should recite the hymn *ayamagne jani*[13]. One should repeat (the hymn) *araṇyāni*[14] in the forests to destroy the fear therein.

90. (One who recites the two hymns)[15] with devotion to

---

1. Cf. *haviṣmatīr imā āpaḥ* Taitt. Sam. 1.3.12.1a.
2. MS. 2.7.13a: 93.1.
3. Taitta. Sam. 1.8.22.2a,
4. Could not be traced.
5. Could not be traced.
6. Could not be traced.
7. Cf. *ahaṃ rudrebhir* RV. 10.125.1a.
8. Cf. *rātriḥ ketunā* Vaj. Sam. 37.21: 38.16; MS. 4.9. 8: 128.14.
9. Could not be traced.
10. Could not be traced.
11. Could not be traced.
12. MS. 4.14.2a: 217.16,
13. Cf. *ayam agne jaritā* RV. 10.142.1a.
14. Cf. RV. 10.146.1a; TB. 2.5.6a.
15. Could not be traced.

(goddess) Brāhmī (the goddess of speech) (and makes use of) *brāhmi* and *śatāvari* (the two herbs) together with water or ghee separately will gain intelligence and wealth.

91. One who desires to conquer his enemy in the battle (should recite the hymn) *māsa*[1]. (The repetition of the hymn) *brahmaṇo'gniḥ saṁvidānaṁ*[2] prevents the death of the child in the womb.

92. After getting pure one should recite the hymn *apaihi*[3], that destroys (the effects of) bad dreams. One gains supreme concentration by the repetition of (the hymn) *yenedaṁ*[4].

93. (The recitation of the hymn) *mayo bhūrvāto*[5] is an excellent means of securing the welfare of the cattle. One will ward off sorcery or jugglery by (the repetition of) this (hymn).

94. One should repeat (the hymn) *mahī triṇāmavaro'stu*[6] for securing one's welfare on his journey. One should repeat (the hymn) *agnaye vidviṣan*[7], which will destroy the enemies.

95-96. The presiding deities of the houses should be worshipped with the hymn *vāstoṣpate*[8]. The procedure relating to the repetition has been told. That relating to the oblation has to be known as different. The (prescribed) fee has to be paid at the end of the oblation. (There will be) expiation of the sin by (offering) an oblation. The oblation done with food appeases by the offer of food and gold as gift.

97-99. The blessings of brahmins will be unfailing. One should bathe outside in every case. Oblations made with the white mustard, barley, grains, milk, curd, ghee and the twigs of the *kṣiravṛkṣa*-s[9], yield all the pleasures. The twigs of thorny (trees), black mustard, blood, poison and stone (are used as oblation) in incantation. *Saktu*[10], milk, curd, food collected as

---

1. Could not be traced.
2. Could not be traced.
3. Cf. RV.10.164.1a.
4. Cf. *Vedic Concordance* p. 802.
5. Taitt. Sam. 7.4.17.1a.
6. Ms. 1.5.4a; 70.7; 1.5.11: 79.9.
7. Could not be traced.
8. Taitt. Sam. 3.4.10.1a.
9. The four trees—*nyagrodha, udumbara, aśvattha* and *madhūka*.
10. The flour of barley first fried and then ground.

alms, fruits and roots are the food while offering an oblation. Thus the use of the hymns of *Ṛgveda* has been explained.

CHAPTER TWO HUNDRED AND SIXTY

The use of the hymns of Yajurveda

Puṣkara said :

1-2. I shall describe the use (of the hymns) of *Yajur* (*veda*), that yield enjoyment and emancipation. Listen (to me) : O Rāma : The great *vyāhṛtis*[1] are considered to be preceded by the syllable *oṁ*. They destroy all sins and yield all pleasures. A wise man should worship the gods with thousand oblations of clarified butter.

3. O Rāma : This confers the desired pleasures. One who desires peace should offer (oblation) with barley. (One should offer) with sesamum for the destruction of sin.

4. (One should offer oblation) with grains and white mustard that will confer all the pleasures. (Offering oblations) with the twigs of *udumbara* (tree) is commended for one who desires cattle.

5. One who desires food (should offer oblation) with curd and one who desires peace (should) with milk. One who desires plenty of gold (should offer oblation) with the twigs of *apāmārga*.

6. One who seeks a maiden should offer oblation of *jāti* flowers that have been strung together in pairs and soaked in ghee. One who desires to have (governorship over) a village should offer (oblations of) sesamum and rice.

7. The oblations (of the twigs) of *śākhoṭa*, *vāsā* and *apāmārga* (trees) (are commended) for bringing (others) under control. O Son of Bhṛgu (Paraśurāma) : (oblation) of twigs mixed with poison and blood (should be made) for causing the death of one after becoming sick.

---

1. The syllables *bhūḥ*, *bhuvaḥ*, *svaḥ*, *mahaḥ*, *janaḥ tapaḥ* and *satyaṃ*.

8-9. One who is angry (should act) perfectly in the above manner in order to kill his enemies. O Brahmin : After having made an image of the king made up of rice one should offer a thousand oblations. The king will thus be subjected to one's control. Flowers (are to be used) by one who desires clothes. (The offering of) *dūrvā* (grass) destroys disease.

10. It is laid down that strong scents (should be used) by one who desires to gain the splendour of a realised soul. Oblation should be offered with the ash of husk and thorns in retaliatory enchantments.

11-12. (In incantation) to cause animosity, the wings of a crow and owl (should be offered). O Brahmin ! One should offer the ghee of a black cow to fire at (the time of) the lunar eclipse and partake of it after having mixed it with the residue of powdered *vacā* (a kind of aromatic root) after incantation a thousand times. This will make him intelligent.

13-14a. A peg of eleven inches made of iron or *khadira* (tree) should be buried in the house of the enemy after repeating (the hymn) *dviṣato vadho'si*[1]. This act of magical incantation for (the destruction of) the enemy has been narrated to you.

14b-15. By the recitation of (the hymn) *cakṣuṣyā*[2] one will get back lost eyesight. (The repetition) of the section (of the hymn beginning with) *upayuñjata*[3] will procure food. One will be free from difficulties by offering oblation of *dūrvā* (grass) (with the recitation of the hymn) *tanūnapāgne sat*[4].

16-18. Oblation made with curd and clarified butter (with the recitation of the hymn) *bheṣajamasi*[5] will cure the sickness of domestic animals. Oblation (made with the recitation of the hymn) *tryambakaṁ yajāmahe*[6] will increase one's fortune. (One who makes an oblation with this hymn) pronouncing the name of a maiden, will secure that maiden. One who repeats

1. Vāj. Sam. 1.28.
2. Cf. *cākṣuṣmatyāya svāhā* TB. 3.10.7.1.
3. Could not be traced.
4. Cf. Bloomfield, *Vedic Concordance* p. 397b.
5. Vaj. Sam. 3.59.
6. Taitt. Sam. 1.8.6.2a.

(this hymn) daily when he is stricken with fear, will get free from fears. By making an oblation with the *dhuttūra* flower along with ghee (repeating this hymn), one will get all the pleasures. O Rāma ! One who makes an oblation with *guggulu* (a fragrant gum resin) (with the recitation of the hymn) will see Śaṅkara (Śiva) in the dream.

19-20. One will get long life by repeating the section *yuñjate mana*[1]. (The repetition of the hymn) *viṣṇorarāṭaṁ*[2] destroys all the obstacles. It is capable of destroying demons. It also confers victory. (The repetition of the hymn) *ayaṁ no agniḥ*[3] yields victory in battle.

21-22. (The hymn) *idamāpaḥ pravahata*[4] (when repeated) while bathing is capable of destroying sins. If one buries an iron nail of ten inches length at the threshold (of the house) of a maiden with (the repetition of the hymn) *viśvakarmannu havis*[5] she will not be given (in marriage) to somebody else. One who makes an oblation with (the repetition of the hymn) *deva-savitah*[6] will get food.

23-24. O Knower of virtue ! The excellent brahmin who desires strength should do oblation with sesamum, barley, rice and (twigs of) *apāmārga* with (the recitation of) *agnau svāhā* (oblations to fire). O Brahmin ! One will win the affection of the people by making a mark (on the forehead) with *gorocanā* (yellow pigment got from the belly of cow) after having made the incantation (of the sacred syllable) a thousand times.

25-28. The repetition of the Rudra (hymns)[7] is capable of destroying all the sins. The oblation (made with that hymn) accomplishes all tasks and ensures peace everywhere. O Bhārgava ! Knower of virtue ! when the goats, sheep, horses, elephants, cows, men, kings, children, women, villages, cities and countries are being attacked or afflicted by diseases, when

---

1. Vāj. Sam. 5.14a; Taitt. Sam. 1.2.13.1a.
2. Vāj. Sam. 5.21; Taitt. Sam. 1.2.13.3.
3. Vāj. Sam. 5.37a; 7.44a; Taitt. Sam. 13.4.1a; 4.46.3a.
4. RV. 1.33.22a; Vāj. Sam. 6.17a.
5. Cf. Bloomfield, *Vedic Concordance* p. 878a.
6. Vāj. Sam. 9.1; 11.7; 30.1; Taitt. Sam. 1.7.7.1; 4.1.1.2.
7. *namas te rudra manyave* Taitt. Sam. 4.5.1.1a; Vāj. Sam. 16. 1a.

there is the outbreak of plague and there is fear from the enemies, then (the offering) of oblation with Rudra hymns with sweet porridge and ghee (will confer) supreme peace.

29-30. One gets free from all sins by offering oblation with pumpkin and ghee (with the Rudra hymns). Excellent man ! One gets free from (the sin of) killing a brahmin by eating the flour of barley, barley or alms in the night and bathing for a month outside. One will get everything by offering oblation with (the repetition of) the hymn *madhuvātā*[1].

31. One will certainly get childern by offering oblation (with the recitation of the hymn) *dadhikrāvṇa*.[2] Similarly (oblation made) with ghee (with the recitation of the hymn) *ghṛtavatī*[3] will give life.

32. (The recitation of the hymn) *svasti na indra*[4] would destroy all difficulties (and the hymn) *iha gāvaḥ prajāyadhvaṁ*[5] would increase the strength.

33-34. A thousand oblations made with ghee (with this hymn) will ward off ill-luck. (Oblations made) with (the twigs of) *apāmārga* and rice (with the recitation of the hymn) *sruveṇa devasya tvā*[6] will without any doubt free one quickly from the deformities inflicted by incantation. One would get gold by (oblations) with the twigs of *palāśa* with (the hymn) *rudra pātu*[7] (Rudra protect).

35. One should offer oblations with rice with (the recitation of the hymn) *śivo bhava*[8]. (The repetition of the hymn) *yāḥ senā*[9] removes the fear of thieves.

36. O Brahmin ! One who makes a thousand oblations with black sesamum with (the recitation of the hymn) *yo asmabhy-*

1. Taitt. Sam. 4.2.9.3a; 5.2.8.6.
2. Taitt. Sam. 1.5.11.4a; 7.4.19.4a.
3. Cf. Taitt. Sam. 4.4.12.5a.
4. RV. I.89.6a; Vāj. Sam. 25.19a; MS. 4.9.27a; 140.1.
5. AV. 20.127.12a; Kāṭh. Sam. 35.5a.
6. Could not be traced.
7. Could not be traced.
8. Vāj. Sam. 11.45a; Taitt. Sam. 4.1.4.2a.
9. Could not be traced.

amayātiyāt[1] will become free from deformities caused by incantation.

37. One will get food by offering an oblation of food with (the recitation of the hymn) *annapate*[2]. The repetition of (the hymn) *haṁsaḥ śuciṣad*[3] (while remaining) in the water destroys sins.

38. (The repetition of the hymn) *catvāri śṛṅgāḥ*[4] (while remaining) in the water will remove all sins. By the repetition of (the hymn) *devā yajña*[5] one will be respected in the world of Brahmā.

39. One will obtain the favour of the Sun by offering oblation with clarified butter with (the repetition of the hymn) *vasanta*[6]. The rites relating to (the use of the hymn) *suparṇo'si*[7] are the same as for the (seven) *vyāhṛtis*[8].

40. One will get released from bondage by repeating *namaḥ svāhā*[9] three times. By repeating (the hymn) *drupadā*[10] three times (while remaining) in the water will destroy all sins.

41. The sacred formula *iha gāvaḥ prajāyadhvaṁ*[11] is capable of sharpening the intellect when oblations are offered with clarified butter, curd, milk and sweet porridge.

42. Oblations made with leaves and fruits with (the recitation of the hymn) *śataṁ yo*[12] confers health, wealth and long life.

43. (The recitation of the hymn) *oṣadhīḥ pratimodadhvaṁ*[13] while mowing and cutting will give returns. Oblations made with sweet porridge (with the repetition of the hymn) *aśvāvat*[14] will secure peace.

---

1. Vāj. Sam. 11. 80a; Taitt. Sam. 4.1.10.3a.
2. Taitt. Sam. 4.2.3.1a; 5.2.2.1.
3. Vāj. Sam. 10.24a; 12.14a; Taitt. Sam. 1.8.15.2a; 4.2.1.5a.
4. Vāj. Sam. 17.91a; MS. 1.6,2a; 87.17.
5. Cf. *devā yajñam nayantu* RV. 1.40.3d; MS. 4·9.1d; 120.10.
6. Vāj. Sam. 10.10; Taitt. Sam. 4.3.3.1.
7. Vāj Sam. 10.4; 17.72; Taitt. Sam. 4.1.10.5; 6.5.3; 5.1.10.5.
8. See note to verse 1 above.
9. Cf. G. Dh. 27. 9.
10. Cf. *drupadād iva* Vāj. Sam. 20. 20a.
11. Kaṭh. Sam. 35. 3a.
12. Tait. Sam. 5.7.2.3c.
13. RV. 10.97.3a; Vāj. Sam. 12. 77a.
14. RV. 9.63. 18b; Vaj. Sam. 8. 63b.

44. One will be released from bondage by (the repetition of) the sacred formula *tasmā*[1]. One will get excellent dress by (repeating the hymn) *yuvā suvāsāḥ*[2].

45. (The recitation of the hymn) *muñcantu mā śapathyāt*[3] is capable of destroying all the enemies. Oblation of sesamum (while reciting the hymn) *mā mā hiṁsīḥ*[4] is capable of destroying enemies.

46. (Oblations of) ghee and sweet porridge (with the repetition of the hymns) *namo'stu sarvasarpebhyo*[5] and *kṛṇudhvaṁ rāja*[6] destroys magic incantations.

47-49. One can control an epidemic in a village or country by making ten thousand oblations of pieces of *dūrvā* grass with (the recitation of the hymn) *kāṇḍāt kāṇḍāt*[7]. One who is suffering from a disease will be cured and the grief-stricken (will become free) from grief (by this). O Rāma ! A person who offers a thousand twigs of *udumbara* (tree) as oblation with (the recitation of the hymn) *madhumānno vanaspatiḥ*[8] will get wealth. One will also get great fortune and victory in litigation.

50-51. One will make the gods rain by offering oblations (of the same) with (the recitation of the hymn) *apāṁ garbhaṁ.*[9] O Knower of virtue ! By making oblations of curd, ghee and honey (with the repetition of the hymn) *apaḥ pinva*[10] one will make it rain heavily. (The repetition of the hymn) *namaste rudra*[11] destroys all misfortunes.

52-53. (The above hymn) is also said to ensure all peace and destroy great sins. One who is afflicted by a disease is protected by (the repetition of the hymn) *adhyavocat.*[12] It is also capable of destroying demons, increasing fame, long life and

1. Cf. RV. 10.9.3a; Taitt. Sam. 4.1.5.1a.
2. RV. 3.8.4a; MS. 4. 13.1a: 199.13.
3. RV. 10.97.16a; Vaj. Sam. 12.90a.
4. Tait. Sam. 1.2.2.2.
5. RV. Kh. 7.55.10a; Tait. Sam. 4.2.8.3a.
6. RV. 7.32.9b.
7. Tait. Sam. 4.2.9.2a.
8. Tait. Sam. 4.2.9.3a.
9. Tait. Sam. 4.1.4.3b.
10. Tait. Sam. 4.3.4,3.
11. Tait. Sam. 4.5.1.1a.
12. Tait. Sam. 4.5.1.2a.

strength. One will be happy by scattering white mustard and repeating this (hymn) on the journey.

54-55a. O Knower of virtue ! One will get long life and undiminishing food by worshipping daily the sun morning and evening unweariedly repeating (the hymn) *asau yastāmro*[1].

55b-56. Weapons are consecrated by the six (hymns) *pramuñca dhanvanas*[2]. It will frighten enemies in battle. One need not entertain any doubt. (The repetition of the hymn) *māno mahāntaṁ*[3] confers peace on children.

57. One should offer oblations of black mustard soaked in pungent oil (with the repetition of) the seven sections (beginning with) *namo hiraṇyabāhave*[4] that will destroy enemies.

58. One becomes a sovereign by offering oblations of a lakh lotuses with (the recitation of the hymn) *namo vaḥ kirikebhyo*[5]. By similar (offerings) of *bilva* (leaves) (one will acquire) gold.

59. One will obtain wealth by oblations of sesamum with (the repetition of) *imā rudrāya*[6]. Oblations with *dūrvā* grass (will make one) free from all diseases.

60. (The hymn) *āśuḥ śiśāna*[7] (is used) in the protection of weapons. O Rāma ! It is said to destroy all the enemies in battle.

61. O Brahmin ! Knower of virtue ! One thousand oblations of clarified butter with (the repetition of) the five (hymns) *rāja sāma*[8] will cure the eye disease (of a person).

62. The oblation (done with the hymn) *śanno vanaspate gehe*[9] will destroy the defects of a building. One will not earn enmity

---

1. Tait. Sam. 4.5.1.3a.
2. Tait. Sam. 4.5.10·2a.
3. Tait. Sam. 4.5.10.2a.
4. Tait. Sam. 4.5.2.1.
5. Tait. Sam. 4.5.9.2.
6. Vaj. Sam. 16.48a.
7. Tait. Sam. 4.6.4.1a.
8. Could not be traced.
9. Could not be traced.

with anyone by offering oblations of clarified butter (with the repetition of) *agna āyūṁṣi*[1].

63. One will gain victory by the oblation of fried paddy (with the hymn) *apāṁ phena*[2]. He who has defective sense-organs will get sound ones by the repetition of (the hymn) *bhadrā*[3].

64. (The hymn) *agniśca pṛthivī ca*[4] (is) an excellent charm. One who repeats the hymn *adhvana*[5] will be victorious in litigation.

65. (The hymn) *brahma rājanyaṁ*[6] accomplishes the task (when repeated) at its commencement. One will be free from disease by the oblation of ghee a lakh times (with the repetition of the hymn) *saṁvatsaro'si*[7].

66. (The hymn) *ketuṁ kṛṇvan*[8] will confer victory in battle. (The hymn) *indro'gnirdharma*[9] ensures fair play in battle.

67. The hymn *dhanvanā gā*[10] is excellent for the bow wielder. The hymn *yuñjīta*[11] is known (to be used) in consecrating (the bow).

68. The hymn *āhiratha*[12] should be used for the consecration of arrows. *Bahvīnāṁ pitā*[13] is said to be the hymn for consecrating quiver.

69. *Yuñjanti*[14] is said to be the hymn for arranging horses. (The hymn) *āśuḥ śiśāna*[15] is said (to be used) while commencing a journey.

---

1. TS. 1.3.14.7a.
2. Cf. *apām phenena* Vaj. Sam. 19.71a.
3. Cf. RV. 8.19.19b.
4. Vaj. Sam. 26.1.
5. Tait. Sam. 1.7.8.1.
6. Cf. *brahma rājanyābhyām* Vāj. Sam. 26.2c.
7. Vaj. Sam. 27.45 or TB. 3.11.1.14.
8. Tait. Sam. 7.4.20.1a.
9. Could not be traced.
10. Tait. Sam. 4.6.6.1a.
11. Could not be traced.
12. Could not be traced.
13. Tait. Sam. 4.6.6.2a.
14. Cf. *Yuñjanti bradhnam* Tait. Sam. 7.4.20.1a.
15. Tait. Sam. 4.6.4.1a.

70. The hymns *viṣṇoḥ krama*[1] (is said to be) excellent for one who boards a chariot. (The hymn) *ājaṅghanti*[2] is said (to be used) for whipping the horses.

71. One should repeat (the hymn) *yaḥ senā abhitvari*[3] when facing the army of the enemy. The war drums are beaten with (the recitation of the hymn) *dundubhya*[4].

72-73. One will become victorious by offering oblations earlier with these hymns. A wise man who offers one crore oblations with (the recitation of the hymn) *yamena dattam*[5] will soon produce a chariot that will give victory in the battle. The ceremonies relating to (the hymn) *ā kṛṣṇa*[6] are similar to that of the *vyāhṛtis* (*bhūḥ* etc.).

74. One will get the composure of mind by the repetition of (the hymn of) *śivasaṅkalpa*[7]. One will get fortune by making five lakh oblations (with the repetition of the hymn) *pañcanadyaḥ*[8].

75. One should wear a golden (plate) after making incantations one thousand times with the hymn *yad ābadhnan dākṣāyaṇā*[9]. It will ward off the enemies.

76. One will not have the fear of thieves by throwing stones and lumps of earth in all the four directions in the house (after repeating the hymn) *imaṁ jīvebhyaḥ*[10].

77. (The hymn) *pari me gāmaneṣata*[11] is excellent for charming. One who has come to kill will be subdued.

78. O Knower of Dharma ! A person will be brought under one's complete control soon by giving him food, betels, flowers and other things charmed (with this hymn).

---

1. Tait. Sam. 1.6.5.2.
2. Tait. Sam. 4.6.6.5a.
3. Could not be traced.
4. Cf. *Vedic Concordance* p. 485b.
5. Tait. Sam. 4.6.7.1a.
6. Tait. Sam. 3.4.11.2a.
7. Could not be traced.
8. Vāj Sam. 34.11a.
9. Vāj Sam. 34.52b.
10. Vāj. Sam. 35.15a.
11. Vāj. Sam. 35.18a.

79-80. (The hymn) *śanno mitra*[1] always confers peace everywhere (when repeated). One will be able to charm the entire world by making oblations of all grains (with the repetition of the hymn) *gaṇānāṁ tvā gaṇapatiṁ*[2] at the junction of four roads. The hymn *hiraṇyavarṇāḥ śucayaḥ*[3] (is used) in consecration.

81-82. (The hymn) *śanno devir abhiṣṭaye*[4] (is) excellent for conferring peace. There is no doubt that one will appease the planets and get their grace by offering oblations of clarified butter in parts (to the respective planets) with (the repetition of) the hymn *ekacakra*[5]. One who makes oblations of clarified butter with the two (hymns) *gāvo bhago*[6] will get cows.

83. (The hymn) *pravādāṁṣaḥ sopat*[7] is used in the propitiatory rite in the house. (The hymn) *devebhyo vanaspate*[8] is prescribed (for use) in the rite for the consecration of a tree.

84. (The hymn) *tad viṣṇoḥ paramaṁ padaṁ*[9] is known to be the *gāyatrī* for (Lord) Viṣṇu. It is capable of destroying all the sins and granting all the pleasures.

CHAPTER TWO HUNDRED AND SIXTY-ONE

The use of the hymns of Sāmaveda

Puṣkara said :

1. I have described the use of (the hymns of) *Yajur* (*veda*). I shall (now) describe the use of (the hymns of) *Sāma* (*veda*). One will get all the pleasures by repeating the *vaiṣṇavī* hymns.

---

1. RV. 1.90.9a; Vāj. Sam. 36.9a.
2. Tait. Sam. 2.3.14.3a.
3. Tait. Sam. 5.6.1.1a.
4. RV. 10.9.4a.
5. Cf. TA. 1.11.7c.
6. RV. 6.28.5a.
7. Could not be traced.
8. MS. 4.13.7a: 208.10.
9. Tait. Sam. 1.3.6.2a.

2. One pleases (Lord) Śaṅkara (Śiva) by repeating the *chāndasi* (Sāman) hymns well. One will get the grace by repeating the *skāndi* and *paitri* hymns.

3. (The repetition of the hymn) *yata indra bhayāmahe*[1] is capable of destroying the harmful effects (of incantations). One who has broken the vow of continence will be released (from the fault) by repeating (the hymn) *agnistigmena*[2].

4. (The repetition of the hymn) *paritoṣaṁ ca*[3] is known to be capable of destroying all sins. One who has sold (a thing) that should not be sold, should repeat (the hymn) *ghṛtavati*[4].

5-6. (The hymn) *adyā no deva savitaḥ*[5] is known to be capable of destroying bad dreams. O Rāma ! The foremost of Bhṛgus ! It is laid down that the girdle may be tied with the remnant of the ghee that has been sprinkled with (the hymn) *abodhyagniḥ*[6] as laid down, in the case of the women who have a miscarriage.

7. Then it should be tied on the wrist of the child that is born, with (the repetition of the hymn) *somaṁ rājānaṁ*[7]. This will make the child free from all diseases.

8-9. By the use of *sarpasāma*[8] one will not have the fear of serpents. A brahmin will not have any fear from weapons by tying the *śatāvari* (a herb) after making a thousand oblations with (the hymn) *mādya tvā vādyate*[9]. One will get plenty of food by making oblation (with the hymn) *dirghatamaso'rka*[10].

10. One who repeats (the hymn) *samamadhyāyanti*[11] will not die of thirst. One will not get a disease by repeating (the hymn) *tvamimā oṣadhiḥ*[12].

---

1. SV. 1.274a; 2.671a.
2. Tait. Sam. 4.6.1.5a; SV. 1.512a.
3. Cf. *parito ṣiñcatā* SV. 1.512a.
4. SV. 1.378a.
5. SV. 1.141a.
6. SV. 1.73a; 2.1096a.
7. Cf. *Vedic Concordance* p. 1033b.
8. Could not be traced.
9. Could not be traced.
10. Could not be traced.
11. Could not be traced.
12. RV. 1.91.22a.

11. One will become free from fears by repeating (the hymn) *devavrata*[1] on the journey. Oblations offered with (the hymn) *yadindro munaye tvā*[2] increase fortune.

12. O Rāma ! Collyrium applied to the eyes (with the hymn) *bhago na citra*[3] will increase fortune. There need be no doubt.

13-14. The repetition (of the hymn) *indreti varga*[4] will also increase fortune. A man who seeks the love of a woman should make her listen to (the hymn) *pari priyā divaḥ kaviḥ*[5]. O Rāma ! There need be no doubt that she will love him in return. (The repetition of the hymns) *rathantara*[6] and *vāmadevya*[7] increases the divine splendour.

15. A child should be fed with the powder of *vacā* soaked in ghee daily with the repetition of (the hymn) *indramidgāthino*[8]. It will give him good memory.

16. There is no doubt that one will get progeny after repeating (the hymn) *rathantara*[9] and offering oblations. The hymn *mayi śrīḥ*[10] has to be repeated for the increase of fortune.

17. The repetition of the eight *vairūpya*[11] (hymns) daily confers fortune. One will get all the desires fulfilled by repeating the *saptāṣṭaka*[12] (hymns).

18. One who worships cows daily morning and evening (with the repetition of the hymn) *gavyoṣuṇo*[13] unweariedly will always have cows in his house.

19. One who offers a *droṇa* (a measure) of barley soaked in

1. Could not be traced.
2. Could not be traced.
3. SV.1.449ab.
4. Could not be traced.
5. SV. 1.476a; 2.285a.
6. Tait. Sam. 1.8.13.1.
7. MS. 4.9.11:132.10.
8. SV. 1.198a.
9. See 14.1.
10. RV.Kh. 5.87.10d.
11. Cf. Tait. Sam. 4.4.2.2.
12. Could not be traced.
13. SV. 1.186a.

ghee into fire (with the repetition of the hymn), *vāta āvātu bheṣajaṁ*[1] as laid down will ward off all spells.

20-21a. Oblations of sesamum with (the repetition of the hymn) *pra daivo dāso*[2] destroys witchcraft. (Repeating the hymn) *abhi tvā pūrva pītaye*[3] followed by the syllable *vaṣaṭ* while offering oblations made with perfumed fuel will yield victory in battle.

21b-24. A wise man should make good figures of elephants, horses and men with flour and represent the chief men of the enemy with oily cakes of flour and cut them into pieces with a knife. Then the knower of the sacred formulas should offer oblations (with these cakes) soaked in mustard oil with wrath while reciting the hymn *abhi tvā śūranonumaḥ.*[4] The wise man gets victory in battle by this act. The hymns *gāruḍa*[5], *vāmadevya,*[6] *rathantara*[7] and *bṛhadratha*[8] are without any doubt said to destroy all sins.

CHAPTER TWO HUNDRED AND SIXTY-TWO

The use of the hymns of Atharvaveda

Puṣkara said :

1. The application of the hymns of *Sāma* (*veda*) has been described. I shall describe to you (the application) of (the hymns of) *Atharva* (*veda*). One gets peace by offering oblations with the hymns of the peace class.

2. One will get rid of all the diseases by offering oblations to (the gods of) the remedial class. One will get free from all sins by offering oblations to (the gods of) the *trisaptiya* class.

---

1. SV. 1. 184a; 2.1190a.
2. SV. 1.51a; 2.867a.
3. SV. 1.256a; 2.923a.
4. SV. 1.233a; 2.30a.
5. Could not be traced.
6. MS. 4.9.11:132.10.
7. See p. 706, note 6.
8. Tait. Sam.2.3.10.2.

3. One will never get fear by offering oblations to (the gods of) the protection class. O Rāma! one will never be born by offering oblations to (the gods of) the *aparājita* (unconquered) class.

4. One will ward off untimely death by offering oblations to (the gods of) the life-giving class. One will get welfare everywhere by offering oblations to (the gods of) the welfare class.

5. One will get united with good fortune (by propitiating the gods of) happiness and armour group. One will remove the defects of a building by offering oblations to the class of deities presiding over the foundations of a house.

6. In the same way one will remove all the defects by offering oblations to (the gods of) the Raudra class. Oblations (are to be offered to) these ten classes in eighteen propitiatory (rites).

7-9. (The goddesses) Vaiṣṇavī, Śānti, Aindrī, Brāhmī, Raudrī, Vāyavyā, Vāruṇī, Kauberī, Bhārgavī, Prājāpatyā, Tvāṣṭrī, Kaumārī, Vahnidevatā, Mārudgaṇā, Gāndhārī, Śānti Nairṛtakī, Śānti Āṅgirasī, Yāmyā and Pārthivī (are the eighteen propitiatory items) that yield all pleasures. The recitation (of the hymn) *yastvā mṛtyuḥ*[1] conquers death.

10. One will never be afflicted by serpents by offering oblations with (the hymn) *suparṇastvā*[2]! (The hymn) *indreṇa dattaṁ*[3] confers all the pleasures.

11. (The hymn) *indreṇa dattam*[4] is capable of destroying all obstacles. The hymn *imā devi*[5] is an excellent all-appeasing (hymn).

12. (The hymn) *devā maruta*[6] confers all the pleasures. (The hymn) *yamasya lokāt*[7] is excellent for removing (the effects of) bad dreams.

1. AV. 3.11.8c.
2. AV. 4.6.4a
3. Tait. Sam. 2.3.10.2b.
4. See note 3 above.
5. Could not be traced.
6. Could not be traced.
7. AV. 19.56.1a.

13. (The hymn) *indraśca pañcavaṇijā*[1] is excellent for profit in trade. Oblations offered with (the hymn) *kāmo me vāji*[2] increase the fortune of women.

14. Oblation offered a lakh times with (the repetition of the hymn) *tubhyameva jariman*[3] and with (the hymn) *agne gobhir na*[4] will promote the intellect.

15. Offering oblation with (the hymn) *dhruvaṁ dhruveṇa*[5] will ensure the acquisition of land. The repetition of (the hymn) *alaktakajīva*[6] will ensure prosperous agriculture.

16. (The hymn) *ahaṁ te bhagna*[7] increases fortune. (The hymn) *ye me pāśāḥ*[8] secures release from bondage.

17. Oblation offered with the repetition of (the hymn) *śapatvahan*[9] destroys enemies. (The hymn) *tvamuttamam*[10] is capable of increasing fame and intellect.

18. (The hymn) *yathā mṛgamati*[11] increases the good fortune of women. (The hymn) *yena cehadiśaṁ*[12] is advantageous for conception.

19. (The hymn) *ayaṁ te yoniḥ*[13] is favourable for progeny. (The hymn) *śivaḥ śivābhiḥ*[14] increases good fortune.

20. (The repetition of the hymn) *bṛhaspatirnaḥ paripātu*[15] secures safety on the journey. (The hymn) *muñcāmi tvā*[16] is said to ward off untimely death.

---

1. Could not be traced.
2. Could not be traced.
3. AV. 2.28.1a.
4. Tait. Saṃ. 2.4.5.1a.
5. AV. 6.87.3b; 7.94.1a.
6. Could not be traced.
7. Could not be traced.
8. Could not be traced.
9. Could not be traced.
10. Could not be traced.
11. Could not be traced.
12. Could not be traced.
13. AV. 3.20.1a.
14. RV. 1.187.3b.
15. AV. 7.51.1a.
16. AV. 3.11.1a.

21. One who masters the *atharvaśiras*[1] becomes free from all sins. I have described to you some procedures relating to some important hymns.

22-24a. The first material for oblations is the twigs of trees suitable for such rites. O Bhārgava ! Clarified butter, rice, white mustard, unbroken rice, sesamum, curd, milk, *darbha* (grass), *dūrvā* (grass), *bilva* (leaves) and lotuses are always said to be the materials that promote peace and prosperity.

24b-25. O Knower of righteousness ! Mustard oil, blood, poison, twigs of thorny (trees) should be used in magic incantations. One who knows the employment should repeat the sage, deity and metre (relating to the hymns).

CHAPTER TWO HUNDRED AND SIXTY-THREE

Appeasing rites for portents

Puṣkara said :

1. The *śrisūkta* of each *Veda* is known to be capable of increasing fortune. The fifteen hymns (beginning with) *hiraṇya-varṇāṁ hariṇīṁ*[2] (are considered to be conferring) fortune.

2. The four hymns *ratheṣvakṣeṣu vṛṣabha*[3] in the *Yajur* (*Veda*) (are said to confer) fortune. The *Sāma* hymns *srāvantiyaṁ*[4] is the *śrisūkta* in the *Sāmaveda*.

3. In the same way, (the hymn) *śriyaṁ dhātarmayi dhehi*[5] in the *Atharvaveda* is said (to be conferring fortune). One who repeats the *śrisūkta* with devotion and offers oblation gets fortune.

4. One will get fortune by offering oblations of lotuses, *bilva* (leaves), clarified butter and sesamum. The *puruṣasūkta*[6] is the same for each one of the *Vedas*. It gives everything.

---

1. The Atharvaṇa hymns.
2. RV. Kh. 5.87.1a.
3. Vidh. 65.7.
4. Cf. *śrāyanta iva*, Vaj. Sam. 33.41a.
5. Āp. Śr. 6.20.2.
6. RV. 10.90.1a.

5. If libation of water is presented with (the recitation of) each one of the hymns, it will make one free from sin. One will destroy his sins by offering flowers to *Viṣṇu* with each one (of the hymns) after bathing.

6. One would get all the pleasures by giving away a fruit with each one (of the hymns) after bathing. By the repetition of the *Puruṣasūkta* major and minor sins are destroyed.

7. One gets everything by repeating the *kṛcchra* (hymns) and offering oblations (with them) after becoming clean by bathing. Three other appeasing (hymns) besides the eighteen appeasing (hymns) are excellent.

8-10. Amṛtā, abhayā and saumyā destory all the calamities. Amṛtā (is governed) by all the gods. Abhayā (is governed) by Brahmā and Saumyā by all gods. Any one (of them will) confer all the pleasures. O Foremost among Bhṛgus! The wristlet with the Varuṇa (hymn) is to be prepared for the *abhayā* appeasement. Similarly *śatakāṇḍa* is (for the wristlet) for *amṛtā* and conch for *saumyā*. In order to accomplish (the desired results) the respective hymns of the deities should be used for the wristlets.

11-13. These are capable of destroying the calamities relating to the heavens, atmosphere and earth. Listen to me! (I shall describe) the supernatural events relating to the heavens, atmosphere and the earth. You learn from me that (the phenomena) relating to the heavens are caused by the ruling asterisms of the day. (Those) of the sky are the fall of a meteor, scorching glow in the directions, the halo around the sun or moon, (the appearance of) fairy towns and rains. (The phenomena) relating to the earth are the extraordinary events affecting the movable and immovable things and earthquake.

14. The portent will not bear any fruit if it rains within seven days. A portent without any appeasement within three years is very dangerous.

15-16a. The images of gods will dance, shake, glow, shout, weep, perspire and laugh. (These are portents.) The changes in the images can be pacified by worshipping (Lord) Prajāpati (Brahmā) and offering oblations.

16b-17. When there is blaze in a country without fire,

with loud noise and without fuel that burns, that country will be tormented by kings. O Son of Bhṛgu ! The change in the fire is appeased with the hymns of Fire (god).

18. When the trees bear fruit out of season, ooze out milk and blood, one should do the appeasing rite for the portents after worshipping (Lord) Śiva.

19-20a. Both excessive rains and draught are considered to give rise to famine. Rain occurring consecutively for three days out of season is known (to be a portent) of danger. The change in (the pattern of) rain is nullified by the worship of Parjanya (Rain god), Moon and Sun.

20b-21. If rivers recede from the cities or come near them, if they flow gushing forth or get dried up, then the Varuṇa hymn should be recited as also in the case of deterioration in the (state of) the reservoirs.

22-23a. The women may deliver prematurely or may not deliver at the appropriate time. They may deliver children with deformities or deliver twins etc. One should worship the women and brahmins in the case of such deviations in the delivery (as above).

23b-25a. If a mare or she-elephant or cow gives birth to twins or to deformed younger or to ones different from the species, it will die within six months. In the case of deformed youngs there will be danger from hostile forces. The recitation and oblation as well as worship of brahmins should be done (in such cases).

25b-26a. If vehicles run without being yoked (to steeds), if (vehicles) yoked (to steeds) do not run, or trumpet sounds (are heard) in the sky, then it forebodes great impending danger.

26b-30a. If wild animals and birds enter village and those of village enter forest; land (animals) enter water and water (animals) enter land, vixens howl at the threshold of a palace, cocks crow at *pradoṣa* (the time preceding the night fall); vixens howl at the residence or at the rising Sun; dove enters the house, carnivorous birds stoop down on the head; bees make sweet (sound); crows mate in sight; strong arches of palace, garden, door-ways, corridor and mansions fall without an obvious cause, it forebodes evil. (It forebodes) the death of the king.

30b-31. If the quarters are filled by dust or smoke, if (the country is) under the influence of the descending node, if spots in the moon and sun are visible, or if the stars and planets are not to be seen, it also indicates fear.

32. Where the fire does not glow, the waterpots ooze, there is the fear of death and witchcraft as the result of the portents. The portent is appeased by the worship of brahmins and gods, recitation of hymns and offer of oblations.

CHAPTER TWO HUNDRED AND SIXTY-FOUR

Worship of gods to ward off the effects of portents and mode of offering the Vaiśvadeva ball

Puṣkara said :

1. I shall describe the mode of worshipping the gods and other rites that destroy (the effects of) portents. One should offer respectful water of libation to (Lord) Viṣṇu with the three (hymns beginning with) *āpo ni ṣṭhā*[1] after having bathed.

2. O Brahmin ! Water for washing the feet (should be offered) with the three (hymns beginning with) *hiraṇyavarṇa*[2]. Water for sipping (is offered with the recitation of the hymn) *śanna āpo*[3] and for bathing with (the hymn) *idamāpaḥ.*[4]

3. Perfumes (are offered) with the three (hymns) *rathe akṣe*[5] and dress with (the hymn) *yuva*[6]. Flowers (are given) with (the recitation of the hymn) *puṣpavatiḥ*[7] and incense with (the hymn) *dhūpo'si.*[8]

---

1. RV. 10.9.1a.
2. RV.Kh. 5·87.1a.
3. AV.1.6.4a.
4. RV. 1.23.22a.
5. *Rathe akṣeṣu*, AV. 6.38.3a.
6. Cf. Bloomfield, *Vedic Concordance* pp. 792-93.
7. RV. 10. 97-3b.
8. Cf. *dhūr asi*, Tait. Sam. 1.1.4.1.

4-6. (The hymn for offering) the lamp is *tejo'si*[1] and for the *madhuparka*[2], *dadhi*[3]. O Foremost among men! The eight hymns (beginning) with *hiraṇyagarbhaḥ*[4] are said to be (used) in offering eatables (to gods), cooked rice, drinks, perfume, chowrie, fan, shoe, umbrella, chariot and seat. Whatever other thing has to be offered should be accompanied by the recitation of (the hymn) of (god) Savitṛ. The *puruṣasūkta*[5] should be repeated and oblations should be offered with the same (hymn).

7. In the absence of an image (of Lord Viṣṇu) (the deity should be invoked) on the altar or in water or in a pot full (with water) or on the banks of a river or in a lotus. One would thus accomplish the propitiation by worshipping (lord) Viṣṇu.

8-12. Then the oblations should be offered to the glowing fire with the entire food being collected and offered with earnestness after cleaning the ground, sprinkling water and spreading sand and *kuśa* grass. (One should say) (obeisance) to Vāsudeva, to the lord, to the master, to the immutable, to the Fire (god), to Soma[6], to Mitra, to Varuṇa and to Indra. O Fortunate one ! Obeisance to Indra and Fire (god), the Viśvedevas[7] and to the lord of the beings. Oh ! Rāma ! Then (one should say) (obeisance) to Anumati[8], to Dhanvantari[9], to Vāstoṣpati[10], to the goddess, to the Fire that accomplishes the sacrificial rite. After having made the oblations (thus) with the names ending in the dative case, a part of the offering is given away as gift.

13-14. O Son of Bhṛgu ! Knower of righteousness ! Takṣa and Upatakṣa towards the east, then the horses and the hairs

---

1. Tait. Sam. 1.1.10.3
2. Consisting of curd, clarified butter, water, honey and candied sugar.
3. Cf. AV. 20.127.9b and TB. 3.7.6.13.
4. RV. 10.121.1a.
5. RV. 10.90.1a.
6. This and the following three are different celestial gods.
7. A particular group of deities ten in number and supposed to be sons of Viśvā.
8. A female deity.
9. The physician of the gods.
10. The deity that presides over the foundation of a house.

(on the south), Nirundhī and Dhūmriṇīkā (on the west) and Asvapantī and Meghapatnī (on the north) are the names of all those (to be worshipped) all around (in a circle).

15-16. The Fire-god and other gods should be located in (the places of) the goddesses. O Son of Bhṛgu ! (goddesses) Nandinī, Subhāgyā, Sumaṅgalī, Bhadrakālī, Sthūṇā, Śrī, Hiṙanyakeśī and Vanaspati are worshipped.

17-22. Offering is made to Dharma and Adharma at the door, Dhruva at the centre of the house, Mṛtyu outside, Varuṇa at a reservoir, the goblins outside (the house), the god of wealth at the house, Indra and companions on the east, Yama and his attendants on the south, Varuṇa and his companions on the west and Soma and his attendants on the north. (Offering) is made to Brahmā and his attendants at the centre. (Offerings) should be made in the sky, above, on the floor and on the earth during the day (for the spirits) that wander during the day and in the night for those that wander during the night. Offering should be made (to the spirits) morning and evening daily outside. Then offering of balls of rice is made (for the manes). It should not be done in the evening.

23-28. Offering is first made to (the dead) father, then to the grandfather and great-gradfather, then to one's mother, paternal grandmother and paternal great-grandmother. The manes should thus be worshipped on the kuśa (grass) having their tips facing the south. The offerings of balls of rice to the crows are made with the repetition of the sacred formula stating 'let the crows partake in the directions of east, west, north-west, south and south-west'. (Similarly) the ball of rice to the dogs is offered (with the repetition of the sacred formula, 'I am offering the ball of rice to the dogs in the family of Sun that are black and of variegated colours. May it protect me always on the path to the next world'). (Then offerings are made to the cows with the following words:) 'Accept this oblation of mine, O cows, the daughters of the celestial cow, that are good for all, holy, destroyer of sins and the mothers of the three worlds'. After having offered the food to the cows and bidding adieu, one should offer the alms. After having worshipped the guests and the poor, the householder should himself eat. One should say, '*Oṁ bhūḥ* oblations. *Oṁ bhuvaḥ* oblations. *Oṁ svaḥ* oblations.

Oṁ bhūrbhuvaḥ svaḥ oblations. *Oṁ* oblations, you are the atonement for sins done by the gods. *Oṁ* oblations, you are the atonement for sins done by the manes. *Oṁ* oblations, you are the atonement for sins done by me. *Oṁ* oblations, you are the atonement for sins done by men. Oblations, you are the atonement for all sins done by the learned men and the ignorant men. Oblations, to Fire god that accomplishes the desires. *Oṁ* oblations to Prajāpati (lord of beings). I have described to you (the mode of) worship of (Lord) Viṣṇu and the offering made to all gods.

CHAPTER TWO HUNDRED AND SIXTY-FIVE

The sacred bathing of the deities

Fire-god said :

1. Listen to me. I shall describe the bathing that accomplishes all objects and that is propitiatory. A wise man should bathe the planets and (Lord) Viṣṇu on the banks of a river.

2. One who is afflicted by fever as well as one who is afflicted by planets causing obstacles (should bathe it) in a temple. One who desires to acquire knowledge (should bathe it) on (the banks of) a tank or in the house and one who desires victory (should do the sacred ablution) at a sacred place.

3. A woman who has a miscarriage should be bathed in a lotus tank, and one whose issue dies after birth should bathe in the presence of an *aśoka* (tree).

4. One who desires to have flowers, one who desires to have progeny and who desires to have a house and other fortunes (should bathe) respectively at a place abounding in flowers, an ocean and in the presence of (the image of Lord) Viṣṇu.

5. Bathing in (the asterisms) *śravaṇa*, *revati* and *puṣya* is meritorious for all. One who wishes to do the ceremonial bathing has to observe a purificatory vow for seven days prior to that.

6-8a. (The herbs) *punarnavā*, *rocanā*, *śatāṅga*, *guruṇitvak*, *madhūka*, the two sorts of *rajani*, *tagara*, *nāgakeśara*, *ambari*, *mañjiṣṭhā*, *māṁsi*, *yāsaka*, *kardama*, *priyaṅgu*, *mustard*, *kuṣṭha*, *balā*, *brāhmi*, saffron and the five things got from a cow should be mixed with the flour of barley and rubbed (on the body). One should then bathe.

8b-11a. (Lord) Viṣṇu should be worshipped on the pericarp of a circle, (Lord) Brahmā on the right side and (Lord) Śiva on the left side. (Lord) Indra and others should be drawn from the east onwards in order together with their weapons and associates. Bathing circles should be drawn in the different directions and the intermediary directions. (Lords) Viṣṇu, Brahmā, Īśa (Śiva), Śakra (Indra) and others and their weapons should then be worshipped and oblation offered. One hundred and eight twigs, sesamum and ghee (are offered) to each one (of the gods).

11b-13. The pitchers *bhadra*, *subhadra*, *siddhārtha*, *amogha*, *citrabhānu*, *parjanya* and *sudarśana* that give prosperity should be placed on the ground. (The gods should be invoked in them as follows) : "May the Aśvins, Rudras, Maruts, Viśvedevas, Demons, Vasus and Munis and other gods get pleased and enter these pitchers."

14-16. The herbs *jayanti*, *vijayā*, *jayā*, *śatāvari*, *śatapuṣpā*, *viṣṇukrāntā*, *aparājitā*, *jyotiṣmati*, *atibalā*, sandal, *uśira*, *keśara*, musk, camphor, *bālaka*, *patraka*, *tvak*, *jātiphala* (nutmeg), clove, earth and the five things got from a cow should be put into the pitcher. Then the person (who desires to have the ceremonial bath) should be made to sit on the auspicious seat and bathed by brahmins.

17-18. Then oblations should separately be offered to the gods with the sacred formulas used in the anointing of kings. Then the final oblation should be made and the fee paid to the preceptor. In olden times (Lord) Indra was able to kill the demons being (thus) bathed by the preceptor. (I) have described (to you) the bathing of the guardians of the directions (that give) victory in the battle and other things.

CHAPTER TWO HUNDRED AND SIXTY-SIX

The mode of performing the ceremonial bathing to wash off obstacles

Puṣkara said :

1-6a. I shall describe the bathing that would be beneficial for those afflicted by (the evil spirit called) Vināyaka. The spirit Vināyaka was commissioned by (Lords) Keśava (Viṣṇu), Īśa (Śiva) and Pitāmaha (Brahmā) as the leader of the attendants in order to frustrate the work of men. One who is possessed by Vināyaka dreams as if he is bathing in water excessively, sees shaven heads, rides the demons (in a dream) and as he goes thinks that he is being followed by others. The fruitless beginning (of a task) leads to frustation and (the body) emaciates without any reason. A girl does not get a (suitable) bridegroom, a married woman does not get progeny, a brahmin does not become a preceptor and a pupil does not get instruction. A trader does not get profit and a cultivator, the produce. A king does not get a kingdom. In such cases a (ceremonial) bath has to be done.

6b-9a. (It should be done) on an auspicious seat in (the asterisms) *hasta*, *puṣya*, *aśvini*, *mṛgaśirṣa* and *śravaṇa*. Levigated powders of white mustard mixed with clarified butter, all herbs and perfumes should be besmeared on the head (of the person concerned). He should be bathed with (the waters in) four pitchers into which all herbs have been put. Earth brought from stables of horses and elephants, anthill and confluence of rivers as well as resin got from a cow, perfumes and *guggulu* should be put (into the pitchers).

9b-17. (The bathing is done with the repetition of the following sacred formulas) "*Sahasrākṣam śatadhāram ṛṣibhiḥ pāvanaṁ kṛtaṁ*[1]. I bathe you with the waters that have been made holy by the sages. May the removers of sins protect you." *Bhagaṁ te varuṇo rājā bhagaṁ sūryo bṛhaspatiḥ bhagamindraśca vāyuśca bhagaṁ saptarṣayo daduḥ*[2]. "May Varuṇa, the Sun, Bṛhaspati,

1. YDh. 1.280a.
2. YDh. 1. 281a.

Indra, Vāyu and the seven sages give you wealth." "May the misfortune that sticks to your hair, the parting line of the hair, head, fore-head, ears and eyes always be removed by the water." Then the preceptor should hold the leaf of the *darbha* (grass) on the left hand and pour the mustard oil on the head of the person that has bathed with a ladle made of *udumbara* (tree). Then oblation should be made holding the *kuśa* grass on the head with the left hand (repeating) the names Mita, Sammita, Śālaka, Kaṇṭhaka, Kūsmāṇḍa and Rājaputra together with (the word) oblation, the sacred formulas for oblation and obeisance. Then after having spread the *kuśa* (grass) everywhere at the crossroads, one should offer cooked and uncooked rice, meat, food, large quantities of raw fish, coloured flower, wine, *mūlaka*, cake, sweet cake of flour, garland of *eṇḍavikā* (?), curd rice, sweet porridge (*pīyasa*), *piṣṭaka* (a cake made of any grain), *modaka* (a kind of sweetmeat in the form of balls) and treacle on a winnowing basket.

18-20. Then Ambikā (mother goddess; consort of Śiva), the mother of Vināyaka, should be worshipped after having offered *dūrvā* (grass), mustard and flowers and the final oblation is made. (The following request is made): O Fortunate one! You give me beauty, fame, good fortune, progeny, wealth and all desired things. The brahmins should be fed and a pair of clothes should be given to the preceptor also. One would get the fruit of his action and wealth after worshipping the (spirit) Vināyaka and the planets.

CHAPTER TWO HUNDRED AND SIXTY-SEVEN

Ceremonial bathing known as Māheśvara and other kinds of ablutions

Puṣkara said :

1. I shall describe the bathing (known as) Māheśvara that has been described by Uśanas (preceptor of demons) to Bali, the king of demons, in olden days and that would promote the victory of a king and others.

2. When the sun has not risen the votary should be bathed on a seat with (the waters of) pitchers (with the repetition of the following words): *Oṁ* obeisance to Lord Rudra and to Bala besmeared with ashes of grey colour. Victory! Victory! Trample down all the enemies of a weak man in wars and arguments. *Oṁ*! Crush down all the (hostile) marchers. Let that god who desires to burn (all the worlds) at the end of the *yuga* (period), and who having terrible form (accept) this worship. Let that god having thousand rays and white (in complextion) protect your life. May that (Lord) Śiva, the destroyer of Tripura[1], who resembles the *saṁvartaka*[2] fire and is of the form of all the gods, protect your life; *likhi, likhi, khili* oblations. After bathing, oblations should be done with sesamum and rice with (the repetition of the above) sacred formulas.

3. After having bathed with the *pañcāmṛta*[3], the trident bearing lord should be worshipped. I shall describe (to you) the other kinds of ablutions that would always be for your victory.

4. Bathing with ghee is said to be excellent for the lengthening of life. (Bathing) with cow-dung would be (conferring) fortune. (Bathing) with cow's urine would destroy the sins.

5. (Bathing) with milk would be (giving) strong intellect and with curd, would further fortune. One would be destroying the sins by bathing with *kuśa* grass and would get all the things by bathing with the five things got from a cow.

6. One would get everything (by bathing) with *śatamūla*. One would destroy the sins (by bathing) with the waters (touched by) the horns of a cow. One would get everything by bathing with *palāśa*, *bilva*, lotus and *kuśa* (grass).

7-8. Bathing with *vacā*, two varieties of *haridrā* and *musta* (is spoken as) excellent for killing the demons. One would gain long life, fame, righteousness and intellect by ablution with washings of gold. It would be auspicious (to bathe) with the

---

1. The three cities of the demons Tārakākṣa, Kamalākṣa and Vidyunmālin.

2. The fire that destroys the universe at the end.

3. The five sweet things—milk, sugar, ghee, curd and honey.

washings of silver and copper. One would gain victory and fortune respectively by bathing with the washings of gems and all perfumes.

9. One would gain health and excellent fortune respectively (by bathing) with water containing fruits and water with *dhātrī*. One would get wealth and fortune respectively (by bathing) with sesamum and white mustard and *priyaṅgu*.

10. (One would gain) wealth (by bathing with water containing) lotus, blue lotus and *kadamba*. (One would gain) strength (by bathing) with the water containing (the twigs of) the *balā* tree. Bathing with the water that has washed the feet of (Lord) Viṣṇu is the best among all kinds of ablutions.

11-13a. (At the time of bathing) one should repeat the hymn *ekakāmāya*[1] alone duly. A band made of (the herbs) *kuṣṭha*, *pāṭhā*, *vacā*, *śuṇṭhi*, conch and iron etc. should be tied round the wrist with (the repetition of) the hymn *ākrandayati*.[2] Lord Hari (Viṣṇu) is the master of all desires. One would enjoy all the pleasures by worshipping Him.

13b-14. By bathing (the image of Lord Viṣṇu) with ghee and milk and worshipping Him, one would get rid of biliousness. By offering an oblation of five kinds of pulses one would get free from dysentry. By bathing (the image) with the five things got from a cow, one would get rid of rheumatism.

15-16. Bathing with *dvisneha* (ghee and water) with intense devotion would remove derangement of phlegm. Ghee, oil and honey (is said to be) the *trirasa* (three fluids mixed together) that is excellent for bathing. Ghee and water mixed for bathing (is said to be) *dvisneha*, Ghee and oil (mixed for bathing is said to be) *samala*. Bath water with honey, the juice of sugar-cane and milk is known to be *trimadhura* (three sweet things).

17-18. Bath water with ghee, juice of sugar-cane, oil and honey (is known to be) *trirasa* (three fluids) (good) for wealth. An unguent of the three white (things)—camphor, *uśīra* (a fragrant thing) and sandal (should be used for bath). Sandal, agallochum, camphor, musk and saffron are the five unguents for (Lord) Viṣṇu that yield all the pleasures.

---

1. Could not be traced.
2. Cf. RV. 6.47.30a.

19. The three fragrant things are camphor, sandal and saffron. Musk, camphor and sandal (used as an unguent) yield all the pleasures.

20-22. Nutmeg, camphor and sandal (are said to be) the three cooling things. O son of Bhṛgu! The five colours are indicated as yellow, blue, white, black and red. Blue lotus, lotus and *jāti* (flowers) (are spoken to be) the three cool things (that are commended) for the worship of (Lord) Viṣṇu. Saffron, red lotuses and red lilies are the three red things. Men would get peace by worshipping (Lord) Viṣṇu well by (showing) incense, lamp, etc.

23. One would duly get all peace by worshipping the planets with the *gāyatrī*[1] (hymn) after offering a lakh or crore oblations of sesamum, clarified butter, barley and other grains in a square sacrificial pit (done) by eight or sixteen brahmins.

CHAPTER TWO HUNDRED AND SIXTY-EIGHT

Mode of worshipping Indra, doing nirājanā (relating to King's expedition) and other rites

Puṣkara said :

1-2. I shall describe the rites to be performed by the kings in the course of a year. On (the day of) the birth-asterism He (Lord Viṣṇu) should be worshipped. The Sun, Moon and other gods should be worshipped every month at the time of sun's entry into one of the signs of the zodiac. Agastya should be worshipped at the time of the rise of Agastya (Canopus). (Lord) Hari (Viṣṇu) should be worshipped for four months. Festivities should be had for fifteen days in connection with the lying down to sleep and waking up from sleep (of Lord Viṣṇu)[2].

1. RV. 3.62.10.

2. These are respectively the periods corresponding to June-July and September-October.

3-5. A mansion should be made ready (by the king) on the east of his army camp in the bright fortnight of the month (ruled by the asterism) Proṣṭhapāda (i.e. Bhādrapada = September-October) for (worshipping) Indra from the first lunar day. The banner of Indra should be raised therein. (Lord) Indra and (his consort) Śacī should be worshipped (therein). Those two and the flag-staff should be led to the proper place accompanied by the sounding of musical instruments on the eighth day. He should fast on the eleventh day, raise the flag staff (on the twelfth day) and worship the flagstaff, as well as the Lord of celestials (Indra) and Śacī in a pitcher covered by a cloth etc. (repeating the following words):

6-12. "O Indra! You flourish! Conqueror of the enemies! Killer of (the demon) Vṛtra! Punisher of the demon Pāka! Lord of lords! Most fortunate one! You have come to the earth. You are the master, the eternal one and one who is bent on the welfare of all the beings. You are a person who has endless lustre and splendour. You are the one who increases fame and victory. May these gods increase your lustre. O Śakra (Indra)! One who causes good rain! May (the Lords) Brahmā, Viṣṇu, Maheśa (Śiva), Kārtikeya (son of Śiva), Vināyaka (son of Śivā), (the twelve) Suns, (the eight) Vasus, (the eleven) Rudras, the Sādhyas, the Bhṛgus, the (different) quarters, group of Maruts, the protectors of the world, planets, the Yakṣas (a kind of semi-divine beings), the rivers, the oceans, (goddesses) Śrī (the consort of Viṣṇu), Earth, Gaurī (consort of Śiva), Caṇḍikā (a form of the consort of Śiva) and Sarasvatī (goddess of speech; consort of Brahmā) increase your radiance. Hail O Indra! Consort of Śacī! May auspicious things accrue to me daily by your victory. Always extend thy grace to the kings, brahmins and people. May the earth abound in grains by your grace. May there be prosperity without any obstacle. May calamities come to an end."

13-16a. After having worshipped Indra with (the above) sacred formulas, one will conquer the earth and reach the heaven. (The picture of) Bhadrakālī (a benevolent form of the consort of Śiva) should be drawn on a cloth on the eighth day of the bright fortnight in the (month of) Āśvina (October-November) for victory. In the same way, the weapon, bow, banner, umbrella, the insignia of the king such as the arms (should be worshipped) with flowers. After remaining awake in the night, the offering should be made. (She) is again worshipped on the second day. O Bhadrakālī ! Mahākālī ! Durgā ! Remover of all difficulties ! Conqueror of the three worlds ! Caṇḍī ! Be successful in (conferring) peace on me !

16b-20. I shall describe the mode of performing the *nirājanā*[1] (rite). A chamber should be got ready in the north-eastern direction. Three arches should be erected therein and the gods should be worshipped daily. The worship should be done from the moment Sun leaves (the asterism) Citrā and enters (the asterism) Svāti and stays therein. (The gods) Brahmā, Viṣṇu, Śambhu (Śiva), Śakra (Indra), Fire-god, Wind-god, Vināyaka and Kumāra (the two sons of Śiva), Varuṇa, Dhanada (god of wealth), Yama (god of death), Viśvedevas (a group of gods) and the eight elephants of Vaisravasa (son of Viśravas) such as Kumuda, Airāvaṇa, Padma, Puṣpadanta, Vāmana, Supratīka, Añjana and Nīla, should be worshipped in the chamber.

21-23. The priest should offer as oblation clarified butter, twigs, white mustard and sesamum. After worshipping eight pitchers, the excellent horses and elephants should be bathed with them. The horses should be bathed (first) and the balls of rice offered. Then the elephants should be led out first through the arches but should not be made to cross the principal gateways etc. Then all should set out. The insignia of the king should be worshipped in the chamber. After having worshipped (Lord) Varuṇa on the west, the offering to the spirits should be made in the night.

24-26. When the Sun has entered (the asterism) Viśākhā, the king should stay in the hermitage. The chariot should be specially decorated on that day. The royal insignia that has been worshipped should be placed in the hands of the respective men. O Knower of righteousness ! An astrologer should then consecrate the elephant, horse, umbrella, sword, bow, war

1. Lustration of arms, a kind of military and religious ceremony, performed by kings or generals before they set out.

drum, flag staff and flag (of the king). After consecration they should be made to be carried on the elephant.

27-30. The astrologer and priest should then ride the elephant. (The king) should ride the consecrated horses and set out through the arch. After setting out he should ride the elephant and go out through the arch. After having offered the oblation, the king riding the elephant and remaining calm should circumambulate (the city) thrice as the collection of fire-brands illuminate the different quarters of space, the fourfold army keep company and the entire army shout (victory). After doing this, (the king) having offered water with the palms should go back to the palace. This is the appeasing rite (called) *nīrājanā* that would make (a king) prosper and kill the enemy.

CHAPTER TWO HUNDRED AND SIXTY-NINE

The sacred formulas for the consecration of the umbrella and other royal insignia

Puṣkara said :

1-3. I shall describe the sacred formulas for (the consecration of) the umbrella and other things, the worship of which (would confer) victory and other things. "O One with great intellect ! One having the splendour of jasmine ! One having the lustre of snow, jasmine and moon ! You be glorious by the true words of Brahmā, Soma, and Varuṇa and the power of the Sun. May you shield the king for the achievement of success and promotion of health in the same way as the cloud covers the earth for its welfare.

4-9a. O Horse ! You were born in the race of the Gandharvas (a kind of semi-divine beings). May you not become a defiler of the race. You be glorious by the true words of Brahmā, Soma and Varuṇa and the power of Fire (god) as well as the splendour of the Sun, the penance of the sages, the continence of Rudra (Śiva) and the strength of the Wind (god). You remember that you are of royal birth. You remember the *kaustubha* gem. May you not incur the sin that would accrue to the killer of a brahmin, or to a patricide or to a matricide or to a person who utters a lie for the sake of (gaining) a land or to a man of the warrior-class who turns his back (upon the battle), although you may swiftly move that way. O Horse! May you not meet with adversity in the battle or on the road. May you be happy together with your master after killing the enemies in the battle.

9 b-13. O Banner of Indra! Suparṇa of great valour has taken his position on you. The lord of birds, Son of Vinatā, One (seated) on the banner of Nārāyaṇa (Viṣṇu), A progeny of (sage) Kaśyapa, One that carried away the nectar, The Enemy of the serpents, the Vehicle of (Lord) Viṣṇu, Immeasurable one, Unassailable in the battle, Destroyer of the enemies of the celestials, One having great strength, One having swift speed, One possessing a huge body, One who drinks the nectar, The winged one, One who has the swiftness of Māruti (son of Wind, Hanumat) is always present in you. You have been fixed by (Lord) Viṣṇu, the lord of lords, for the sake of Indra. May you always give me victory, prosperity and strength. (You) protect the warriors together with their horses, armours and weapons. You burn our enemies.

14-23. Kumuda, Airāvaṇa, Padma, Puṣpadanta, Vāmana, Supratīka, Añjana and Nīla[1] are the eight (elephants) of divine origin. Their sons and grandsons constitute eight forces. You remember Bhadra, Manda, Mṛga and Saṅkīrṇa that have been born in the different forests and have become great elephants. May the (eight) Vasus, (eleven) Rudras, (twelve) Ādityas, the group of Maruts protect you. O King of elephants! Protect the master! May the obligation be discharged! (Lord) Indra, the lord of the celestials, riding the Airāvata (the elephant of Indra) and wielding the (weapon) thunderbolt following you, protect you. May you gain victory in the battle and march always in good state. May you get the strength of Airāvata (elephant of Indra) in the battle. May

1. Supposed to guard the quarters.

you get wealth from Soma, strength from Viṣṇu, splendour from Sun, speed from wind, firmness from mountain, victory from Rudra and fame from Lord Purandara (Indra). May the elephants protect you in the battle. May the quarters in the company of Aśvins (the two physicians of the gods) and Gandharvas (semi-divine beings) protect you in all the directions. May the Manus (the first representative of man-kind), Rudras, Vāyu, Soma, the great sages, Nāgas (serpents), Kinnaras (semi-divine beings), Gandharvas (semi-divine beings), Yakṣas (semi-divine beings), the hosts of spirits, planets, goblins with Ādityas, the Lord of the goblins with the (divine) mothers, Indra, Skanda (son of Śiva) the commander-in-chief (of the celestials) and Varuṇa resting in you burn all the enemies. May the king gain victory.

24-28a. May the festoons used by the enemy for decoration everywhere, fall down being struck by your splendour. In the same way as you have shone at the time of killing (the demon) Kālanemi,[1] the destruction of Tripura[2], the battle with Hiraṇyakaśipu[3] and the killing of all the demons, may you shine now. You remember the opportune moment. May the enemies of the king be destroyed quickly. (May the enemies) be conquered by different kinds of terrible diseases and weapons. May (the names) Pūtanā, Revatī, Lekhā and Kālarātṛī that we have read (as terrible forces) burn all the enemies quickly with your help.

28b-33. (O sword!) You have been created by the god of gods, the trident-bearer, (Lord) Śarva (Śiva) out of the essence of the world at the great sacrifice in which everything was offered. The destroyer of the enemies! Remember the foremost form of Nandaka (the sword of Lord Kṛṣṇa). One having a dark complexion like the petals of blue lotus! Dark one! Destroyer of bad dreams! (Lord) Brahmā has declared the following as your eight names : asiḥ, viśasanaḥ, khaḍgaḥ, tīkṣṇadhārаḥ, durāsadaḥ, śrīgarbhaḥ, vijayaḥ and dharmapālaḥ. Kṛttikā is your asterism. Lord Maheśvara (Śiva) is

1. A demon killed by Viṣṇu.
2. The three cities destroyed by Śiva.
3. A demon killed by Viṣṇu.

your preceptor. Gold is your body. Janārdana (Viṣṇu) is your lord.

34. O Armour! You cause (the enemy forces) to feel ashamed in the battle. I will have fame in the army today. O Sinless one! Protect me, worthy of being protected by you! Obeisance to you.

35-38. O War drum! You cause the hearts of enemies to tremble by your sound. You act in such a way that you may achieve victory for the king's army. Just as the excellent elephants get delighted on (hearing) the sound of the (colliding) clouds, in the same way (let us) rejoice on (hearing) your sound. You bring us joy. Just as the rumbling clouds cause fright in women, so also let our enemies get frightened by your sound in the battle. (These) should always be worshipped with sacred formulas. They should be employed for victory etc. Every year (Lord) Viṣṇu should be anointed with ghee and water. The king should be given the ablution by an astrologer and priest.

CHAPTER TWO HUNDRED AND SEVENTY

A hymn to Viṣṇu that destroys Evil

Puṣkara said :

1. O Foremost among brahmins! This (hymn) Viṣṇu-pañjara was prescribed by Brahmā for the protection of Śiva, who was desirous of destroying Tripura in olden days.

2. It was told by Vāgīśa (Bṛhaspati, the preceptor of the celestials) to Indra, who was making efforts to kill (the demon) Bala. I shall describe its form. You listen to that which will give you victory.

3-4. (Lord) Viṣṇu is stationed in the east bearing the disc. (Lord) Hari (is stationed) in the south bearing the mace. (Lord) Viṣṇu (remains) in the west bearing the bow. (Lord) Viṣṇu (is stationed) to my north bearing the sword. (Lord) Hṛṣīkeśa is in the angular points and (Lord) Janārdana in the inter-spaces. (Lord) Hari (is stationed) on the earth in the form of a tortoise and (Lord) Narasiṁha (man-lion form of Viṣṇu) in the sky (above) me.

5. This sharp-edged and stainless Sudarśana disc (of Viṣṇu) revolves. His garland of rays is imperceivable. "May you kill the evil spirits and those who wander in the night."

6. This mace has the lustre of the flames given out by the Sun. It is capable of destroying the demons, goblins, spirits and female spirits.

7. May the bow of Vāsudeva (Viṣṇu), that is striking suddenly, kill all my enemies, such as birds, men, *kūṣmāṇḍa* and the spirits of the dead.

8. Those who have been shaken by the shining lustre of the stroke of the sword, let those assembed (enemies) be subdued at once, like serpents by Garuḍa (vehicle of Viṣṇu).

9-12. May the *kūṣmānḍas*, *yakṣas*, demons, the night wanderers, spirits of the dead, Vināyakas, cruel men, *jambhagas* (jackals ?), birds, lions and other animals, serpents and others become good being struck by the sound of the conch of Viṣṇu. Those that take away my thinking faculty, those men who affect my memory, those who affect my strength and splendour, those who cast their shadow, those who affect my pleasures, those who destroy my traits, may those *kūṣmāṇḍas* get destroyed by the sound of the disc of (Lord) Viṣṇu.

13. May my intellect, mind and sense-organs be healthy by the singing of (the glory of) lord of lords, Vāsudeva.

14. May (Lord) Janārdana, Hari, be behind me, in my front, on the south and north and at the angular points. One that makes obeisance to (the Lord) Janārdana, one worthy of worship, Īśāna, endless and undecaying will not have grief.

15. Just as (Lord) Hari is the Supreme Brahman, that Keśava is above the form of the universe. May my three kinds of inauspiciousness get destroyed by the truth of singing the name Acyuta (undecaying).

CHAPTER TWO HUNDRED AND SEVENTY-ONE

The different recensions of the Vedas

Puṣkara said :

1. The number of hymns of the *Ṛg* (*veda*), *Yajur* (*veda*), *Sāma* (*veda*) and *Atharva* (*veda*) that yield all (the desires) and confer the four ends of the human life[1] is one lakh.

2. (The *Rgveda*) is divided into two branches, Sāṅkhyāyana and Āśvalāyana. The *brāhmanas* (of this *Veda*) (contain) two thousand one hundred and ten hymns.

3. The *Rgveda* is considered as the authority by the Dvaipāyanas and others. The hymns of the *Yajurveda* number one thousand nine hundred and ninetynine.

4-5. Their branches are one thousand eightysix. The branches of the *Yajur* (*veda*) are (known as) Kāṇvī, Mādhyandinī, Kathī, Mādhyakaṭhī, Maitrāyaṇī, Taittirīya and Vaiśampāyana.

6-8a. The first (branch) of the *Sāmaveda* is known as Kauthuma and the second as Atharvaṇāyanī. The songs of this *Veda* consist of *āraṇyaka*, *uktha* and *ūha*. The extent of the (*Sāmaveda*) is said to be a collection of nine thousand four hundred and twentyfive.

8b-9a. Sumantu, Jājali, Ślokāyani, Śaunaka, Pippalāda, Muñjakeśa and others (are those who represent the branches) of *Atharva* (*veda*).

9b-10. The Lord (Viṣṇu) in the form of (sage) Vyāsa divided the ten thousand and six hundred hymns and one hundred *Upaniṣads* into different recensions. (Lord) Viṣṇu also made the divisions of the Epics and *Purāṇas*.

11-12. The bard Lomaharṣaṇa got it from Vyāsa. Sumati, Agnivarcas, Mitrayu, Śiṁśapāyana (Śāṁśapāyana ?), Kṛtavrata and Sāvarṇi were his disciples. Śāṁśapāyana and others were the makers of the collection of Purāṇic texts.

13. The *Brahma* (*purāṇa*) and other *Purāṇas* are eighteen. (They are known to be) learning relating to (Lord) Hari

1. Righteousness, material prosperity, pleasures and beatitude.

(Viṣṇu). (Lord) Hari remains in the form of learning in the great *Purāṇa* (called) *Agni*.

14. One would get enjoyment and emancipation by worshipping and praising Him, who is immanent, transcendent and bears the gross and subtle forms.

15. (That) all-pervasive, triumphant (lord) wishing for prosperity is of the forms of Fire, Sun etc. (Lord) Viṣṇu, that is the mouth of the gods in the form of the Fire (god), is the supreme state.

16. The embodiment of sacrifices is praised in the *Vedas* and *Purāṇas*. The *Āgneya-purāṇa* is the greatest of the forms of Viṣṇu.

17-22. The composer and listener of the *Āgneya-purāṇa* is (Lord) Janārdana (Viṣṇu). Hence the *Āgneya-purāṇa* is great as that made up of all the *Vedas*. It is of the form of all learning, meritorious, of the form of all knowledge and excellent. It is of the form of all the beings and of (Lord) Hari (Viṣṇu). (It is meritorious) for the men who read and listen to (its narration). It gives knowledge to those who seek knowledge. It yields material prosperity to those who seek material prosperity. It confers kingdom on those who desire to have kingdom. It yields righteousness to those who seek righteousness. It confers heaven on those who seek heaven. It blesses those who seek progeny with progeny. It gives cows to those who seek cows. Those who seek a village would be blessed with a village. Those who desire pleasures would be getting pleasures. It gives all good fortune. It gives good qualities and fame to men. Those who seek victory would get victory. It gives all things to those who seek everything. Those who desire emancipation would be blessed with emancipation. The *Agnipurāṇa* destroys the sins of sinners.

CHAPTER TWO HUNDRED AND SEVENTY-TWO

The meritoriousness of making gifts of the different Purāṇas

Puṣkara said :

1-2. (The *Purāṇa*) that was narrated by Brahmā to Marīci in olden days in fifty thousand verses (is said to be) *Brahmapurāṇa.* One who desires to attain heaven should write and give it as a gift on the full moon day in (the month of) *Vaiśākha* (May-June) together with water and a cow. The *Padma purāṇa* that contains twelve thousand verses should be given (on a similar day) in (the month of) *Jyeṣṭha* (June-July) together with a cow.

3-4a. (Sage) Parāśara narrated the *Vaiṣṇavapurāṇa* based on the accounts of the *Varāhakalpa*[1] in twenty thousand verses. One who makes a gift (of the same) together with water and a cow in (the month of) *Āṣāḍha* (July-August) would reach the place of (Lord) Viṣṇu.

4b-5. The *Vāyavīya* (*purāṇa*) (that contains) fourteen thousand (verses) (is) dear to (Lord) Hari (Viṣṇu). The Wind god has narrated the righteous way in this (*Purāṇa*) with reference to (the incidents of) the *Śvetakalpa.* It has to be copied and given as a gift to a brahmin together with the molasses and a cow (on the full moon day) in (the month of) *Śrāvaṇa* (August-September).

6-7. It is said to be the *Bhāgavata* (*purāṇa*) in which the virtues have been explained with reference to the *gāyatrī*[2] (*mantra*) and also the killing of the demon Vṛtra during the *Śārasvatakalpa* has been described. It should be given as a gift in (the month of) *Proṣṭhapadī* (September-October) together with a golden lion. It contains eighteen thousand (verses).

8-9a. It is said to be the *Nāradīya* (*purāṇa*) consisting of twenty five thousand (verses) in which (the sage) Nārada described the virtues based on the *Bṛhatkalpa.* One can have the supreme attainment by making a gift (of the same) (on a full moon day) in (the month of) *Āśvina* (October-November) together with a cow.

---

1. There are thirty-two *kalpa* periods each equal to 432 million years of mortals.

2. RV. 3.62.10.

9b-10a. The *Mārkaṇḍeya* (*purāṇa*) (contains) nine thousand (verses) in which there is a discussion of righteousness and unrighteousness relating to the enemies. It should be given as a gift (on the full moon day) in (the month of) *Kārttika* (November-December).

10b-11. That (*Purāṇa*) is *Āgneya* that was spoken by the Fire-god to (sage) Vasiṣṭha. (It contains) twelve thousand (verses) and imparts all knowledge. It should be copied and offered as a gift in (the month of) *Mārgaśirṣa* (December-January). It yields everything.

12. The *Bhaviṣya* (*Purāṇa*) (contains) fourteen thousand (verses). It had its origin from the Sun. (Lord) Bhava (Śiva) narrated it to Manu. It should be offered as a gift in (the month of) *Pauṣya* (January-February) together with molasses etc.

13-14a. The *Brahmavaivarta* (*purāṇa*) was narrated by Sāvarṇi (Manu) to (sage) Nārada (dealing) with the history of Rathantara and the boar (manifestation of Viṣṇu) in eighteen thousand (verses). One who gives it in (the month of) *Māgha* (February-March) as a gift would reach the world of Brahmā.

14b-15. The *Liṅga* (*Purāṇa*) is that in which the great Lord (Śiva) residing in the fiery *liṅga* in the *Āgneyakalpa* described the virtues in eleven thousand (verses). One who makes a gift of the same in (the month of) *Phālguna* (March-April) together with sesamum and cow would have the vision of (or attain to) Śiva.

16-17a. The *Varāha* (*purāṇa*) was narrated by (Lord) Viṣṇu in fourteen thousand (verses). The account of the boar (form of Viṣṇu) was propagated by (Lord) Viṣṇu on the earth (assuming the form) of a man. (One who makes a gift of it) together with a golden (image of) eagle in (the month of) *Caitra* (April-May) would reach the place of (Lord) Viṣṇu.

17b-18a. The great *Skānda* (*purāṇa*) was narrated by (Lord) Skanda in eighty-four thousand (verses) on the virtues in the *Tatpuruṣa kalpa*. One should make a gift (of the same).

18b-19a. The *Vāmana* (*purāṇa*) narrates the story of (Lord) Hari (Viṣṇu) relating to *Dhaumakalpa* in ten thousand (verses) dealing with the virtues and material prosperity should be given (as a gift) during autumnal equinox.

19b-20a. The *Kūrma* (*purāṇa*) was narrated by the tortoise (form of Lord Viṣṇu) in eight thousand verses in connection with (the story of) Indradyumna in the nether world. It should be given (as a gift) together with a golden (image of) tortoise.

20b-21a. The *Matsya* (*purāṇa*) was narrated by (Lord Viṣṇu in the form of a) fish to Manu at the beginning of the *kalpa* (period). It should be given (as a gift) at the time of the equinox together with a golden (image of) fish.

21b-22a. The *Garuḍa* (*purāṇa*) was narrated by (Lord) Viṣṇu in the *Tārkṣakalpa* describing the birth of Garuḍa (the vehicle bird of Lord Viṣṇu) from the universal egg. It should be given (as a gift) together with a golden (image of) *haṁsa* (swan).

22b-23a. The *Brahmāṇḍa* (*purāṇa*) is that in which (Lord) Brahmā described the greatness of the universe in twelve thousand (verses). It should be given (as a gift) to a brahmin.

23b-26. The reciter of the (*Mahā*) *bhārata* should be honoured with clothes, perfumes, garlands and other things after the completion of each *parvan* (each one of the eighteen divisions) and brahmins should be fed with sweet gruel. After (the recitation of) each *parvan* is complete cows, land, village, gold and other things should be given (as gift). After (the recital of the text) of *Bhārata* is complete, a brahmin and the *Saṁhitā* texts should be worshipped. Then the book should be wrapped in silken cloth and kept at a sacred place. (Lords) Nara and Nārāyaṇa[1] and the books should be worshipped with flowers and other things. The recitation should be completed by making gifts of cows, food, land and gold and feeding (the brahmins).

27-29. Great gifts should be made and different kinds of gems should be given. Two or three *māṣakas* (a particular weight of gold) should be given every month. It is laid down that gift (should be given) to the reciter at the commencement of the solstice. O Brahmin! The reciter should be worshipped by all

1. Originally regarded as identical but in mythology and epics considered as distinct beings, Arjuna being identified with Nara and Kṛṣṇa with Nārāyaṇa.

the listeners. One who makes a gift of the Epics and *Purāṇas* (in the above manner) after worship would get long and healthy life and would attain emancipation and heaven.

CHAPTER TWO HUNDRED AND SEVENTY-THREE

The description of the solar race

Fire-god said:

1-4. I shall describe to you the genealogies of the solar and lunar races and of other kings. (Lord) Brahmā was born from the (navel) lotus of (Lord) Hari (Viṣṇu). (Sage) Marīci was the son of (Lord) Brahmā. (Sage) Kaśyapa was born from Marīci and Sun from Kaśyapa. He (Sun) had three wives—Saṁjñā, Rājñī and Prabhā. Rājñī was the daughter of Raivata. She gave birth to a son (called) Revanta. Prabhā (gave birth) to Prabhāta through the Sun. Saṁjñā, the daughter of Tvaṣṭṛ (Viśvakarman) (gave birth) to a son (called) Manu. The twins Yamunā and Yama were born (to Rājñī). Chāyā gave birth to Sāvarṇi, Śani, Tapatī and Viṣṭi. Saṁjñā gave birth to Vaivasvata Manu and again the Aśvins[1].

5-6. Vaivasvata Manu had eight sons best of all but not equal to him—Ikṣvāku, Nābhāga, Dhṛṣṭa, Śaryāti, Nariṣyanta, Prāṁśu, Karuṣa and Pṛṣadhra. They were of great prowess and lived in Ayodhyā.

7. Ilā was the daughter (of Manu). Purūravas (was born) to her through Budha. That Ilā (again) became Sudyumna (a male) after delivering Purūravas.

8-10a. The three kings Utkala, Gaya and Vinatāśva were from Sudyumna. The country of Utkala was given to Utkala, the western part (of the earth) to Vinatāśva and all the quarters to the foremost king Gaya (with his capital at) Gayāpurī. Sudyumna obtained Pratiṣṭhāna by the words of

1. For an account relating to Saṁjñā and Chāyā See *Liṅg.* P. 65. 3-14.

Vasiṣṭha. After getting the kingdom, Sudyumna gave it away to Purūravas.

10b-11. Śakas (were) the sons of Nariṣyanta. Ambarīṣa, a devotee of (Lord) Viṣṇu (was the son) of Nābhāga and a protector of the people. The race of Dhārṣṭaka (was) from Dhṛṣṭa. Sukanya and Ānarta (were the sons) of Śaryāti. King Vairohya (was the son) of Ānarta.

12-16. Kuśasthalī became the domain of Ānarta. The virtuous Raivata, known as Kakudmin was the eldest among the hundred sons of Reva. He got the kingdom of Kuśasthalī. He heard the science of music from Brahmā in the company of his daughter. In moment of the god passed ages of the world of mortals. He returned to his city hurriedly surrounded by the Yādavas. He made the beautiful Dvāravatī (Dvārakā) having many doors (as his capital) guarded by the Bhojas, Vṛṣṇis and Andhakas led by Vāsudeva and others. He gave away (his daughter) Revatī of spotless beauty in marriage to Baladeva. Then he performed penance on the peak of the Sumeru mountain and reached the abode of (Lord) Viṣṇu.

17. Nābhāga had two sons, that were *Vaiśyas*, who became brahmins (later on). Kārūṣas (were born) from Karūṣa, who were of the warrior caste that were invincible.

18. Pṛṣadhra became a *śudra* on account of killing the cow of his preceptor. Vikukṣi, the divine ruler, was born from Ikṣvāku, the son of Manu.

19-20. Kakutstha was born from Vikukṣi and Suyodhana was his son. Pṛthu was his son. Viśvagāśva was the son of Pṛthu. His son was Āyus. Yuvanāśva was his son. Śrāvanta was born from Yuvanāśva. The city of Śrāvantikā in the east (was his capital).

21. Bṛhadaśva was born from Śrāvanta. Kuvalāśva was the next king. He got the name Dhundhumāra (as he killed a demon) named Dhundhu[1] in olden days.

22. The three kings Dṛḍhāśva, Daṇḍa and Kapila (were the sons) of Dhundhumāra. Haryaśva and Pramodaka (were born) from Dṛḍhāśva.

---

1. See *Vi. P.* IV. 2 40.

23. Nikumbha (was born) from Haryaśva and Saṁhatasva from Nikumbha. Akṛśāśva and Ranāśva were the two sons of Saṁhatāśva.

24. Yuvanāśva (was the son) of Raṇāśva. Māndhātṛ (was born) from Yuvanāśva. Purukutsa was (born) from Māndhātṛ. Mucukunda (was his) second (son).

25. Trasadasyu and Sambhūta[1] (were born) from Purukutsa through Narmadā. Sudhanvā was (born) from Sambhūta. Then Tridhanvā (was born) from Sudhanvā.

26. Taruṇa (was born) from Tridhanvā and Satyavrata (was) his son. Satyaratha (was born) from Satyavrata. Hariścandra (was) his son.

27-29. Rohitāśva (was born) from Hariścandra. Vṛka was (born) from Rohitāśva[2]. Bāhu (was born) from Vṛka and Sagara from Bāhu. His dear (wife) Prabhā was the mother of sixty thousand sons. (His other wife) Bhānumatī[3] (gave birth) to Asamañjasa from that king by the grace of the pleased (sage) Aurva. The sons of Sagara were burnt by Viṣṇu (Lord Viṣṇu in the form of sage Kapila) as they were digging up the earth. Aṁśumān (was born) from Asamañjasa. Dilīpa was (born) from Aṁśumān.

30. Bhagīratha (was born) from Dilīpa. He brought down the Ganges (from the heaven). Nābhāga (was born) from Bhagīratha and Ambarīṣa from Nābhāga.

31. Sindhudvīpa (was born) from Ambarīṣa. Śrutāyu is known to be his son. Rtuparna was (born) from Śrutāyu. Kalmāsapāda (was) his son.

32. Sarvakarmā (was born) from Kalmāṣapāda. Anaraṇya was (born) from him. Nighna (was born) from Anaraṇya, Anamitra (from Anaraṇya) and Raghu (from Anamitra).

33. Dilīpa was (born) from Raghu. Aja (was) the (next) king (born) from Dilīpa. Dīrghabāhu (was born) from Aja and Kāla and Ajāpāla were (born in order).

---

1. Differs from *Vi. P.* IV. 3. 17 Anaraṇya was born from Trasadasyu.

2. The list here omits certain names. See *Vi. P.* IV. 3. 25.

3. The names of the wives of Sagara differ from *Vi. P.* IV. 4. 1.

34-35. Then Daśaratha was born. He had four sons who were all partial manifestations of (Lord) Nārāyaṇa (Viṣṇu). Rāma was the eldest among his (sons). That foremost of the Raghus was the ruler at Ayodhyā and the Killer of (the demon) Rāvaṇa. (Sage) Vālmīki composed his life accounts after hearing that from (sage) Nārada.

36. Kuśa and Lava, the furtherers of the family, (were) the sons of Rāma through Sītā. Atithi was born from Kuśa. Niṣadha (was) his son.

37. Nala was born from Niṣadha. Nabha was born from Nala. Puṇḍarīka was (born) from Nabha. Then Sudhanvā was born.

38. Devānīka (was born) from Sudhanvā and Ahīnāśva was his son. Sahasrāśva (was born) from Ahīnāśva and Candrāloka was born then.

39. Tārāpīḍa (was born) from Candrāloka. Candraparvata (was born) from him. Bhānuratha (was born) from Candragiri (parvata). Śrutāyu was his son. These are known to be the descendants of the Ikṣvāku family that bore (the name of) the Solar race.

CHAPTER TWO HUNDRED AND SEVENTY-FOUR

Description of the Lunar race

Fire-god said :

1. I shall describe the Lunar race. It would destroy the sin of one who reads it. Brahmā was born from the navel-lotus of (Lord) Viṣṇu. (Sage) Atri was the son of Brahmā. (Soma was born) from Atri.

2-5. Soma performed the Rājasūya (sacrifice) and gave away (the suzerainty over) the three worlds as the fees (for the priest). When the final (bathing) was finished, the wives of the mortals who desired to look at his (beautiful) form served him being tormented by the arrows of the god of love. (Goddess) Lakṣmī deserted (lord) Nārāyaṇa. Sinīvālī, Dyuti,

Puṣṭi, Prabhā, Kuhū, Kīrti, Vasu and Dhṛti respectively deserted Kardama, Vibhāvasu, the undecaying Dhātā, Prabhākara, Haviṣmān, (the husband) Jayanta, Mārīca Kaśyapa and (husband) Nandī and entertained Soma alone then.

6-7. Soma also bestowed his affection on them as if they were his wives. The husbands of these (women) were not able to curse him or (punish him) with the weapons, although he had done a misdeed, as he had obtained suzerainty over the seven worlds by means of his penance.

8-10. Being influenced by their submission his mind faltered. Soma seduced hastily the glorious Tārā, the wife of Bṛhaspati (the preceptor of the celestials) and thus insulted the son of Aṅgiras (Bṛhaspati). On account of this (incident) there was the battle well-known as Tārakāmaya (involving the celestials) between the celestials and the demons causing great destruction to the world. Brahmā (intervened and) prevailed upon Uśanas (preceptor of the demons) (to shed his wrath) and entrusted Tārā to (the care of) Aṅgiras (Bṛhaspati).

11. Guru (Bṛhaspati) finding her pregnant said to her "Shed the child in the womb". The child that was delivered was effulgent and said "I am the son of Moon".

12-13. Thus Budha was born from Soma. Purūravas was his son. The nymph Urvaśī deserted heaven and was enamoured of him. O Great sage ! The king spent fiftynine years with her.

14. There was only one fire in days of yore which was made into three by him.[1] Purūravas practised *yoga* and reached the world of the Gandharvas.

15. Urvaśī (wife of Purūravas) gave birth to the kings Āyus, Dṛḍhāyus, Aśvāyus, Ghanāyus, Dhṛtimān, Vasu, Divijāta and Śatāyus[2].

16-19. Nahuṣa, Vṛddhaśarman, Raji, Darbha and Vipāpmā were the sons of Āyus. Raji had a hundred sons known as Rājeyas. Raji having obtained a boon from (Lord) Viṣṇu killed

1. For a detailed account see *Vi. P.* IV. 6. 77-94.

2. Sons are said to be only six in the *Purāṇas* and *MBh.*—Āyu, Dhīmān, Amāvasu, Dṛḍhāyu, and Śatāyu. See *MBh.* Ādi. 75.24-25.

the demons on the request of the celestials. He gave the status of a son to Indra and bestowed his kingdom on him and ascended the heavens (to fight with the demons). But the kingdom of Indra was usurped by the wicked sons of Raji. Bṛhaspati deluded the sons of Raji and restored that (kingdom) to Indra by means of performing the appeasing (rites) of the planets. Then they (the sons of Raji) became the followers of their own *dharma*.

20. Nahuṣa had seven sons—Yati, Yayāti, Uttama, Udbhava, Pañcaka, Śaryāti and Meghapālaka.

21-23. Yati, even as a boy, contemplated on (Lord) Viṣṇu and attained Him. Then Devayānī, the daughter to Śukra (the preceptor of the demons), became the wife of Yayāti. Then Śarmiṣṭhā, the daughter of Vṛṣaparva (became the wife) of Yayāti and had five sons. Devayānī gave birth to Yadu and Turvasu. Śarmiṣṭhā, the daughter of Vṛṣaparva (gave birth) to Druhya, Anu and Pūru. Yadu and Pūru, among them, (became) the founders of dynasties.

CHAPTER TWO HUNDRED AND SEVENTY-FIVE

Description of the dynasty of Yadu

Fire-god said :

1. Yadu had five sons—Nīlāñjika, Raghu, Kroṣṭu, Śatajit and Sahasrajit and Sahasrajit was the eldest among them.

2. Śatajit had three (sons)—Haihaya, Reṇuhaya and Haya. Dharmanetra (was the son) of Haihaya. Saṁhana (was the son) of Dharmanetra.

3. Mahimā was (the son) of Saṁhana. Bhadrasenaka (was born) from Mahimā. Durgama was (born) from Bhadrasena. Kanaka was (born) from Durgama.

4. Kṛtavīrya, Kṛtāgni, Karavīraka and Kṛtaujas were the four (sons) of Kanaka. Arjuna (Kārtavīryārjuna) (was born) from Kṛtavīrya.

5-9. Suzerainty over the seven continents of the earth, (possession of) thousand arms and invincibility by the enemy in the battle and certain death at the hands of (Lord) Viṣṇu in case of leading an unrighteous life were conferred on (Kārtavīrya) Arjuna who was doing penance. That king Arjuna performed ten thousand sacrifices. By the remembrance of him (his name) there was no loss of property in the kingdom. The kings would not certainly attain the position of Kārtavīrya by (doing) sacrifices, (giving) gifts, (performing) penances, by valour and by learning. Among the hundred sons of Kārtavīrya (the following) five (were) foremost—Śūrasena, Śūra, Dhṛṣṭokta, Kṛṣṇa and Jayadhvaja. (Jayadhvaja) was a great king among the Āvantayas.

10-11. Tālajaṅgha (was born) from Jayadhvaja. The sons of Tālajaṅgha formed the five branches of the Haihayas—Bhojas, Āvantas, Vītihotras, Svayaṁjātas and Śauṇḍikeyas. Ananta was (born) from Vītihotra. Durjaya (was) king from Ananta.

12. I shall describes the race of Kroṣṭu in which (Lord) Hari Himself was born. Vṛjinīvān (was born) from Kroṣṭu. Svāhā was (born) from Vṛjinīvān.

13. Ruṣadgu (was) the son of Svāhā and Citraratha (was) his son. Śaśabindu (was born) from Citraratha. He was a great monarch and a staunch devotee of (Lord) Hari.

14-15. Among the ten thousand intelligent, handsome, wealthy and radiant sons of Śaśabindu, Pṛthuśrava was the foremost. Suyajñaka was his son. Uśanas (was) the son of Suyajña. Titikṣu (was) the son of Uśanas.

16-18. Marutta was (born) from Titikṣu. Kambalabarhiṣa (was born) from him. (Rukmakavaca was born from him). Fifty (sons) were (born) from Rukmakavaca (among whom) Rukmeṣu, Pṛthurukmaka, Havis, Jyāmagha and Pāpaghna (were) most prominent. Jyāmagha was a hen-pecked husband. Vidarbha was (born) from Jyāmagha through Sevyā. Kauśika, Lomapāda and Kratha (were) his sons. From the excellent Lomapāda, Kṛti (was born) and Cidi (was) the son of Kauśika. His successor kings were hence known as Caidyas.

19. Kunti (was born) from Kratha, the son of Vidarbha.

Dhṛṣṭaka (was the son) of Kunti. Nidhṛti (was the son) of Dhṛṣṭa. His (son was) known as Udarka. Vidūratha (was his son).

20. Vyoma (was) the son of Daśārha (Vidūratha). It is said that Jīmūta was (born) from Vyoma. Vikala was the son of Jīmūta. Bhīmaratha (was) his son.

21. Navaratha (was born) from Bhīmaratha. Dṛḍharatha was (born) then. Śakunti (was born) from Dṛḍharatha. Karambhaka (was) from Śakunti.

22. Devarāta was from Karambha. Devakṣetra was his son. (A son) by name Madhu (was) from Devakṣetra. Dravarasa was from Madhu.

23. Puruhūta was from Dravarasa. Jantu was his son. Sātvata, the Yādava king of good quality, (was) the son of Jantu.

24. Bhajamāna, Vṛṣṇi, Andhaka and Devāvṛdha were the four (sons) of Sātvata. Their races were renowned.

25-26. Bāhya, Vṛṣṭi, Kṛmi and Nimi were (the sons) of Bhajamāna. Babhru was from Devāvṛdha. The following verse is sung about him: "We hear his virtues sung close by (in the same way) as we had heard from a distant place. Babhru is the foremost among men and (considered) by the celestials as equal to Devāvṛdha."

27. Babhru (had) four sons. (Those were) kings and devotees of (Lord) Vāsudeva (Hari). (They were Kuhura, Bhajamāna, Śini and Kambalabarhiṣ.

28. Dhṛṣṇu (was the son) of Kuhura. Dhṛti (was) the son of Dhṛṣṇu. Kapotaromā was from Dhṛti. Tittiri (was) his son.

29. Nara (was) the son of Tittiri. Candanadundubhi (was) his (son). Punarvasu (was) his son. Āhuka (was) the son of Āhukī (wife of Punarvasu).

30-33. Devaka was born from Āhuka and Ugrasena was born then. Devavān and Upadeva are known to be the sons of Devaka. They had seven sisters. (Devaka) gave them in marriage to Vasudeva. They were Devakī, Śrutadevī, Mitradevī, Yaśodharā, Śrīdevī, Satyadevī and Surāpī. Ugrasena had nine sons among whom Kaṁsa was the eldest, (the others being) Nyagrodha, Sunāman, Kaṅku, Śaṅku (the protector of earth), Sutanū, Rāṣṭrapāla, Yuddhamuṣṭi and Sumuṣṭika.

34. Vidūratha, the chief among the charioteers (was) the son of Bhajamāna. The powerful king Śūra was the son of Vidūratha.

35. Śoṇāśva and Śvetavāhana (were) the two sons of that mighty monarch. Śamī, Śatrujit and others were the five sons of Śoṇāśva.

36-37. Pratikṣetra (was) the son of Śamī and Bhojaka (was the son) of Pratikṣetra. Hṛdika (was) the son of Bhoja. Hṛdika had ten sons—Kṛtavarmā, Śatadhanvā, Devārha, Bhīṣaṇa and others. Kambalabarhis (was born) from Devārha. Asamaujas was (then born from Kambalabarhis).

38-39. Sudaṁṣṭra, Suvāsa and Dhṛṣṭa were (born) from Asamaujas. Gāndhārī and Mādrī were the wives of Dhṛṣṭa. Sumitra was born to Gāndhārī. Mādrī gave birth to Yudhājit. Anamitra and Śini (were the descendants) from Dhṛṣṭa. Devamīḍhuṣa (was born) then.

40-43. Nighna (was) the son of Anamitra. Prasenaka and Satrājit (were the sons) of Nighna. When Prasena was wearing the *syamantaka* jewel got from Sun god by Satrājit and wandering in the forest, a lion killed him and carried away the gem. The lion was killed by Jāmbavān (the king of bears) and Jāmbavān was conquered by (Lord) Hari (Viṣṇu). He got the jewel and Jāmbavatī (the daughter of Jāmbavān) and went to the city of Dvārakā (on the western coast of India in Gujarat). (He) gave (the gem) to Satrājit. Śatadhanu killed him (Satrājit). The famous Kṛṣṇa killed Śatadhanu, recovered the gem and entrusted the gem to Akrūra in the presence of Bala (deva) and the Yādava chiefs.

44. Kṛṣṇa thus got rid of the false accusation on him that he had killed Satrājit. One who reads (this account) would go to the heaven. Satyabhāmā (the daughter of Satrājit) became the wife of Kṛṣṇa.

45. Śini was born from Anamitra. Satyaka (was) the son of Śini. Sātyaki was born from Satyaka. Dhuni was (born) from Yuyudhāna (Sātyaki).

46. Yugandhara (was) the son of Dhuni. Svāhya was (born from him). He was invincible in battle. Ṛṣabha and Kṣetraka (were) his (sons). Śvaphalkaka (was born) from Ṛṣabha.

47. Akrūra (was) the son of Śvaphalka. Sudhaṁvaka (was born) from Akrūra. Vasudeva and others (were born) from Śūra. Pṛthā (Kuntī) was the wife of Pāṇḍu.

48. Yudhiṣṭhira was born to Kuntī (wife) of Pāṇḍu, from Dharma (god of virtue), Vṛkodara (Bhīmasena) from Vāya (Wind god), Dhanañjaya (Arjuna) from Indra and Nakula and Sahadeva to Mādrī (the other wife of Pāṇḍu).

49-51. (Bala) rāma, Sāraṇa and Durdama (were born) to Rohiṇī from Vasudeva. Susenaka was born first. to Vasudeva through Devakī. (The other sons were) Kīrtimān, Bhadraṣena, Jārukhya, Viṣṇudāsaka and Bhadradeha. Kaṁsa killed these six childern. Then Bala (rāma), Kṛṣṇa, Subhadrā, that speaks sweet and Cārudeṣṇa (were born). Sāmba and others were the sons of Jāmbavatī from Kṛṣṇa.

CHAPTER TWO HUNDRED AND SEVENTYSIX

The manifestations of Lord Viṣṇu

Fire-god said :

1-2. (The patriarch) Kaśyapa manifested as Vasudeva and Aditi (his wife) as the excellent Devakī. Kṛṣṇa was born to Devakī and Vasudeva being endowed with penance for the sake of the protection of righteousness, removal of unrighteousness, protection of the celestials and others and the destruction of the demons and others.

3-5a. Rukmiṇī, Satyabhāmā, Satyā, Nāgnajitī, Gāndhārī, Lakṣmaṇā, Mitravindā, Kālindī, Jāmbavatī, Suśīlā, Mādrī, Kauśalyā, Vijayā, Jayā and others were the sixteen thousand wives (of Kṛṣṇa) among whom Satyabhāmā served (Lord) Hari (Kṛṣṇa).

5b-6. Pradyumna and others were born to Kṛṣṇa through Rukmiṇī, Bhīma and others through Satyabhāmā, Sāmba and others through Jāmbavatī and thus were among the one hundred thousand sons of that wise man.

7-9. Yâdavas were eighty thousand that were protected by (Lord) Kṛṣṇa. Pradyumna (son of Kṛṣṇa) had Aniruddha, who was fond of war, as his son through Vaidarbhī. The mighty Yādavas Vajra and others (were the sons) of Aniruddha. Thus there were three crores and sixty lakhs of Yâdavas. He (Kṛṣṇa) appeared for the destruction of the demons that afflicted men. (Lord) Hari (Viṣṇu) is born as a mortal in order to regularise the duties (of men).

10. There were twelve battles between the celestials and the demons for the sake of their (legitimate) portions. The first (war of Viṣṇu was in) the man-lion form. The second war (was) as a dwarf.

11. The battle (fought) as the boar (was) the next one. The fourth one was for the churning of the nectar. The sixth one was the battle involving all the celestial bodies for the sake of resuscitation.

12. (The seventh one was the destruction of) the three cities. (The eighth one was for) the destruction of (the demon) Andhaka. The ninth one (was) the killing of (the demon) Vṛtra. The deadly (poison of) hālāhala was conquered (in the tenth one). (The demom) Kolāhala (was subdued in the next one).

13. (The next one was) the form as the man-lion, the protector of the celestials in olden days, that pierced the chest of (the demon) Hiraṇyakaśipu with his nails and made Prahlāda the king.

14. In (the dispute between) the celestials and the demons, (the Lord) was born of Kaśyapa and Aditi as a dwarf, deceived the powerful (demon) Bali and restored the kingdom to Indra.

15. The manifestation as a boar (was made by Lord Viṣṇu) and the demon Hiraṇyākṣa was killed, protecting the celestials thus. He lifted up the earth that got submerged and was praised by the celestials.

16. (The mount) Mandara was made the churning rod, (the serpent) Vāsuki as the string and (the ocean) was churned by the celestials and the demons. The ambrosia (that was obtained) was given to the celestials.

17. The celestials were in the same way protected at the time of the battle of the stars after preventing Indra, Guru, the

celestials and demons (from a combat) and thus the Lunar race was made to flourish.

18. (The sages) Viśvāmitra, Vasiṣṭha, Atri and Brahmā protected the celestials in the battle after warding off the demons that were having infatuation and hatred.

19. Lord Hari (Viṣṇu) was the refuge of (Lord) Īśāna (Śiva) that had (Lord) Brahmā as the charioteer of the earth, the chariot. The protector of the celestials and the destroyer of the demons burnt the three cities.

20. (Lord) Rudra (Śiva) was attacked by (the demon) Andhaka desirous of carrying away Gaurī (consort of Śiva). (Lord) Hari, who was fond of (his beloved) Revatī killed the demon Andha.

21. (Lord) Viṣṇu became the foam of the water at the time of the battle between the celestials and the demons and killed (the demon) Vṛtra that afflicted the celestials, and protected the virtues of the celestials.

22. (Lord) Hari, (manifested as) Paraśurāma, conquered the demons such as Śālva and protected the celestials after killing the wicked *kṣatriyas* (kings).

23. Madhusūdana (the destroyer of demon Madhu) took away the demon of Hālāhala poison from Maheśvara and destroyed the fear of the celestials.

24. The demon Kolāhala was conquered by Him at the battle of the celestials and demons. All the celestials were protected by (Lord) Viṣṇu by protecting righteousness.

25. The kings, princes, sages and the gods are the manifestations of (Lord) Hari, whether (their names) have been narrated or not (in the traditional list).

CHAPTER TWO HUNDRED AND SEVENTY-SEVEN

The narration of the lineage of Aṅga

Fire-god said :

1. Varga (was) the son of Turvasu. Gobhānu was his son. Traiśāni was (born) from Gobhānu. Karandhama (was the son) of Taraiśāni.

2. Marutta was (born) from Karandhama. Duṣyanta (was) his son. Varūtha was (the son) of Duṣyanta. Gāṇḍīra (was born) from Varūtha.

3. Gāndhāra (was born) from Gāṇḍīra. The mighty five peoples—Gāndhāras, Keralas, Colas, Pāṇḍyas and Kolas (were born) then.

4. Druhyu and Babhrusetu[1] (were the sons of Gāndhāra). Purovasu (was born) from Babhrusetu. Then Gāndhāra (was born) and Dharma from Gāndhāra. Ghṛta was (born) from Dharma.

5. Viduṣa (was born) from Ghṛta. Pracetas (was born) from him. He had a hundred sons (among whom) Ānadra, Sabhānara, Cākṣuṣa and Parameṣuka (were foremost).

6. Kālānala (was born) from Sabhānara. Sṛñjaya, was born from Kālānala. Purañjaya (was the son) of Sṛñjaya. Janamejaya was his son.

7-8. Mahāśāla (was) his son. Mahāmanas was his son. O Brahman ! Uśīnara (was) from him. He had then a son Nṛga through (his queen) Nṛgā, (a son) Nara through (his queen) Narā and (a son) Kṛmi (through) Kṛmi. Suvrata was born (to him) through Dṛṣadvatī.

9. Pṛthudarbha, Vīraka, Kaikeya and Bhadraka were the four sons of Śibi. There were prosperous regions in their names.

10. Titikṣu was born from Uśīnara. Ruṣadratha (was born) from Titikṣu. Paila was (born) from Ruṣadratha. Sutapā (was) the son of Paila.

11. The great ascetic Bali (was born) from him. Aṅga, Vaṅga, Mukhyaka, Puṇḍra and Kaliṅga (were the sons) of Bali. Bali, the ascetic, (generated them) by means of his power.

---

1. Given as two separate names and subsequent names also differ. See *Vi. P.* IV. 17.

12. Dadhivāhana was (born) from Aṅga. Diviratha (was the next) king after him. Dharmaratha (was born) from Diviratha. Citraratha (was) his son.

13. Satyaratha (was born) from Citraratha. Lomapāda (was) his son. Caturaṅga (was born) from Lomapāda. Pṛthulākṣa (was) his son.

14. Campa was (born) from Pṛthulākṣa. Haryaṅgaka was from Campa. Bhadraratha was from Haryaṅga. Bṛhatkarman (was) his son.

15. Bṛhadbhānu was born from him. Bṛhātmavat (was) from Bṛhadbhānu. Jayadratha was from him. Bṛhadratha (was born) from Jayadratha.

16. Viśvajit (was born) from Bṛhadratha. Karṇa was from Viśvajit. Vṛṣasena (was the son) of Karṇa. Pṛthusena was his son. These are the kings born in the race of Aṅga. Describe me the race of Puru.

CHAPTER TWO HUNDRED AND SEVENTY-EIGHT

The description of the lineage of Puru

Fire-god side :

1. Janamejaya was (born) from Puru. Prācīnavān was his son. Manasyu was from Prācīnavān. Vītamaya (was) the (next) king from him.

2. Śundhu was from Vītamaya. Bahuvidha was the son of Śundhu. Saṁyāti (was) from Bahuvidha. Rahovādī[1] (was) his son.

3-4. Bhadrāśva (was) his son. Bhadrāśva had ten sons—Ṛkṣeyu, Kṛṣeyu, Sannateyu, Ghṛteyu, Citeyu, the noble Sthaṇḍileyu, Dharmeyu, Sannateyu (?), Kṛteyu and Matināra.

5. Taṁsurodha, Pratiratha and Purasta were the sons of Matināra. Kaṇva was (born) from Pratiratha. Medhātithi was from Kaṇva.

1. Names differ from *VI. P.* IV. 19.

6-8. Duṣyanta, Pravīra, Sumanta and Vīra (were) the four (sons) from Taṁsurodha. Bharata was (born) from Duṣyanta through Śakuntalā. The descendants known as Bhāratas were mighty. When the sons of Bharata were lost on account of the wrath of the mother, then the Maruts (gods) brought Bharadvāja, son of Bṛhaspati and made (him) to meet (Bharata). Vitatha was born as a consequence of rituals (done by Bharadvāja).

9-11. That Vitatha also generated five sons—Suhotra, Suhotṛ, Gaya, Garbha and the great Suketu. Kapila had two sons—Kauśika and Gṛtsapati. The brahmins, warriors, tradesmen were the sons of Gṛtsapati. The Dīrghatamas were the sons of Kāśi (Kauśika ?). Dhanvantari was (born) then. Ketumān was his son.

12. Hemaratha (was born) from Ketumān. He was well-known as Divodāsa. Pratardana (was) from Divodāsa. Bharga and Vatsa (were born) from Pratardana.

13. Anarka was from Vatsa. Kṣemaka was born from Anarka. Varṣaketu (was) from Kṣemaka. Vibhu is remembered (to be) from Varṣaketu.

14. Ānarta was the son of Vibhu. Sukumāraka (was the son) of Vibhu. Satyaketu (was born) from Sukumāra. Vatsabhūmi (was born) from Vatsaka.

15. Bṛhat (was) the son of Suhotra. Ajamīḍha, Dvimīḍha and the brave Purumīḍha were the three sons of Bṛhat.

16. The valorous Jahnu was born to Ajamīḍha and Keśinī. Ajakāśva was born from Jahnu. Balākāśva (was) his son.

17. Kuśika (was the son) of Balākāśva, and Gādhi, the Indra, (was born) from Kuśika. Satyavatī (was) the daughter of Gādhi and Viśvāmitra his excellent son.

18-20. Devarata and Katimukha were the sons of Viśvāmitra. Śunaḥśepa (known also as) Aṣṭaka (was) the other (son). Śānti was born as son to Ajamīḍha through Nīlinī. Purujāti (was born) from (Su) Śānti. Bāhyāśva (was born) from Purujāti. The five kings Mukula, Sṛñjaya, Bṛhadiṣu, Yavīnara and Kṛmila (were) from Bāhyāśva. They were known as the Pāñcālas.

21-23. (The descendants) of Mukula, (known as) the Maukulyas were brahmins endowed with property. Cañcāśva was born from Mukula. Cañcāśva had the twins—Divodāsa and Ahalyā. Śatānanda (was born) from Śaradvata through Ahalyā. Satyadhṛk (was born) from Śatānanda. Then a pair, Kṛpa and Kṛpī, (were born from Satyadhṛk). Maitreya (was born) from Divodāsa and then Somapa (from Maitreya). Pañcadhanus (was born) from Sṛñjaya. Somadatta was his son.

24. Sahadeva (was born) from Somadatta. Somaka (was born) from Sahadeva. Jantu was from Somaka. Pṛṣata (was) the son of Jantu.

25. Drupada (was) from Pṛṣata. Dhṛṣṭadyumna (was) from him. Dhṛṣṭaketu was his son. Ṛkṣa was born to Ajamīḍha through Dhūminī.

26. Saṁvaraṇa was born from Ṛkṣa. Kuru (was) then (born) from Saṁvaraṇa. He migrated from (the city of) Prayāga and founded (the kingdom of) Kurukṣetra.

27. Sudhanvā, Sudhanu, Parikṣit and Arimejaya (were the sons) of Kuru. Suhotra was from Sudhanvā. Cyavana was born from Suhotra.

28-29. Seven other sons such as Bṛhadratha, Kuśa, Vīra, Yadu, Pratyagraha, Bala and Matsyakālī, were born through (his queen) Girikā by propitiating (the sage) Vasiṣṭha. Kuśāgra was from King Brhadratha. Vṛṣabha was born from Kuśāgra and Satyahita was his son.

30. (His son was) Sudhanvā, Ūrja was his son. Sambhava was (born) from Ūrja. Jarāsandha (was) from Sambhava. Sahadeva was his son.

31. Udāpi (was born) from Sahadeva. Śrūtakarmaka (was born) from Udāpi. The righteous Janamejaya was the descendant of Parikṣit.

32. Trasadasyu (was born) from Janamejaya. Suratha, Śrutasena, Ugrasena and Bhīmasena (are) the names of the sons of Jahnu.

33. Janamejaya had two sons Suratha and Mahimān. Vidūratha was born from Suratha. Ṛkṣa was born from Vidūratha.

34. Bhīmasena was the son of Ṛkṣa[1] the second. Pratīpa (was) from Bhīmasena. Śantanu (was the son) of Pratīpa.

35. Devāpi, Bālhika and Somadatta (were born) from Śantanu. Somadatta, Bhūri, Bhūriśravas and Śala were born from Bālhika.

36-38. Śantanu had Bhīṣma through Gaṅgā and Vicitravīryaka through Kālī (Satyavatī). Kṛṣṇa Dvaipāyana begot Dhṛtarāṣṭra, Pāṇḍu, and Vidura through the wife of Vicitravīrya. Yudhiṣṭhira, Bhīmasena and Arjuna were the three sons of Pāṇḍu through Kuntī and Nakula and Sahadeva through Mādrī by divine agency. Saubhadra (Abhimanyu born to Subhadrā) (was the son) of Arjuna. Parikṣit (was born) from Abhimanyu.

39-40. Draupadī was the wife of the Pāṇḍavas. Through her Prativindhya was born to Yudhiṣṭhira, (Śrutasena) from Bhīmasena, Śrutakīrti from Dhanañjaya (Arjuna), Śrutavarmā from Sahadeva and Śatānīka was the (son) of Nakula. Ghaṭotkaca was another (son) of Bhīmasena through Hiḍimbā.

41. These are the past and future kings. There is no count of their numbers. O Brahmin! They have gone along with the passage of time. Lord Hari (Viṣṇu) is really the time. Hence one should worship Him. Hence one should offer oblation to fire intended for Him that would yield all the desires.

CHAPTER TWO HUNDRED AND SEVENTY-NINE

The description of the potent remedies

Fire-god said :

1. I shall describe the science of medicine, that was propounded by lord Dhanvantari to Suśruta, the essence that would revive the dead.

Suśruta said :

2. Describe to me the science of medicine that would cure

1. See verse 25 for Ṛkṣa, the first.

the diseases of men, horses and elephants and also the potent combinations and potent charms that would revive the dead.

Dhanvantari said :

3-7. One that is having fever should be made to fast by the physician protecting his strength and then feed him with gruel made of fried paddy and dry ginger. The patient having thirst at the end of the fever (should be given) water boiled with *musta* (cyprerus rotundus), *parpaṭa* (oldenlandia), *uśira* (the fragrant root of a plant), sandal, *udicya* (a kind of perfume) and dry ginger. After six days, (the patient) may be made to drink pungent food certainly. After the disorder has subsided, (medicated) oil should be rubbed (on the body). Then purgative should be given. Old *nivāra* (rice grown without cultivation), *ṣaṣṭika* (a kind of rice), red paddy and *pramodaka* (a kind of rice) and similar things and barley converted into any form are the favourite (food) at (the time of) fever. Green gram, *masūra* (a kind of pulse), chick-pea, horse-gram, saussurea, *āḍhaka* (a kind of pulse), *nāraka* (?), *karkoṭaka* (a kind of paddy), *kaṭolbaka* (?), snake-gourd, neem together with the fruits, *parpaṭa* and pomegranates (could safely be used by a patient) having fever.

8. An emetic is commended in the case of downward hemorrhage and a purgative in upward (hemorrhage). The six constituents[1] except the dry ginger (should be given) as the drink.

9-10. Flour of barley, wheat, fried paddy, barley, *Śāli* (a kind of rice), *masūra*, *makuṣṭha* (a kind of rice), chick-pea, green-gram and eatables (made) of wheat mixed with ghee and milk are beneficial. Honey and the juice of *vṛṣa* (a kind of drug) are good. Eating old *śāli* rice is beneficial in dysentry.

11. The food that does not cause excessive (motion), and that mixed with the barks of *lodhra* (a kind of tree) are commended. One should avoid taking food that causes excess of wind. One should always make (extra) efforts in (treating) the enlargement of spleen.

12. (Those suffering from dropsy) should take fried barley with milk. *Vāstūka* (chenopodium album) mixed with ghee,

1. These are *musta, parpaṭaka* etc. noticed in verse 4 above.

wheat, *śāli* rice and bitter things are beneficial for those having dropsy.

13-14a. Wheat, *śāli* rice, green gram, cow's urine, *ṛkṣa*, *khadira*, *abhayā*, *pañcakola* (the five spices—long pepper etc.), venison, neem, *dhātri* (a variety of myrobalan), snake-gourd, the juice of citron, nutmeg, dried radish and *saindhava* (a kind of rock-salt) (are good for dropsy).

14b-16. Water (boiled) with *khadira* is commended as a drink for those affected with leprosy. (Similarly) *masūra* (a kind of pulse) and green-gram (with water should be given) for drinking. Old *śālī* rice may be eaten. The juice of venison (mixed) with neem and *parpaṭaka* and vegetables, *viḍaṅga* (embelia ribes), black pepper, *musta*, *kuṣṭha*, *lodhra*, natron (are also good). Paste of red arsenic and *vacā* (a kind of aromatic root) with (cow's) urine cures leprosy.

17-19a. Cakes, *kuṣṭha*, *kulmāṣa* (black barley) and barley etc. are beneficial for diabetes. Things made out of cooked barley, green gram, horse-gram, old *śāli* rice, vegetables that are bitter and astringent, bitter green things, oils (extracted) from sesamum, *śigru* (the leaves of a kind of tree), *vibhītaka* (a kind of myrobalan) and *iṅgudi* and greengram, barley, wheat and grains stored for a year (are also good).

19b-21. The juice of venison is commended as food for those suffering from pulmonary consumption. Horse-gram, green-gram, black pepper etc. and dry radish compounded with venison or cakes or bird's flesh or compounded with curd and pomegranade juice, dressed with the juice of citron, honey, grapes and *vyoṣa* (dried ginger, long and black pepper) and cooked barley, wheat and *śāli* rice should be given as food to an asthma patient.

22. Decoction made of the ten kinds of drugs (such as *bṛhatī* etc.), *bala*, *rāsnā* and horse-gram should be drunk with cakes in order to get relief from breathing (difficulty) and hiccough.

23. One should take dry radish, horse-gram, *mūla* (the root of long pepper) and juice of venison mixed with cooked barley, wheat and *śāli* rice and old *uśira*.

24. One who is having a swelling should eat molasses

together with *pathyā* (the long pepper) or molasses with dry ginger. Both buttermilk and *citraka* (a kind of root) are excellent remedies for diarrhoea.

25-26. Old barley, wheat, *sāli* rice, juice of venison, green-gram, *āmalaka* (one variety of myrobalan), dates, grapes, jujube fruits, honey, clarified butter, milk, *sakra*, neem, *parpaṭaka*, *vṛṣa*, buttermilk and *ariṣṭa* are always commended for rheumatic patients.

27-28a. Purgatives should be given to those having heart disease. Long pepper is beneficial for those having hiccough. Buttermilk, gruel made from the fermentation of boiled rice, spirit distilled from molasses together with cold water (are also beneficial). *Muktas*, natron and wine are commended in any distemper due to drunkeness.

28b-30a. A person who has been injured (on the chest) should drink lac together with honey and milk. Wasting diseases could be cured by eating the essence of meat and by protecting the digestive power. One should eat red *śāli*, *nīvāra* and *kalama* varieties of rice, cooked barley, meat, vegetables, natrum and *śaṭi*.

30b-31. In the same way *pathyā* (is beneficial) for piles. Its scum (should be used) with buttermilk and water. *Musta* should be repeatedly used. Ointment with turmeric and *citraka* should be applied. Modified forms of boiled barley, *śāli* rice, *vāstūka* (chenopodium album) and natrum (are also beneficial).

32. Water-melon, cucumber, and wheat mixed with milk, (juice of) sugarcane and ghee are commendable for painful discharge of urine. Scum and wine etc. (are commended) for drinking.

33-34. Fried paddy, flours of fried barley, honey, flesh roasted on a stick, brinjal and gourd are drinks for remedying vomitting. Cooked *śāli* rice, water and milk simply heated or boiled (would be beneficial for the same). Pills of *musta* and molasses held in the mouth would remove thirst.

35-37a. Modified forms of cooked barley, cakes made of dried radish, vegetables, snake-gourd and tender shoots of cane would remedy the stiffness of thigh. One should take food consisting of old wheat, barley, *śāli* rice together with soup made of green-gram *āḍhaka* and *masūra* (different kinds of pulses), sesamum, juice of venison, *saindhava* (a kind of rock-salt), ghee, grapes, dried ginger, *āmalaka* (a kind of myrobalan) and black pepper.

37b-38. One who is having a dry spreading itch (should use) juice of pomegranate together with candied sugar, honey and grapes. Red paddy, wheat, barley, green-gram and other such light (eatables are also beneficial). *Kākamārī*, shoots of cane, *vāstūka* and natrum (may also be used).

39. Water, candied sugar and honey are commended for remedying acute gout. *Dūrvā* (a kind of grass) soaked in ghee is beneficial in nasal diseases.

40. Oil made up of the juice of *bhṛṅgarāja* (a kind of shrub) or the juice of *dhātri* (a variety of myrobalan) (may be used) as sternutatory in all diseases relating to the head.

41-42. O Brahmin ! The eating of sesamum and drinking cold water and eating cold food are said to strengthen teeth and also give supreme satisfaction. Gargling with sesamum oil would also strengthen teeth. The powdered *viḍaṅga* (mixed with) goat's urine is used in destroying all worms.

43. The fruits of *dhātrī* (a variety of myrobalan) and clarified butter are excellent as an ointment for head for the destruction of all diseases relating to head. The food should consist of oily and hot things.

44. Filling ear with oil or the urine of goat is excellent for the destruction of pain in ear. O Brahmin ! All kinds of oysters (may also be used).

45-48. A wick made by compounding red chalk, sandal, lac and buds of *mālati* (a kind of jasmine flower) would cure the whiteness in eye. *Vyoṣa* (dried ginger), long pepper and black pepper) mixed with the *triphalā* (the three myrobalans taken collectively), and water with blue vitriol would cure all eye diseases. The collyrium of blue vitriol will also produce the same result. (If collyrium) fried in ghee, ground on a stone together with *lodhra*, sour gruel and natrum is sprinkled, it would be beneficial in all the diseases of eyes. Application of ointment of red chalk and sandal is commended for the external eye. One should always use *triphalā* (the three kinds of myrobalans) for curing the diseases of the eyes.

49-51a. One who desires to have a long life should take (a mixture of) honey and clarified butter every night. Milk and ghee boiled with the juice of *śatāvari* are known to be the givers of vitality. Similarly *kalambikās*, black-gram, milk and ghee increase vitality. *Triphalā* is known to be the giver of long life (when used) with *madhuka* as before. (The same) together with the juice of *madhuka* would arrest all senile degeneration.

51b-52. O Brahmin ! Ghee heated with *vacā* would destroy the defects due to goblins. Food offered to manes would give intellect and secure all objects. A decoction made of the paste of *balā* is beneficial when besmeared.

53. Oil together with *rāsnā* and *sahacaya* (is good) for deranged wind. Food that does not cause excessive phlegm is commended for abscess.

54. Flours of fried barley made into balls as well as *amlā* are commended (for making the abscess) to ripen. The pulverised neem (is used) to make (the ripened abscess to) open and for healing.

55. The treatment of women after delivery consists mainly of offering oblations to all the creatures. The use of amulet for women after the delivery as well as for animals is always beneficial.

56-60a. Chewing the leaves of neem is the remedy for one bitten by a snake. The (shoots of) palmyrah, *keśya*, old oil, old barley and old ghee (are also good for the same). A fumigation with the plumes of peocock with ghee (is good) for one bitten by a scorpion. A plaster of the seeds of *palāśa* ground with the juice of *arka* (plant) (is also beneficial). Black pepper or yellow myrobalan with the three kinds of myrobalans (is beneficial) for one bitten by a scorpion. If the juice of arka (plant), gingelly oil, flesh and molasses in equal proportion is drunk, it would at once destroy the poison due to (the biting of) a dog that is difficult to cure. The root of rice (if ground) with equal part of *trivṛt* (three kinds of myrobalans) and clarified butter and drunk, it would destroy quickly the poisons due to snakes, and other insects even if they are very powerful.

60b-61. (A mixture of) sandal, *padmaka*, *kuṣṭha*, *latāmbu* (?), *uśira*, *pāṭalā*, *nirguṇḍi*, *śārivā* and *selu* (?) would destroy the poison due to spiders. O Brahmin ! Molasses and dried ginger are commended as eliminator (of toxic matter) from head.

62. Nothing excels oil or ghee for anointing, as a drink or as diuretic. Fire is the best sweating agent. Cold water is the best astringent.

63. The *trivṛt* (the three myrobalans) is the best purgative. So also *madana* is the best emetic. Oil, clarified butter, and honey are the best remedy for (deranged) wind, biles and phlegm, as diuretic, and emetic.

CHAPTER TWO HUNDRED AND EIGHTY

The remedies for all the diseases

Dhanvantari said:

1a. Diseases are considered to be (of four kinds such as), relating to the body, relating to the mind, arising accidentally and arising naturally.

1b-2a. Fever, leprosy and the like (are considered) to be relating to the body. Anger etc. are considered to be relating to the mind. Those that are due to a blow etc. (are known) as accidental. Hunger, old age and the like (are known) as natural.

2b-3. One should give ghee, molasses and salt along with gold to a brahmin on a Sunday in order to get rid of the diseases relating to the body and those that are accidental. One who makes a gift of oil for bathing to a brahmin on a Monday would become free from all diseases.

4. Oil should be given on Saturday. One who makes a gift of food with cow's milk in the (month of) *Āśvina* (October-November), (would also get rid of the diseases). One who bathes the *liṅga* (representative symbol of Lord Śiva) with ghee and milk would become free from diseases.

5. One should offer unto fire *dūrvā* (grass) dipped in the three sweet things (sugar, honey and clarified butter) with (the recitation of) the *gāyatrī* (*mantra*). One should bathe and make the offering in that asterism in which one got the disease.

6. A hymn to (Lord) *Viṣṇu* would remove the diseases that are mental. Listen to me. (I shall describe) the defects (of the humours) wind, bile and phlegm as well as the ingredients of the body (such as blood).

7. O Suśruta ! The food that is eaten gets two forms after leaving the stomach. A part becomes secreted and the other, the constituent fluid of the body.

8. The part that is secreted is the impurity such as feces, urine, sweat, rheum of the eyes, the mucus of the nose, the ear-wax and the bodily impurity.

9-10a. From the constituent fluid, serum (is formed) which again is turned into blood. Flesh (is formed) from blood and then fat and bones from fat. Sap (is formed) from bones and then semen. From semen, complexion and strength (are got).

10b-11a. One should render treatment (to a patient) after examining (the nature of) the country, the disease, the strength, the stamina, the season and the nature (of the patient). Then the strength of the remedy (should also be examined).

11b-14. One should reject the *rikta*[1] days, Tuesdays and Saturdays and baneful (combination) (and begin treatment) after worshipping (Lord) Hari (Viṣṇu), a cow, a brahmin, the Moon and the Sun and the celestials. O Learned one ! Listen to this sacred formula (that has to be recited) before commencing the treatment. "May (the gods) Brahmā, Dakṣa, Aśvins, Rudra, Indra, the Earth, the Moon, the Sun, the Wind, the Fire, the sages, the collection of herbs and the hosts of spirits protect you. Let this medicine be like the elixir of life of the sages, the nectar of the gods and the ambrosia of the outstanding serpents."

15-16. A country abounding in trees and having plenty of water is known as *anūpa* (marshy) and would produce (excess of) wind and phlegm. (A country) that is devoid of (the above features) (is known as) *jāṅgala* (rural or picturesque). A country that has trees and water in moderate proportion is known as *sādhāraṇa* (ordinary). (The country known as) *jāṅgala* (produces) excessive bile. The *sādhāraṇa* (type) is known as moderate.

---

1. The fourth, ninth and fourteenth days of a lunar fortnight.

17. It is said that wind is dry, cool and unsteady, bile is hot like the three kinds of astringents and phlegm is steady, acid, unctuous and sweet.

18. They get increased by things having the same (qualities) and get abated by things having the opposite (qualities). Things that have sweet, sour and saline taste generate phlegm and destroy wind.

19. Those that are pungent, bitter and astringent produce wind and destroy phlegm. Similarly those that are pungent, sour and saline are known to increase bile.

20. Those that are bitter, sweet and astringent destroy bile. This is not the effect of the taste but only of its chemical action.

21. O Suśruta ! Those that are stimulant and hot destroy phlegm and wind. Those that are cold destroy bile. They (the herbs) exert their influence according to their qualities.

22. It is said that phlegm gets collected, deranged and subsided in winter, spring and summer respectively.

23. O Suśruta ! wind is said to get collected, deranged and subsided in the nights of summer, rainy season and autumn (respectively).

24. Bile is said to get collected, deranged and subsided in the rainy season, autumn and fore-winter (respectively).

25. The three (seasons)[1] beginning with the rainy (are said to be) *visargas*. The three (seasons)[2] beginning with winter and ending with summer (are) *ādāna*.

26-31a. The *visarga* relates to the moon and the *ādāna* is stated to be relating to the fire. The moon going round the three seasons such as the rainy etc. by turns produces the three tastes—sour, saline and sweet in order. The sun going round the three seasons such as winter and the like increases the three tastes—bitter, astringent and pungent flavours in order. As the duration of night increases, the strength of men also increases. When they decrease, (the strength) also decreases. During the beginning, middle and end of nights, eating, days and one's

1. Rainy season, autumn and fore-winter.
2. Winter, spring and summer.

age, phlegm, bile and wind get deranged. They are said to get collected before the beginning of their derangement and get appeased after their derangement.

31b-34a. O Brahmin ! All the diseases are caused by excessive eating or not eating or forcing or retaining the flow (of urine etc.). Two parts of the belly should be filled with food, one part with drink and one part should be left free for the wind etc. to work. A remedy is only that which is the opposite of the cause of a disease. This is what should be done. I have described to you the essence.

34b-36a. (Though) it is said that phlegm, bile and wind have their places above and below the umbilical region and the regions of the anus and the buttocks (respectively) in the body, they are capable of coursing through the entire body. Especially wind (can do so). Heart is at the centre of body and it is known to be the place of mind.

36b-39a. It is said that a man of windy temperament would be emaciated, have scanty hair, be fickle-minded, garrulous, have uneven wind, and feel flying in the air in his dream. A man of bilious temperament is said to be having ultimely grey hair. He would be irritable and would perspire copiously. He would be fond of sweets and would see glowing things in dream. A phlegmatic man would have strong body and firm mind. He would be brilliant. He will have glossy hair on the head. He would see clear water in dream.

39b-40a. O The foremost among the sages ! Men of windy, bilious and phlegmatic temperaments are known to be *tāmasa* (inactive), *rājasa* (passionate) and *sāttvika* (virtuous) (respectively).

40b-43a. *Raktapitta* (haemoptysis) (is caused) by excessive coition and engaging in doing hard (physical) work. The wind in the body gets deranged on account of eating bad food or on account of grief. O Brahmin ! Bile gets deranged on account of internal heat, eating hot food, making a journey as well as due to fear. Phlegm gets deranged due to excessive drinking of water, eating heavy food and lying down after eating. A lazy man also gets his phlegm deranged.

43b. After knowing the diseases caused by (humours) wind

and the like from their characteristics, one should remedy them (as below).

44. The characteristics of the disease due to the (deranged) wind are—pain in the bones, bitter taste in the mouth, parched state of feeling in the mouth, yawning and bristling of the pair.

45. A disease due to (deranged) bile is marked by yellowness in the nails, eyes and veins, bitter taste in the mouth, thirst and burning heat (in the body).

46. The characteristics of disease due to phlegm are languor, flow of water (from the mouth), heaviness (of the body), sweet taste in the mouth and longing for heat.

47. (Eating of) oil and hot food, anointing the body with oil and bathing and drinking of oil and the like would appease (deranged) wind. Clarified butter, milk, sugar and the rays of the moon and the like would counter (deranged) bile.

48. The oil of the three myrobalans together with honey and doing exercises etc. would remove (deranged) phlegm. Contemplation on (Lord) Viṣṇu and His worship would appease all the diseases.

CHAPTER TWO HUNDERD AND EIGHTY-ONE

The description of the characteristics of the different tastes and the qualities of the herbs

Dhanvantari said :—

1. Listen to me ! I shall describe the tastes and the other characteristics and merits of the herbs. A physician who knows the properties of the herbs, such as taste, strength and flavour, will be able to save kings and other people.

2. O One possessing powerful arms ! The tastes such as sweet, sour and saline are stated to come from the moon. The tastes—bitter, astringent and pungent—are (known to be) from fire.

3. The herbs have three flavours—bitter, sour and saline. The strength (of the herbs) is said to be of two kinds—hot and cold.

4-5a. O Foremost among the brahmins ! The effect of the herbs is indescribable. Those that are sweet, astringent and bitter are said to be having cold potency. The rest are stated to be hot.

5b-6. Although *guḍuci* has the bitter taste, it is hot on account of its high potency. O One who shows respect ! *Pathyā*, though an astringent, is (considered) hot. Although meat is sweet, it is said to be hot.

7. The saline and sweet tastes would become sweet flavour. The sour things that are hot are also said to become so. The rest would have pungent flavour.

8. One has to determine the drugs that have got modified in their potency and flavour from their efficacy. Honey, although sweet, is said to be pungent in flavour.

9. (The herb) should be boiled with water, sixteen times its proportion, until it comes down to four times the proportion. This is the general rule for (preparing) a decoction wherever (something else) has not been stated.

10-12. The decoction (thus prepared) (should be composed) of water alone. In a decoction prepared with oil, it should be four times that of the drug. A wise man should take equal quantity (of water) to that of the herb. Then the herb and oil should be added. Oil should be one-fourth the measure of the substance. The herb that is free from water would be (known as) extraction in oil. The process of preparing decoctions of the herbs in oil has been explained. O Suśruta ! (The method of preparation) of the lambative is also similar.

13-15a. The decoction that is clear and having little medicinal ingredient would be as above described. (The dosage) for pulverised drugs is stated to be an *akṣa* (a particular measure of weight equal to 16 *māṣas*) and four *palas* (a particular weight) for the decoction. This measure is said to be middling. There is no hard and fast rule about the dosage. O Fortunate one ! The measure of the dosage has to be decided according to the age, time, strength, digestive power, place, herb and disease.

15b-16a. Those tastes are known to be *saumyāḥ* which increase the quality of the ingredients. Those that are *madhurāḥ* are specially known to increase the quality.

16b-17a. That substance which has the qualities in equal proportion to the defects would be for betterment. The opposite would subdue the effect.

17b-20. O Foremost among men ! There are said to be three functions in this body, such as, eating, sleeping and coition. One has to pay attention to these always. One would get destroyed if there is no indulgence or is over-indulgence (in any one of these). An exhausted body has to be strengthened. Obesity of a person should be reduced. The middle type has to be protected. These are considered to be the three different types of bodies. Gratification and non-gratification are said to be the two courses of action. One should moderately eat (food) that is good (for health) after the food already taken had been digested.

21-24a. O Foremost among men ! The remedies are classified into five groups—juice, levigated powder, the distilled, the cold and decoction. Juice is known to be that got by pressing. Levigated powder is got by pulverising the drug after heating. The distilled is that got after boiling. The cold one is that allowed to cool the previous night. Decoction is that distilled immediately after boiling. There are one hundred and sixty ways of doing so. One who knows the ways would become inconquerable. That person is skilled in the preparation of mixtures.

24b. The purity of food is for the sake of digestion. A good digestion is the root cause of the strength of men.

25-30a. One should eat the three myrobalans together with the rock-salt, that would give good complexion to a king. (One would get similar benefit by using) the juice of venison together with rock-salt or curd or small quantities of milk. One whose constitution is windy should eat (a food) that has either more juice or the same proportion of juice. It is said that massaging (the body) (should be done) in summer. In winter it should be in equilibrium. It is known to be of middling type in the spring. The intense massaging in the summer is first done on the skin and then on the muscles, veins, blood and the body.

The bones would get strengthened and become fleshy. A wise man should massage well the shoulders, arms, shanks, knees, collarbones and the chest as before as if (one is attacking) an enemy. After having massaged the joints well, one should stretch them slowly without making a violent jerk.

30b-33. One should not do any physical exercise while the food still remains undigested nor after taking food, nor after drinking (water). One should never do any exercise in the half of the *prahara*[1] after a quarter part of the day. One should bathe in cold water (only) once. Bathing in trepid water would remove fatigue. One should not forcibly retain the breath in the heart. Physical exercises would remove the (excessive) phlegm. Massaging would remove the (excessive) wind. Bathing would remove the excessive bile. (One should not) expose his body to sunlight or enjoy the company of women (after doing exercises). Men should not do exercises affecting one's body under the sunlight.

CHAPTER TWO HUNDRED AND EIGHTYTWO

Description of horticulture

Dhanvantari said :

1. Now I shall describe the science of medicine relating to trees. It is good to have a *plakṣa* (tree) on the north, a banyan tree on the east, a mango (tree) on the south and a holy fig tree on the west.

2-4a. (It is better) to have thorny trees on the south near the house. A garden should be near the house. Blooming sesamum plants should be gathered and the trees should be planted after worshipping a brahmin and the moon. The five fixed asterisms *svāti*, *hasta*, *rohiṇī*, *śravaṇa* and *mūla* are commended for planting the trees.

1. An eighth part of a day.

4b.-5. (The trees) should be planted such that they are fed by rivers or should be made to be on the banks of a tank. (The asterisms) *hasta*, *magha*, *anurādhā*, *aśvini*, *puṣya* and *jyeṣṭhā* as well as *śatabhiṣak* and the three *uttaras* (*uttaraphālguṇi*, *uttarāṣāḍha* and *uttarabhādrapada*) (are good) for beginning (the construction) of tanks.

6-7a. It should be done after worshipping (lords) Varuṇa, Viṣṇu and Parjanya. (Trees such as) *ariṣṭa*, *aśoka*, *punnāga*, *śiriṣa*, *priyaṅgu*, plantain, *jambū*, *bakula* and pomegranate (should be planted) as above.

7b.-9. The planted trees should be watered morning and evening in the summer season, on alternate days in the winter season and in the night in the rainy (season) if the earth has become dry. (Trees planted) twenty cubits apart are (deemed as) excellent and sixteen (cubits) apart are (deemed as) medium. There should be minimum twelve cubits (distance) in between one tree and the other. Trees (planted) densely would not bear fruits. They should first be pruned with a cutter.

10. (The trees) should be sprinkled with cold water mixed with a paste of *viḍaṅga* and ghee. If the fruits get destroyed, (cold water should be sprinkled) with (a paste of) horse-gram, black-gram, green-gram, barley and sesamum.

11-12. One should always sprinkle cold water with ghee for (getting abundant) fruits and flowers. Sprinkling with the excrements of sheep and goat and pulverised barley, sesamum allowed to be soaked in meat and water for seven nights would also increase the bearing of fruits and flowers in all the trees.

13. Sprinkling with the washings of the fish would also increase the growth of the trees. Fish and meat mixed with the *viḍaṅga* and rice would make (them) bear fruits. This would universally control the diseases of all the trees.

CHAPTER TWO HUNDRED AND EIGHTYTHREE

The remedial herbs for all the diseases

Dhanvantari said :

1. A decoction of *siṁhi*, *śaṭi*, two kinds of *niśā* (turmeric) and *vatsaka* is commended for all types of infantile dysentery as well as defects due to mother's milk.

2. One should lick pulverised *śṛṅgi*, *kṛṣṇā* and *atibalā* together with honey. (Otherwise) *ativiṣā* alone would remove the cough, vomitting and fever of a child.

3-5a. *Vacā* should be taken by children together with clarified butter, or with milk or with oil. The child should drink *yaṣṭikā* or *śaṅkha* flower together with milk. This would improve speech, complexion, longevity, intellect and beauty of the child. *Vacā*, *agniśikhā*, *vāsā*, dried ginger, *kṛṣṇā* (long pepper), turmeric, *yaṣṭi* and rock salt should be given to a child in the morning for drinking. It would develop the memory.

5b-6a. A decoction of *devadāru*, *mahāśigru*, the three myrobalans and *payomuca* made into a paste with long pepper and honey would remove all worms.

6b-7. The juice of the three myrobalans, *bhṛṅga* and *viśva* soaked in honey, clarified butter, goat's milk and cow's urine is beneficiai in the diseases of children. The juice of *dūrvā* (a kind of grass) when inhaled is excellent remedy for bleeding of the nose.

8. (Similarly) filling the ear with the juice of garlic, ginger and *śigru* (would remedy the bleeding of the ears). Extracts of ginger and nutmeg in oil would remove intestinal colic and also the diseases of the lips.

9. The outer skin of the nutmeg, dry ginger, pepper, long pepper and turmeric would remove the urinary defects. A paste of mustard made into a decoction in milk dissolved in oil would remove toothache.

10. The coriander water, coconut, cow's urine, betelnut and dry ginger made into a decoction and used for gargling would remedy the defects in the tongue.

11. The juice of *nirguṇḍikā* with the paste of *lāṅgali* prepared in oil when inhaled would destroy *gaṇḍamālā* and *galagaṇḍa*.

12. One should rub (the affected part of the skin) with the leaves of *arka*, *pūtikā* and *snuhī* together with cow's urine. (By this one would destroy) all the defects of the skin.

13. *Vākuci* and sesamum eaten for one year is a cure for leprosy. *Pathyā*, *bhallātaki* and a lump of molasses in oil would also conquer leprosy.

14. One suffering from piles should drink buttermilk together with the powders of *yūthikā*, *vahni*, turmeric, the three myrobalans and *vyoṣa* or should take *abhayā* with molasses.

15. One suffering from a urinary ailment should take a decoction of the (three) myrobalans, a variety of turmeric and *viṣa* or the juice of the emblic myrobalan or the paste of turmeric with or without honey should be used.

16. A decoction of *vāsā* mixed with castor oil would remove acute gout. The drinking (of the juice) of long pepper would cure enlarged spleens.

17-20. One who has an abdominal disorder should take black pepper that has been soaked well in the milk of *snuk* or should drink milk mixed with the paste of *rucya*, *dantya*, *agniviḍaṅga* and *vyoṣa*. The *granthika*, *ugra*, mustard, long pepper and *viḍaṅga* soaked in ghee (and allowed to remain) in buttermilk for a month would remove diarrhoea, piles, jaundice, enlargement of spleen and worms. The decoction of the three myrobalans, *amṛtā*, *vāsā*, *tiktabhūnimbaja* together with honey would remove jaundice with acidity. One who is having acute gout should drink a potion of *vāsā* together with molasses and honey. Or (one may drink) milk in which *varī*, grapes, *balā* and dried ginger have been dissolved.

21. One who is suffering from consumption should lick (the compounded powders of) *varī*, *vidārī*, *pathyā*, the three (kinds of) *balās*, *vāsaka* and *śvadaṁṣṭra* together with honey and clarified butter.

22. The essence of the bark of *pathyā*, *śigru*, *karañja* and *arka* together with honey and rock salt would cure abscess as well as (help) ripening of the intestines.

23-24. Anointing a wound with *trivṛt*, *jivati*, *dantī*, *mañjiṣṭhā*, the two varieties of turmeric, *tārkṣaja* and neem leaves is commended for fistula. An ointment of pulverised *rugghāta*, turmeric, shellac mixed with ghee and honey, and *vāsa* would be an antiseptic and arrest its spread.

25. Oil boiled with *śyāmā*, *yaṣṭi*, turmeric, *lodhra*, *padmaka*, *utpala*, sandal and black pepper, and distilled in milk would heal a wound.

26. Burnt ashes of the leaves of black holy basil and cotton, nutmeg, rock-salt and turmeric made into a paste and boiled in oil in a copper vessel would be a good remedy for ulcers.

27. *Kumbhisāra* mixed with milk should be heated in fire and applied on the wound. It could also be cured by sprinkling with the chops of coconut and ghee.

28. Dried ginger, *ajamoda*, rock-salt and bark of tamarind in equal proportions together with mustard in the same proportion should be drunk with butter-milk or hot water. It would cure dysentery.

29. In the case of dysentery that is longstanding and accompanied by constipation, discharge of blood and pain, one should be made to drink water boiled with *vatsaka*, *ativiṣā*, dried ginger, *bilva* and *musta*.

30. One suffering from any type of colic should drink warm water saturated with rock-salt burnt in charcoal. Alternatively (one may take a mixture of) rock-salt, asafoetida, long pepper and mustard in the same way.

31. *Kaṭurohiṇi*, long pepper, *ātaṅka* and powdered fried paddy made into a paste with honey that is filtered through a cloth and held in the mouth would remove thirst.

32-33. A decoction of *pāṭhā*, *dārvi* (a variety of turmeric), skin of nutmeg, grapes and the three kinds of myrobalans together with honey if gargled would remedy sore-mouth. A decoction of long pepper, *ativiṣa*, *tiktendra*, *dāru*, *pāṭhā* and *payomuc* boiled with (cow's) urine (taken with) honey would remove all throat affections.

34. Drinking of a decoction of *pathyā*, *gokṣura*, *dusparṣa*, *rājavṛkṣa* and *śilābhit* together with honey would remedy painful discharge of urine.

35. A decoction of bamboo bark and *varuṇa* would remove stone in the bladder. One who is suffering from elephantiasis should take the decoction of *śākhoṭaka* together with honey and milk.

36. Oil made with blackgram and the milk extracted from the bark of *arka* (as well as) rock-salt mixed with honey would be remedy for the diseases of leg. Clarified butter similarly (would cure) *jālakukkuṭaja*.[1]

37. Powder of dried ginger, natron and asafoetida mixed with the juice of dried ginger boiled with ghee would remove sickness and this decoction is known to be efficacious in improving digestion.

38. One who is having enlargement of spleen should drink buttermilk together with juices that aid digestion such as natrum, *agni* and asafoetida, or with *viḍa* and *dīpyaka*.

39. A decoction of emblic myrobalan, snake-gourd and greengram together with clarified butter would cure dry spreading itch. Dry ginger, *dāru* and *navā* made into a decoction with milk together with the urine of a cow also (would remove swelling).

40. Decoction of dry ginger, pepper, long pepper, *kṣāra* and the three myrobalans would remove swelling. (Similar effect is had by using) treacle, *śigru* and *trivṛt* together with pulverised rock-salt.

41. A decoction of *trivṛt* and the three myrobalans together with treacle would act as a purgative. A decoction of *vacā* and three kinds of myrobalan with milk would be an emetic.

42-44. One hundred *palas* (a measure of weight) each of the three myrobalans soaked in the essence of *bhṛṅgaja* mixed with ten parts of *viḍaṅga* and iron filings and twentyfive *palas* of *śatāvarī*, *guḍūcī* and *agni* should be licked with honey, clarified butter and sesamum oil. (One would be) free from aging and greying of hair. He would live a hundred years free from all diseases. The three myrobalans with honey and sugar is capable of destroying all diseases.

45-46a. Taking mustard together with honey, ghee, pepper, the three myrobalans, *pathyā*, *citraka*, dry ginger, *guḍūcī*, *muśalirajc* and treacle would remove disease and make (one live) for three hundred years.

46b-48a. The *japā* flower (dried) and made into a powder and then into a ball should be put in water. The oil of the

1. A disease of the leg.

paste with water would be like ghee. By the incense (of the above) one that is old would see things as variegated. One would see as before by the incense of *mākṣika*.

48b-49. If camphor, oil (extracted) from leech and frog and root of *pāṭali* are ground well and anointed on the two feet, one could walk on the fire after arranging and raising of the grass (?) and provide entertainment to the spectators.

50-51. (The scope of medicine) is stated to fall under six heads such as poison, (influence of) stars, ailments (in general), violent deaths, minor (ailments) and love potents. It leads to two kinds of accomplishments. Sacred formulas meditation, medicine, conversation, *mudrā* (postures of the hand) and sacrificial worships are the means therein. The four goals (of life) have been narrated. One who reads (the same) would reach heaven.

CHAPTER TWO HUNDRED AND EIGHTYFOUR

Narration of sacred formulas that are medicinal

Dhanvantari said :

1. The syllable '*oṁ*' and others confer longevity, health and heaven. The syllable '*oṁ*' is the foremost sacred syllable and one becomes immortal by repeating the same.

2. The *gāyatrī* (*mantra*) is the supreme sacred formula. One gets enjoyment and emancipation by repeating the same. The formula "*Oṁ*, Salutations to (Lord) Nārāyaṇa" shall accomplish all things.

3-6a. (The sacred formula) "*Oṁ*, Salutations to (Lord) Vāsudeva" yields all (things). The formula "*Oṁ hrūṁ*, obeisance to (Lord) Viṣṇu" is the foremost medicine. The celestials and demons became prosperous and free from sickness by (repeating) this (formula). It is benevolent for the beings. The *dharma* (*mantra*) is a great remedy—"Virtue, one who does virtuous deeds, and virtuous." One becomes free from blemishes with these *dharma* (*mantras*). "Conferer of prosperity, lord of prosperity, abode of prosperity, bearer of wealth, the abode of wealth, lord of prosperity, the supreme prosperity"—One would obtain prosperity by (the repetition of) these (words).

6b-7a. "One who loves, bestower of desires, desire, the governor of desires, Hari, happiness, consort of Lakṣmī" are the names of (lord) Hari, (which should be repeated) for (gaining) pleasures.

7b-8. "Rāma (one that makes us pleased), Paraśurāma (the Rāma, with the battle-axe), Nṛsiṁha (the man-lion form of lord Viṣṇu), Viṣṇu, Trivikrama (the lord that measured three spaces with three strides)" are the names that are to be repeated by those who desire to conquer. One who desires to acquire knowledge should repeat daily the name "Puruṣottama" (foremost among beings).

9. (The repetition of the name) Dāmodara (one having a string around the belly, denotes lord Kṛṣṇa) would remove bondage. (The repetition of the name) Puṣkarākṣa (lotus-eyed) would cure eye-disease. (The name) Hṛṣīkeśa (the lord of the sense-organs) would remove fear. This has to be repeated while preparing medicines.

10-11. The name 'Acyuta' (the changeless one) is an immortal one and confers victory in the battle. One who begins to cross a water-course (should repeat the name) Narasiṁha (man-lion form of Viṣṇu). One who desires to have welfare in the east and other directions should remember "Cakrin (the bearer of the disc), Gadin (the wielder of the mace), Śārṅgin (the bearer of the bow), and Khaḍgin (the bearer of a sword)". (One should repeat) the name 'Nārāyaṇa' at all times. (The repetition of the name) Nṛsiṁha (man-lion form of Viṣṇu) would remove all fear.

12. (The repetition of the name) "Garuḍavāhana" (one having the eagle on the banner) would remove poison. The name "Vāsudeva" (son of Vasudeva) has to be repeated always. One should repeat (the names) 'Ananta' (endless) and 'Acyuta' (changeless) while storing grains etc. and while going to sleep.

13. (One should repeat) 'Nārāyaṇa' when getting a bad dream and (the term) 'Jalaśāyin' (one who reposes on the water) when there is outbreak of fire etc. One who desires to

gain knowledge (should repeat the name) Hayagrīva (one having the neck of a horse, denotes a form of Viṣṇu). (One who desires) to gain progeny (should repeat the word) Jagatsūti (the progenitor of the universe). (The name) Balabhadra (the elder brother of lord Kṛṣṇa) (should be repeated) during acts of valour. This single name accomplishes things.

CHAPTER TWO HUNDRED AND EIGHTYFIVE

The accomplished recipes that would revive the dead

Dhanvnantari said :

1. I shall describe to you the infallible recipes that would revive the dead. They were expounded to me by (the sage) Ātreya. They are divine and are capable of curing all diseases.

Ātreya said :

2. A decoction of the five roots, such as those of *bilva*, (is an excellent remedy) for fever due to (deranged) wind. Otherwise (a decoction of) the root of long pepper, *guḍūci* and dry ginger is purifying.

3-4. (A decoction of the herbs) emblic myrobalan, mustard, black pepper and *vahni* would cure all fevers. *Bilva*, *agnimantha*, *śyonāka*, *Kāśmari*, *pāṭalā*, *sthirā*, *trikaṇṭaka*, *pṛśniparṇi*, *bṛhati* and *kaṇṭakārikā* are remedies for fever, indigestion, pain on the sides (of the body) and cough. The root of *kuśa* (grass) (should also be added to this).

5. *Guḍūci*, *parpaṭi*, *musta*, *kirāta* and dry ginger should be given in fever due to (deranged) wind and bile. This is known as *pañcabhadra* (the five beneficial things).

6. A decoction made of *trivṛt*, *viśāla*, *kaṭukā*, the three myrobalans and *āragvadha* is a purifier, loosens the bowels and has to be drunk to get relief from all fevers.

7. *Devadāru*, *balā*, *vāsā*, the three myrobalans, *vyoṣa*, *padmaka*, and *viḍaṅga* with an equal proportion of candied sugar made into a powder would conquer five kinds of cough.

8-9. *Daśamūli, śaṭi, rāsnā*, long pepper, *bilva, pauṣkara, śṛṅgita*, emblic myrobalan, *bhārṅgi guḍūci, nāgavalli* and barley compounded well and a decoction prepared from that should be drunk. It would remedy cough, diarrhoea, (pain) on the sides, hiccough and difficult breathing.

10. The three kinds of salts (as well as) *madhuka* together with honey, long pepper together with sugar, and *nāgara* together with treacle would remove hiccough.

11. *Kāravya, jāji*, pepper, grapes, hog-plum, pomegranate, natrum, treacle and honey would remedy all kinds of loss of appetite.

12. One should be made to drink the juice of *śṛṅgavera* (ginger) together with honey. It would remedy loss of appetite, difficult breathing and cough. It would also remedy catarrh and excess of phlegm.

13. (The root of) banyan, *śṛṅgi*, red earth, (the bark of) *lodhra*, pomegranate, *madhuka* and honey should be taken with the scum. It would remove thirst and arrest vomitting.

14. *Guḍūci, vāsaka, lodhra* and long pepper together with honey would remedy fever accompanied by thirst, cough and expectoration of phlegm together with blood.

15. Likewise the juice of *vāsaka*, the juice of *tāmraja* mixed with honey, and pepper infused in the juice of the *śirīṣa* flower would also be beneficial.

16. (The pulse called) *masūra* removes all kinds of pain. (The washings) of rice would remove excess of bile. *Nirguṇḍi, śārivā, śelu* and *aṅkola* would remove poisons.

17. Dry ginger, *amṛtā, kṣudrā, puṣkara* and *granthika* made into powder should be taken with decoction of long pepper when one suffers unconsciousness and intoxication.

18. Asafoetida, natrum and *vyoṣa* (dry ginger) and pepper (each weighing) two *palas*, an *āḍhaka* (a measure) of ghee soaked in four parts of cow's urine would remedy insanity.

19. *Śaṅkha* flower, *vacā* and *kuṣṭha* soaked in the juice of *brāhmi* destroys long-standing epilepsy and insanity. It is also excellent for improving memory.

20-25a. The ghee made up of the five products got from a cow has also similar effects. The same with mustard is a remedy for leprosy. Snake-gourd, the three myrobalans, neem, *guḍūci*, *dhāvani*, *vṛṣa* and *karañja* boiled with ghee destroys leprosy and is known as *vajraka* (potent remedy). Neem, snake gourd, *vyāghri*, *guḍūci* and *vāsaka* should be taken ten *palas* each and pounded well. (The mixture) should then be heated in water vessel (with water) till it is reduced to one fourth (of its original volume). It should then be soaked in one *prastha* (a measure) ghee and boiled with the three myrobalans. This ghee is known as *pañcatiktaka* (five bitter things). This ghee is capable of curing leprosy. This excellent recipe would cure eighty varieties of diseases due to (deranged) wind, forty (diseases) due to (deranged) bile, twenty (diseases) due to (deranged) phlegm as well as cough, catarrh, piles, wounds and other diseases just as the sun (would remove) darkness.

25b-26a. One should sprinkle a wound with the decoction of the three myrobalans and the juice of *bhṛṅgarāja* for the cure of the venereal disease.

26b-28a. The powder of the leaves of snake-gourd and the five particles of the skin of pomegranate should be pounded with *gaja* (a variety of pepper) and the powder of the three kinds of myrobalans. Oil boiled with the three myrobalans, grains of iron, *yaṣṭi*, *mārkava*, blue lotus, pepper and rock-salt would remedy vomitting when used for bathing.

28b-29a. Oil boiled with milk, juice of *mārkava*, two *prasthas* each of *madhuka* and *utpala* made into one *guḍava* (a measure), if used as sternutatory would arrest greying of hair.

29b-30. The two compounds—neem, snake-gourd, the three kinds of myrobalans, *guḍūci*, *khadira* and *vṛṣa* as well as *bhūnimba*, *pāṭhā*, the three kinds of myrabolans, *guḍūci* and red sandal would remedy fever, leprosy, tumour and the like.

31. A decoction prepared from snake-gourd, *amṛta*, *bhūnimba*, *vāsā*, *ariṣṭaka*, *parpaṭa* and bark of *khadira* would appease the fever due to tumour.

32. The *daśamūli*, *chinnaruhā*, mustard, *dāru*, *punarnavā*, *śigru* and dry ginger are beneficial for (remedying) fevers, abscess and swelling.

33-34. Besmearing with (a paste of) *madhūka* and neem leaves would clean the wounds. A decoction of the three myrobalans and the leaves of *khadira*, *dārvi*, *nyagrodha*, *atibalā*, *kuśa* (grass), neem, and *mūlaka* are beneficial in cleaning (wounds). The juice of *karañja*, *ariṣṭa* and *nirguṇḍi* would destroy the parasites of wounds.

35. Besmearing with a paste (made up) of *dhātaki*, sandal, *balā*, *maṅgā*, *madhuka*, blue lotus, *dārvi* and *meda* mixed with clarified butter would heal a wound.

36. *Guggulu*, the three myrobalans, dry ginger, pepper and long pepper in equal proportions mixed with ghee would heal wounds due to affected arteries and painful fistula.

37. The yellow myrobalan boiled in cow's urine with oil and salt should be used every morning. It would remove excess of phlegm and wind.

38. A decoction of dry ginger, pepper, long pepper and the three myrobalans should be drunk with alkali and salt as a purgative in (deranged) phlegm and wind. It arrests the increase of phlegm.

39. The decoction of long pepper, the root of long pepper, *vacā*, *citraka* and dry ginger should be drunk to remedying constipation.

40. One should drink the great remedy—*rāsnā*, *guḍūci*, root of castor and *devadāru* in case of rheumatism (that affects) all the limbs, joints, bones and marrow.

41-43. Otherwise one may drink a decoction of *daśamūla* together with dry ginger and water. By the use of a decoction of dry ginger and *gokṣuraka* every morning one would get back digestive power that has been impaired and would get relief from rheumatic pain in the hip. The oil extracted from the roots, leaves and branches of *prasāriṇi*, an extracted juice or paste or powder or decoction of *guḍūci* would relieve one from acute gout when used for a long time.

44-45a. Long pepper and castor-oil may be used. One would conquer quickly acute gout accompanied by burning sensation by drinking snake-gourd, the three varieties of myrobalans, *tīvrakaṭuka* and *amṛta* boiled with mustard or treacle.

45b-46. Rheumatic pain would be relieved at once by (drinking) *guggulu* in warm water or drinking *guḍūci* with the three myrobalans in water together with *balā*, *punarnavā*, castor seed, the two kinds of *bṛhati*, *gokṣura*, asafoetida and salt.

47-50a. A *kārṣika* (a measure of weight) each of the root of long pepper, the five kinds of salts, long pepper, *citraka*, dry ginger, the three varieties of myrobalans, *trivṛt*, *vacā*, two sorts of alkali, *śādvala*, *danti*, *svarṇakṣiri* and *viṣāṇikā* (should be ground well) and *kola* (a measure of weight) measure of pill should be drunk with jujube. (This would remedy) swelling. It is an excellent remedy with *trivṛt* for indigestion and enlargement of the abdomen etc. Milk together with *dāru*, *varṣābhū* and dry ginger would be excellent for removing swelling. Sprinkling with a decoction of *arka*, *varṣābhū* and *bhūnimba* would remove swelling.

50b-51. Piles would go without any doubt if the clarified butter boiled with three parts of ashes of dry ginger, pepper and long pepper mixed with *palāśa* dissolved in water is used. *Viṣvakṣena*, lotus flower and *nirguṇḍī* boiled with salt would also have similar results.

52-53a. Oil (prepared) with *viḍaṅga*, *anala*, rock-salt, *rāsnā*, *agrakṣāra* and *dāru* boiled with four times water saturated with a pungent material would remove inflammation of the glands of the neck and would remedy goitre if used as an unguent.

53b-54a. Decoction of *śaṭī*, *kunāga* and *valaya* together with the juice of *kṣira* boiled with the paste of *payasyā*, long pepper and *vāsā* would be beneficial for consumption.

54b-55. (A compound of) *vacā*, *viḍ*, mustard, dry ginger, asafoetida, *kuṣṭha*, *agni dipyaka* (mixed in the proportion of) two, three, six, four, one, seven parts and a fiftieth part respectively, if drunk would destroy tumours in the abdomen, (abdominal) colic and coughs.

56. Pills made of *pāṭhā*, *nikumbha*, pepper, dry ginger, long pepper, the three kinds of myrobalans and *agni* boiled with cow's urine would remedy abdominal tumour, spleen and the like.

57. *Vāsā*, margosa, snake-gourd and the three myrobalans would destroy (deranged) wind and bile. Powdered *viḍaṅga* if licked with honey would destroy worms.

58-59a. The yellow myrobalan together with *viḍaṅga*, rock salt, *kṣāra* (alkaline salt) and cow's urine (will also produce the same effect). The barks of *śallaki*, jujube, rose apple, *piyāla*, mango and *arjuna* (trees) soaked in honey and taken with milk separately would arrest haemorrhage.

59b-60a. Equal proportions of the juice of *bilva*, mango (bark), *dhātakī*, *pāṭhā*, dry ginger and *mocā* when taken with treacle or butter-milk would arrest severe dysentery.

60b-61a. The drinking of a decoction of *aṅgerī*, *kola*, curd water, dry ginger and *kṣāra* (an alkaline salt) together with ghee would remove pain due to inflammation of anus.

61b-62a. *Viḍaṅga*, *ativiṣā*, *musta*, *dāru*, *pāṭhā* and *kaliṅga* (taken) together with black pepper would cure dysentery (accompanied by) swelling (of the limbs).

62b-63. One would live for a hundred years happily by eating two yellow myrobalans (everyday) together with sugar, rock-salt and dry ginger or long pepper, honey and treacle. The same would be the result of taking the three kinds of myrobalans and long pepper together with honey and clarified butter.

64. One should lick powdered emblic myrobalan soaked in (the juice of) the same with honey, clarified butter and sugar and drink milk if desirous of enjoying women.

65-66. Powdered black gram, long pepper, *śāli* (a variety of rice), barley and wheat in equal proportion should be fried with long pepper. One should eat them and drink sweet milk with sugar. (Such a person) would gain strength to enjoy women ten times like a sparrow.

67. *Maṅgā*, *dhātakī* flower, *lodhra* and blue lotus should be given to women together with milk. It would remedy *pradara* (a disease) of women.

68-69a. (A mixture of) *bīja*, *kauraṇṭaka*, *madhuka*, white sandal, the roots of lotus and blue lotus, sugar and sesamum is excellent for arresting miscarriage and causing pregnancy.

69b-70. An unguent of *devadāru*, *nabha*, *kuṣṭha*, *nalada* and dry ginger mixed with sour gruel and oil would remedy headache. If rock salt mixed with water is poured (into the ear) after gently heating and filtering through a cloth, it would remove ear-ache.

71. The juice of garlic, ginger, *śigru* or plantain (may be taken) separately. One may drink them with (the mixture of)

balā, *śatāvari*, *rāsnā* and *amṛtā* together with *sairiyaka* (?).

72-74a. Clarified butter together with the three myrobalans is an excellent remedy against blindness. One should drink ghee boiled with the three myrobalans, dry ginger, pepper, long pepper and rock-salt. It would strengthen eyesight, loosen bowels, strengthen heart, stimulate digestion and remedy cold. The filament of blue lotus together with cowdung and water is (known as) collyrium. It would be beneficial for day or night blindness.

74b-77. *Yaṣṭimadhu*, *vacā*, long pepper and seeds of *kuṭaja* made into a paste mixed with a decoction of neem is a good emetic. Glossy and greasy barley water should be given as a purgative. If it is (used) otherwise it would impair the digestion, make the body heavy and cause loss of appetite. A pulverised (compound of) mustard, rock-salt and long pepper should be drunk with warm water. This is an excellent purgative that would remedy all diseases. This is known as *nārāca* (destructive). The infallible compositions that have been expounded by Ātreya to the sages are capable of curing all diseases and are declared by Suśruta as conferring all boons.

CHAPTER TWO HUNDRED AND EIGHTYSIX

Collection of medical recipes

Dhanvantari said :

1. I shall describe the recipes of medicines that would conquer death, confer longevity and cure diseases. The three myrobalans and *amṛtā* together with honey and clarified butter would cure disease and would make one live for three hundred years.

2. (One who uses) one *pala*, half a *pala* or a *karṣa* (a measure of weight) (would enjoy) the full span (of life). One who uses the oil of *bilva* as sternutatory for a month (would live) for five hundred years and (would become) a poet.

3-4. (The use of) sesamum and *bhallātaka* would overcome

disease, premature death and senility. One would overcome leprosy by (using) a decoction of five parts of powdered *vākuci* with the waters of *khadira* for six months. (Otherwise) powder of *nilakuruṇṭa* may be used (for the same). One who eats *khaṇḍadugdha* together with milk or honey (would live for) a hundred years.

5. One who uses a *pala* (weight) of honey, clarified butter and dried ginger in the morning would conquer death. One who drinks milk with the powder of *māṇḍaki* would overcome old age and live long.

6. One who drinks milk with a *karṣa* of *uccāṭa* and honey would conquer death. One would overcome disease and death (by using) *nirguṇḍi* together with honey, clarified butter or milk.

7. One should drink a *karṣaka* of the oil of *palāśa* together with honey for six months. Milk may be drunk afterwards. This would make one live for five hundred or a thousand (years).

8-9a. One should drink the juice of the leaf of *jyotiṣmatī* and the three myrobalans together with milk. Similarly a *pala* (weight) of the pulverised *śatāvari* together with honey and clarified butter or *nirguṇḍi* with honey, clarified butter and milk would overcome disease and death.

9b-10. Five parts of pulverised neem boiled with the decoction of *khadira* (used) with a *karṣa* (weight) of the juice of *bhṛṅga* would make one overcome disease and become immortal. One who drinks milk after taking *rudantī* with clarified butter and honey would conquer death.

11. One should take a *karṣa* (weight) of the powder of yellow myrobalan boiled with the juice of *bhṛṅgarāja* together with ghee (or) honey. He would live for three hundred years and conquer disease.

12-14. (One would live) for five hundred years (by using) a *karṣa* (weight of) *vārāhikā*, juice of *bhṛṅga*, oxide of iron, *śatāvari* together with clarified butter. Powdered *kārta* (gold filings) and *śatāvari* boiled with (the juice of) *bhṛṅgarāja* (used with) honey and clarified butter would make one live for three hundred years. Mango, *amṛtā*, *trivṛt* in equal proportion (and) sulphur purified with the juice of *kumārikā* (are made into pills). (One who uses) two (such) pills together with clarified butter would live for five hundred years. A *pala* (weight) of *aśvagandhā* used with oil, clarified butter and treacle would make one (live for) a hundred years.

15. Drinking a *pala* (weight) of pulverised *punarnavā* or *aśoka* together with honey, clarified butter and milk would remove one's ailment.

16. One who uses the sesamum oil with honey as sternutatory will live for a hundred years (retaining) the black hue of the hair. One would live for a hundred years by drinking a *karṣa* (weight) of *akṣa* together with honey, clarified butter and milk.

17. After taking mustard with treacle, ghee and sweet things etc., one who eats rice mixed with milk would have black hair, be free from disease and live for five hundred years.

18. One who drinks a *pala* (weight) of pulverised *kūsmāṇḍikā* together with honey, clarified butter and milk and eats rice mixed with milk for a month would live for a thousand years without any disease.

19. The powder of *śālūka* together with the juice of *bhṛṅga*, honey and clarified butter would make one live for a hunderd years. A *karṣa* (weight) of the oil of *kaṭutumbi* (used) as a sternutatory would make one live for two hundred years.

20. The use of the three myrobalans, long pepper and dried ginger would make one live for three hundred years. If the same is compounded with *śatāvarī* it would make one strong and live for one thousand years.

21-24. Pills should be made with *citraka*, dried ginger, *viḍaṅga*, iron oxide, *bhṛṅgarāja*, *valā*, the five kinds of neem, *khadira*, *nirguṇḍī*, *kaṇṭakārī* and *vāsaka* boiled with *varṣābhū* or its juice. This powder together with ghee or honey or treacle or water is an excellent compound. It should be consecrated with the formula "*Oṁ hrūṁ sa*". It would be a recipe for reviving the dead and overcoming disease and death. The collections of recipes were made use of by the celestials, demons and sages. (I shall describe) the science of medicine relating to the elephants (that) was narrated by (sage) Pālakāpya to the king Aṅga.

CHAPTER TWO HUNDRED AND EIGHTYSEVEN

The treatment of the diseases of elephants

Pālakāpya said :

1-3. O Lomapāda ! I shall describe to you the characteristics of the elephants and the treatment (of their diseases). Those that have long trunks, deep breath and are of enduring type are commended. Those that have twenty or eighteen nails, those that exude rut (even) in winter, those that have an elevated right tusk, those that have wide ears resembling the cloud, with minute dot like (marks) on the skin should be maintained. Those that are short and have bad features should not be maintained.

4-5. (Similarly it is not advisable to capture) the she-elephants that bear the foetus on their sides and those that are stupid. The elephant that has (good) complexion, good nature, strength, appearance, beauty, firmness and speed would conquer enemies in the battle. The elephants add beauty to the army camp and the army.

6a. A king could gain victory by the diligent (employment) of elephants.

6b-7. In the case of all the fevers (of elephants), they should be anointed. Bathing them after anointing them with ghee or oil would remove the wind (in the body). The shoulders should be treated by the kings as indicated in the case of the fevers (of elephants).

8. O Brahmins ! Cow's urine together with ghee and the two varieties of turmeric (are commended) for jaundice. An infusion (with the above remedy) soaked in oil is commended for constipation.

9-10. *Vāruṇī* (a kind of liquor) mixed with five kinds of salts should be given for drinking. An elephant should be fed with balls of (mixture of) *viḍaṅga,* the three myrobalans, dried ginger, pepper and long pepper and salt in the case of fainting. He should be made to drink honey and water. The head should be anointed with oil for headache. A sternutatory is also commended.

11. The diseases affecting the legs of an elephant should be treated by anointing with oil. Then it is laid down that they should be cleansed with the paste of sediments of oil.

12. An elephant that is suffering from shivering should be fed with the juice of the flesh of peacock and *tittiri* (partridge) mixed with long pepper and pepper.

13. A morsel comprising tender *bilva*, *lodhra*, *dhātaki* together with sugar should be given to an elephant suffering from dysentery.

14. Ghee mixed with common salt should be given as sternutatory in the case of numbness of the trunk. (Otherwise) long pepper, dried ginger and the cumin-seed boiled in the rice or barley gruel together with *musta* grass (could be given).

15-16a. The juice of the flesh of a pig should be given for ear-ache. Oil boiled with the ten kinds of roots, the horse beans, tamarind and *kākamācī* would remove the pain due to stiffness of the neck caused by fetters.

16b-17. Ghee mixed with the eight kinds of salts made into a paste should be given for drinking in the case of retention of urine. Otherwise a decoction of the seeds of *trāpuṣa* (may be given). An elephant should be made to drink a decoction of the bark of neem or *vṛṣa*.

18-19. Cow's urine and *viḍaṅga* are commended for worms in the intestines. Milk boiled with dried ginger, long pepper, grapes and sugar is (an excellent) drink for curing the wounds. The juice of the flesh is also good. Rice and green gram boiled together and mixed with dried ginger, pepper and long pepper is commended for loss of appetite.

20. Oil mixed with *trivṛt*, dried ginger, long pepper and pepper, *agnidanti*, *arka*, *śyāmā*, milk and bigger variety of long pepper would remedy the enlargement of spleen.

21-22a. All sorts of disorders that arise could be remedied by means of loosening, enema, anointment, application of oil, drinks and oily enemas. One could be given *yaṣṭika* with *śārada* (a kind of beans) together with the soup of green gram for drinking.

22b. Besmearing with tender *bilva* is commended in the diseases (known as) *kaṭu*.

23. *Viḍaṅga, indrayava,* asafoetida, *sarala* and the two varieties of turmeric could be given in the form of balls in the forenoon to remedy all kinds of colics.

24. The main meal for them should be composed of (the rice varieties known as) *ṣaṣṭika, vrihi* and *śāli.* (The meals) consisting of barley and wheat are (considered as) mediocre. The other kinds (of food) are (deemed as) inferior for the elephants.

25. Barley and sugarcane increase the strength of the elephants. Dried barley would derange the humours of the elephants.

26. Drinking of milk is commended for an elephant that is emaciated on account of rutting. The juice of flesh that has been cooked with the substances that are stimulants is good.

27. In the event of severe injury in the war, balls of (flesh of) crows, hens, cuckoos and owls (could be given) mixed with honey.

28. An incense (consisting) of pepper, fish, *viḍaṅga,* alkaline salt, juice of *koṣātaki* and turmeric ensures victory in the battle for the elephant.

29. (A liniment consisting of) long pepper, rice, oil, honey of different kinds applied along the eyelids is commended as sharpening the eyesight.

30-31a. Feces of a sparrow and a pigeon, the resin of the *kṣira* tree and the liquor (known as) *prasannā* are the excellent collyrium. Such a collyrium applied on the eye would make the elephant destructive in the battle.

31b-32a. Blue lotuses, *musta* and *tagara* made into a paste with water in which rice has been washed is an excellent cooling agent for the eyes.

32b. (Once in a month) the grown-up nails should be cut. (They) should be bathed with oil once in a month.

33. The bed of an elephant would be powdered dry cow dung. It is commended that (the elephants) should be anointed with clarified butter in the autumn and summer.

CHAPTER TWO HUNDRED AND EIGHTYEIGHT

The diseases of the horses and the management of the horses

Dhanvantari said :

1. I shall describe the essence of (science relating to) the management of horses and the treatment of their diseases. In order to achieve dharma, artha (virtue) and kāma (enjoyment and prosperity) (a king) should acquire (good) horses.

2. (The asterisms) *aśvinī*, *śravaṇa*, *hasta* and the three *uttaras* (*uttarāṣāḍha*, *uttaraphālgunī* and *uttarabhādrapada*) are commended for the first ride on the horses.

3. The early winter, winter and spring are commendable for riding the horses. The riding of the horses in the summer, autumn and rainy season is forbidden.

4-6a. One should not whip the horses severely or with other kinds of sticks or at an improper place. One who rides a horse at a place abounding in nails, thorns and bones, on a rugged ground, on a sandy and muddy ground and spoilt by pits and falls without knowing the temper (of the steed) and without the saddle would be carried away by the horse even as he is seated on its back.

6b-7a. There may be an excellent person among the learned, a fortunate one who knows the behaviour (of the horse) and is able to ride without any instruction on account of his practice and application.

7b-12a. The different gods are assigned on (the different parts of) the body of the horse that has been consecrated, and faces the east, commencing with the syllable *oṁ* and ending with 'obeisance' with the respective *bīja*[1] in order. (Lord) *Brahmā* (is assigned) in the mind, (Lord) Viṣṇu in the strength, Vainateya (vehicle bird of Viṣṇu) in valour, the Rudras on the sides, Guru in the intellect, the Viśvedevas in the vital parts (of the body), the Moon and the Sun in its glances and eyesight, the two Aśvins (the celestial physicians) on the ears,

1. The mystical letter forming the essential part of the mantra of a deity.

the Fire (god) on the stomach, *Svadhā* in the sweat, the (goddess of) speech on the tongue, Wind (god) on speed, the vault of the heaven on the back, all the mountains on the tip of the hoof, the asterisms in the pores of the hairs, the digit of the moon in the heart, the Fire-god in the lustre, the goddess of love on the buttocks, the lord of the world on the forehead, the planets in the neighing, *Vāsuki* (a foremost serpent) on the chest.

12b. One who is to ride (the horse), should fast, worship the horse and recite (the following mystic words) in the right ear (of the horse).

13-19. "Oh ! Horse ! You are a Gandharva prince ! You listen to my words. You are born in the family of Gandharvas. Do not become a defiler of the family. O Horse ! Remember your creed by the true words of the brahmins, of Soma, of Garuḍa, of Rudra, of Varuṇa, by the strength of Pavana (Wind-god) and by the radiance of the Fire-god. You remember that you are the son of a paramount sovereign. You remember the promise (you had made at the time of churning the ocean). You remember the daughter of the ocean (Goddess Lakṣmī). You remember the *kaustubha* jewel. You were born in the divine family at the time of the churning of the milky ocean by the celestials and the demons. You keep up your promise. You were born in the family of horses. You become my eternal friend. O Friend ! You listen to this well. You be ready as my vehicle. You be victorious. You protect me and bring me success in the battle. In olden days the demons were destroyed by the celestials riding on your back. I will now ride on you and conquer the army of the enemy."

20. After having repeated (the above prayer) into the ears (of his steed) the rider should confuse the enemy, saddle the horse and ride (the horse). (This would give him) victory in the battle.

21. Generally the defects in the horses are produced in their bodies. The excellent riders should convert them into good qualities with much effort.

22. The good qualities that are due to the ability of the riders would appear as natural.

23. Other riders would destroy even the natural qualities. Some know the good qualities. Some others know their defects. One is fortunate who knows (the qualities as well as the defects in) a horse. A stupid one is he who does not know both.

24. Even though one is a good judge, he is not commended if he does not know how to manage a horse, does not know the means (at the time of an emergency), acts rash, is of irritable nature and engages in excessive punishing at the vulnerable points.

25. One who knows the means (of handling an emergent situation), one who knows the temper (of the horse), one who is pure, one who removes the defects and takes the (good) qualities is always an expert in all acts (engaging the horses).

26. One who has entered the riding ground holding the bridle should ride his steed either from his right or left.

27. An excellent horse should not be whipped at once after mounting. Whipping causes fright and fear would produce confusion.

28. The rider should conduct (the horse) in a gallop in the morning holding the rein. (He should conduct the horse) slowly in the evening holding the rein but without handling it.

29. (The following are the four political expedients) : stroking is said to be conciliation, isolation (from the other steeds is) division, whipping with the whip and other things (is) punishment and biding time (is reckoned as) gift.

30-31. Each succeeding one should be employed when each preceding one fails. While riding a horse, (the bridle) should be placed without touching the tongue. The reins with hundreds of threads should be entered at the tip of the mouth. (The horse) should be made to forget (that) and then one may ride. One should (ride) slowly if the reins have become loosened.

32. If the tongue of the horse is ulcerated, the joint on the tongue should be released. The tight hold should be released till the horse does not give up its jumping.

33-36. The cuirass should be tied when the steed is released. (A horse) that has a raised face by nature should have its cuirass made loose by the foremost rider and then mounted with a sportive look. One that would make the left fore-leg (of the steed) joined with the left rein, would get the hinder-leg seized. By that the right one (also controls). One that practices in this way with the left rein, the two feet (would be controlled). Then the foot would be held from the left itself. If the fore-feet are released, one would become firmly seated.

37. The left fore-leg should be tied with the rein to the left hind-leg (of a horse) of mischievous habit. It should be ridden by holding the left rein.

38. The nature of the horse is to turn round its face again. It is not on account of tying the legs of the horses thus.

39. After having looked at a trusted horse and after having taken a firm seat on the saddle, (the horse) should be made to touch his leg with the face by holding (the rein). Such a (posture known as) *lokana* is beneficial.

40. The rein is clasped after pulling and firmly pressing with the legs. It is said to be *vakkana* if the two legs are bound.

41. It is considered as *moṭana* if there is binding of the legs with the rein and letting it go by freeing the fore-legs.

42. A wise man should know the loss of consciousness and destruction for a horse and the fourth rule, namely, the *moṭana*, is laid down.

43. A horse whose leg does not touch the ground in a small circle, that foot should be restrained by means of *moṭana* and *vakkana*.

44. It is said to be *saṅgrahaṇa* when it is held with exertion and when one goes slowly holding it after fastening well on the seat.

45. After striking on the side by kicking (the horse) that has distracted mind while one remain on the seat, the rein is drawn and held by the foot. It is known as *grāhya-kaṇṭaka-pāyanam*.

46. If a horse stands on the feet and hurts the rear legs, it is known as *khalikāra* (hurting).

47. It is known as *gahana* (intensified), if (the horse), that is in any one of the motions[1], is held after striking with a stick or with the leg as desired.

1. The trot, the gallop or the canter.

48. It would be *ucchvāsana* (exhalation), if the horse is hurt and taken through a quadrangle by means of a different bridle by cheering.

49. It is considered to be *mukhavyāvartana* (turning the face away), if the nature (of a horse) to turn its face and move towards the place (from which it has been taken out), is restrained and held.

50. After restraining by any one of the three (ways) in order, it should be controlled by taking to the courses such as the circles and the like in order.

51. A wise man should relax and ride a horse that raises its head from its knee onwards. One should rise a horse till its limbs are light.

52. A horse that is soft at its shoulder, light at its face and flexible at its joints, when it becomes controlled by the rider, then it should be tamed.

53-54a. The hinder leg should not be freed when (the horse) becomes quiet. Then it should be drawn forward with the hands by means of the bridle. The horse stands with the part about the hips becoming normal, the neck raised, and face on level.

54b-56. If (the horse) keeps the hinder legs on the ground and the fore legs lifted up and runs very fast, one should hold the bridle with the fist and stop it. If the horse does not stop when suddenly pulled thus and if it shakes its body, it should be stopped by taking it in a circular path. The horse that casts off the shoulder should be stopped by means of the bridle.

57. The cowdung, salt and (cow's) urine boiled with mud is besmeared on the body as a remedy for bites of flies, etc.

58. The scum of boiled rice should be given by the rider to (the horses) belonging to the *bhadra* and other breeds. The bites of tiny insects make the horse feel indolent and hungry.

59. A horse should be trained in such a way that it would become tamed. Horses would perish if they are made to run much. They do not get practice if not made to run. If the faces become white, (the horses) should be made to run.

60-61a. After having pressed the horse well with the two knees (one should ride the horse) with a firm fist. *Gomūtra*, *kuṭilā, veṇi, padmamaṇḍalā,* and (*padma*) *mālikā* are well known as the *pañcolūkhalikā.*

61b-62a. Similarly *saṅkṣipta, vikṣipta, kuñcita, yathācita, valgita* and *avalgita* are said to be six kinds of phases (of a horse). The path would be hundred *dhanus* (a measure of length equal to four cubits) or eighty or ninety (*dhanus*).

63. (Horses are said to be of four varieties such as *bhadra, manda, mṛga* and *saṅkirṇa.*) The (type of horse known as) *bhadra* could be trained well, the *manda* variety, (by making use of) a stick. (The type) of horse (known as) *mṛga* (is classified) taking the shank of a deer (as the basis). The above characteristics would be found mixed in the *saṅkirṇa* class.

64-65a. The horse that eats sugar, honey, and fried rice and has a good aroma is said to be clean and belonging to the brahmin class. The horse that belongs to the warrior class would be lustrous, meek and clever. (If the above qualities are found in lesser proportions it is known as the *vaiśya* class.) (The horse that is) impure, unsteady, dull, ugly, foolish and wicked (is said to belong to) the *śūdra* (class).

65b-66. The horse that would show saliva when being held by the bridle, should be driven in phases by holding and loosening the rein. I shall describe (to you now) the characteristics of the horses etc. as expounded by (the sage) Śālihotra.[1]

CHAPTER TWO HUNDRED AND EIGHTYNINE

The characteristics of the horses and the treatment of the diseases of the horses

Śālihotra said :

1-5. O Suśruta ! I shall describe the characteristics of the horses and the treatment of the diseases. A horse with lesser number of teeth, one devoid of teeth, one that is having dread-

1. Śalihotra is credited with the authorship of works on veterinary science.

ful appearance, one that has a black palate and black tongue, one that is born as a twin, one that has no testicle, one that has a cleft-hoof, one that has a horn, one that is tricoloured, one that has the colour of a tiger, one that has the colour of an ass, one that has the colour of ash, one that is not having a good colour, one that has a hump, one that has white patches (on the skin), one that is (often) ridden by the crows, the voice of which resembles that of an ass, one whose eyes resemble those of a monkey, one that has black manes, one whose anus is black, one whose nostrils have a black hue and are pointed, one that has the colour of a *tittiri* (bird), one that has unequal legs having white patches on the foot, one that is devoid of fixed rings and has rings indicating inauspiciousness, should be avoided.

6. The pairs of curls of hair on the skull, *uparandhra* (flanks), head, chest, forehead and neck of a horse are (deemed to be auspicious.

7. The curls of hair at the corner of the mouth, forehead, the root of the ear, the throat, root of the forelegs, neck are auspicious. (The curls of hair) at other (places) are inauspicious.

8. The horses which resemble the colour of a parrot, *indragopa* (a kind of insect), moon and a crow and those which have a golden colour and are glossy are always commendable.

9. One should dismiss all the hopes of conquest where the horses of the kings have long necks, broad eye-corners and auspicious short ears.

10. A horse or an elephant which is guarded confers good and confers misery otherwise. Those horses are excellent and are *gandharvas* which increase the fortune and progeny.

11a. A horse is offered as an oblation in the *aśvamedha* (a horse-sacrifice) on account of its purity.

11b-13a. A morsel composed of *vṛṣa*, neem, *bṛhati*, *guḍūci*, *mākṣikā*, *siṁhā* and *gandhakari* anointed on the head (of a horse) or asafoetida, root of *puṣkara*, *nāgara* with sour *vetasa*, long pepper and *saindhava* (a kind of rock salt) with hot water would remove the pain (in the stomach).

13b-14a. A decoction of dried ginger, *ativiṣā*, *mustā*, *ananta* and *bilva* leaves would remove all kinds of dysentery if given as a drink.

14b-15a. A horse would become free from fatigue by drinking a potion composed of goat's milk, *pariyaṅgu* and *sāriva* (?) with profuse (quantity of) sugar.

15b-16a. Oily emetic is to be given for the horse in a *droṇikā* (an oval basin of wood). It should penetrate the sinews of the viscera. It would make it feel comfortable.

16b-17a. A ball of pomegranate, the three myrobalans, dried ginger, pepper and long pepper with equal proportion of molasses should be given to the horses. It would cure the harassing cough.

17b-18a. The juice of *vṛṣa* together with *priyaṅgu*, *lodhra* and honey should be given to a horse for drinking. Or the five *kola* etc.[1] (should be given) with milk. It would cure the cough.

18b-19a. It is beneficial to give emetics at first in all the kinds of diarrhoea. Then anointing with oil, rubbing with fragrant unguents, besmearing medicated oil, giving sternutatory and besmearing with unguents should be done in order.

19b. The process of treatment for horses afflicted by fever is with water only.

20. Anointing with the roots of *lodhra* and *karañja*, *mātuluṅga*, *agni*, dried ginger, *kuṣṭha*, asafoetida, *vaśā* and *rāsnā* would cure swelling.

21-22. A horse which drinks *mañjiṣṭhā*, *madhuka*, grapes, *bṛhatī*, red sandal, the seeds and roots of wild cucumber, *śṛṅgāṭaka* and *kaśeruka* boiled with goat's milk and then cooled together with sugar and abstains from food would become free from passing of blood in the urine.

23. Anointment with *kaṭutaila* of the affected parts (of a horse) is commended in the case of swelling in the wrist, cheek or throat or stiff-neck.

24-25a. (A horse) that is affected by stiff-throat would have probably swelling in the region of the throat. A sternutatory with mustard, *vahni*, rock-salt, juice of holy basil, black pepper and asafoetida (is given).

---

1. The five spices such as the long pepper, etc.

25b-26a. Besmearing a paste of two varieties of turmeric, *jyotiṣmatī*, *pāṭhā*, black pepper, *kuṣṭha*, *vacā* and honey mixed with molasses and (cow's) urine is beneficial in paralysis of the tongue.

26b-27a. Paste made with sesamum, *yaṣṭi*, turmeric, neem leaves mixed with honey and clarified butter is a remedy for ulcers.

27b-28a. The horses which limp on account of whipping and feel extreme pain should be fomented with oil. It would remove the pain quickly.

28b-29a. The same procedure as in the case of ulcers (is to be followed) in the case of a hurt or deranged state of the humours or one caused by whipping. A decoction of the barks of *aśvattha*, *udumbara*, *plakṣa*, *madhūka* and *vaṭa* with profuse quantity of water in comfortable heat would cure the ulcers.

29b-31. Oil prepared with a decoction of *śatāhvā*, dried ginger, *rāsnā*, *mañjiṣṭhā*, *kuṣṭha* rock-salt, *devadāru*, *vacā*, two varieties of turmeric and red sandal mixed with *guḍūci* and milk is used for smearing, as emetic and sternutatory and as unguents in all cases when there is oozing of blood at the eye-corners (of a horse) suffering from eye-disease caused by leeches.

32-33. Decoction of the barks of *khadira*, *udumbara* and *aśvattha* mixed with equal parts of emblic myrobalan, *durālabhā*, *tiktā*, *priyaṅgu*, saffron and *guḍūci* is beneficial in case of a limping one (horse), a wound of the tendon, or of an ear or a dry tumour.

34a. In the case of a fast developing derangement of a humour, it is desired that it is broken at once.

34b-35a. Rubbing with cowdung, *mañjikā*, *kuṣṭha*, turmeric, sesamum and mustard ground with cow's urine would remedy itching.

35b-36a. A decoction of the above mixed with honey and cooled should be given through the nostrils together with sugar and *aśvakarṇa*. It would remedy the haemoptysis.

36b-37a. Salt should be given to the horses on every seventh day. The liquor *vāruṇī* should be given to them as an additional drink after they had eaten as above.

37b-38a. (A decoction) with *jīvanīya, madhura, mṛdvikā,* sugar, long pepper and *padmaka* should be given as a substitute drink in the autumn.

38b-39a. (A decoction made) with *viḍaṅgā,* long pepper, coriander, *śatāhvā, lodhrā,* rock-salt and *citraka* (should be given) to horses as a substitute drink on the advent of winter.

39b-40a. A substitute drink in the spring would be with the herbs *lodhrā, priyaṅgu, mustā,* long pepper and dried ginger mixed with honey. This would remedy (the deranged) phlegm.

40b-41a. Wine together with the potent herbs *priyaṅgu,* long pepper, *lodhrā* and *yaṣṭi* together with molasses should be given as the substitute drink in summer.

41b-42a. A substitute drink on the advent of the rainy season would be (decoction made of) stick of *lodhrā,* salt, long pepper and dried ginger mixed with oil.

42b-44. The horses should be given ghee to remedy the (deranged) bile in the summer, increase of the blood in the autumn and loosening of the feces in the rainy season. The horses which have excess of phlegm and wind should be given oil to drink. Any evil consequence of the abuse of oil (should be remedied) by making them dry (to remove fat). Food consisting of barley with butter-milk for three days would make them shed (excess fat).

45. Clarified butter in the autumn and summer, oil in the cold and spring (seasons) and through the syringe in the advanced winter is desired to be the restraining (remedy).

46. Food that is heavy and that would increase the phelgm, exercise, bathing, hot (sun) and wind are prohibited for a horse which has been given oil to drink.

47. Horses should be bathed and made to drink only once on the advent of the rains. On an extremely stormy day drinking only once is commended.

48. When heat and cold are blended in a season, (horses) should be made to drink twice and bathe once. In the summer they should be bathed and led to drink thrice and should be allowed to plunge (into the water) for a long time.

49-50. Four *āḍhakas* (a measure) of barley without the husk should be given (to the horses). They may also be given bengal gram, *vrihi* (a kind of paddy) and green gram. In a whole day and night (a horse may be fed) ten and a half *tulās* (weight) of barley and eight *tulās* of dried (grains) or four (parts) of *vyoṣa*[1] (dried ginger).

51-52. *Dūrvā* (a kind of grass) would remedy (the deranged) bile, barley (would remedy) the cough, mustard, the congestion of phlegm and *arjuna* (would set right) breathing. So also *māna* (?) (would rectify) loss of strength. The horse that takes a meal of *dūrvā* (grass) would not be affected by diseases due to (deranged) wind, bile, phlegm or their combined action.

53-54. Vicious horses should be tied with two ropes on each side to posts behind them at a distance of a *dhanus* (four cubits). They may stay in places (stables) where (hay) has been strewn and the ground has been fumigated. Barley should be placed therein. The place should be well-lit and protected well. Animals such as the goats and monkeys as well as cocks should be kept in the stables of horses.

CHAPTER TWO HUNDRED AND NINETY

Propitiatory rites for curing the ailments of horses

Śālihotra said :

1. O Suśruta ! Listen to me. I shall describe the three kinds of propitiatory rites for the horses—the daily, the periodical and optional (rites) that would cure the diseases of the horses.

2. After having worshipped Śrīdhara (a form of Viṣṇu), Śrī (consort of Viṣṇu) and Uccaiḥśravas, the chief among the horses, on an auspicious day, one should offer ghee as oblation with (the recitation of the formula) Sāvitra (Gāyatrī).

3-6a. Then fees should be paid to the brahmins. Then the horses would increase. The propitiatory rite (should be done)

---

1. The reading *vapuṣmataḥ* in the veṅk. edn. does not fit in.

on the fifteenth (lunar) day of the bright fortnight in the (month of) *aśvayuk* (October-November). It should especially be done outside (the stable). (Lord) Varuṇa (water-god) should be worshipped. (A mystic) diagram should be drawn and (the image of) the goddess (placed at the centre) should be surrounded by branches (of trees). Pitchers filled with all flavours and covered by cloth should be placed at the cardinal points. After offering oblations of barley and clarified butter, the horses and the Aśvin gods[1] should be worshipped. Fees should be paid to the brahmins. Listen to me! (I shall now describe) the periodical (rites).

6b-8. One should worship (Lord) Viṣṇu, (goddess) Śrī (Lakṣmī), (Lord) Brahmā, (Lord) Śaṅkara, (Lord) Soma (Moon), (Lord) Āditya (Sun), the Aśvin gods, Revanta and Uccaiḥśravas (the horse of Indra) in the (constellations) Capricorn etc. for the horses with lotuses. The guardian deities of the cardinal points (should be worshipped) on the petals. Pitchers (should be dedicated) for each one of the (above) deities (and worshipped) on the altar at the auspicious place. After having fasted, oblations of sesamum, unbroken rice, clarified butter and white mustard should be made a hundred times for everyone of the gods. This act would ward off the diseases of the horses.

CHAPTER TWO HUNDRED AND NINETYONE

Propitiatory rites for curing the ailments of elephants

Śālihotra said :

1. I shall describe the propitiatory rites that would destroy the deseases of elephants. One should worship (Lord) Viṣṇu, (goddess) Śrī and the elephant (Airāvata) of Indra on the fifth (lunar) day.

---

1. a pair of celestial gods believed to have been born to Sun through a nymph in the form of a mare.

2-5a. (Similarly one should worship) Brahmā, Śaṅkara (Śiva), Viṣṇu, Śakra (Indra), Vaiśravaṇa (god of wealth), Yama (god of death), Moon, Sun, Varuṇa (Water-god), Wind-god, Fire-god, the Earth, the Sky, Śeṣa (the serpent couch of Lord Viṣṇu), the mountains and the eight elephants which guard the cardinal points such as Virūpākṣa, Mahāpadma, Bhadra, Sumanasa, Kumuda, Airāvata, Padma, Puṣpadanta, Vāmana, Supratīka and Añjana[1]. Oblation should then be made and fees paid (to the brahmins). The elephants which are sprinkled with the propitiatory water would multiply. Listen to me ! I shall describe the periodical rites.

5b-7a. In a lotus diagram (drawn) on the ground outside the city at the constellation Capricorn etc. of the elephants or at the north-eastern (angular point), (Lord) Viṣṇu should be worshipped at the centre, (goddess) Lakṣmī in the filament, (gods) Brahmā, Bhāskara (Sun), the earth and then (Lord) Skanda (son of Śiva), the sky, (Lord) Śiva, the Moon and Indra and his weapons on the petals in order.

7b-8a. (The weapons) such as the thunder-bolt, spear, rod, club, noose, mace, spike and the lotus should be worshipped on the periphery of the outer circle (of the diagram). The Sun and the pair of Aśvins should be worshipped at its centre.

8b-11. The eight Vasus and the Sādhyas (a class of celestials) (should be worshipped) at the petals at the southern and the south-western ends. The celestials, (the sages) Āṅgirasa and others, the Bhṛgus and the Wind-god (should be worshipped) at the north-western (petal), the Viśvedevas at the southern (petal) and the Rudras at the north-eastern (petal). The gods should be worshipped at the outer periphery of the exterior circle. The sages who composed the aphorisms, (goddess) Vāṇī (Sarasvatī, goddess of speech), the rivers and mountains (should be worshipped) on the east etc. The great spirits should be worshipped at the angular points such as the

1. Airāvata, Puṇḍarika, Vāmana, Añjana, Puṣpadanta, Sārvabhauma and Supratīka are the standard names of the elephants of the cardinal points. The text here reads additional names.

north-east and the like. The lotus, disc, mace and conch (which form) the four sides (enclosing) the circle (should be worshipped).

12-14. Pitchers (should be placed) at (each one of) the four entrances (at the east etc.) and banners on (the angular points such as) the south-east etc. Four ornamental arches (should be erected at the entrances). The elephants Airāvata and others (should be invoked to guard the entrances). Separate containers with herbs (should be placed) on the east and other directions for the gods. After having offered a hundred oblations with clarified butter and worshipped the elephants, one should circumambulate them. After having worshipped the elephant, fire-god and the gods at the outer periphery, the worshippers would go home. Fees should be paid to the brahmins as well as the physicians of the elephants.

15-20. An astrologer should then mount the famale elephant and utter in its ear. After having done the propitiatory rite in this eternal king of elephants, one should recite the (following) mystic words : "O ! Fortunate one ! The king has made you the chief among the elephants. The king would worship you with perfumes, flowers and excellent attendants. Then the people would worship you by his order. The king has to be protected by you in the battle, on the way and in the house. Abandoning your animal nature you remember your divine nature. In olden days, at the time of the battle between the celestials and demons, the celestials created the divine elephant. The elephant called Ariṣṭa that was born to Airāvata (elephant of Indra) inherited the splendour of the divine elephants. O King of elephants ! You attain that splendour endowed with divinity. May you be blessed with virtues ! You protect the king in the battle."

21. The king should (then) mount (the elephant) that has been consecrated thus. Excellent warriors bearing weapons should follow it.

22. Again in a lotus diagram (drawn) outside (the shed) on the ground, the guardians of the cardinal points and others should be worshipped. Bala (deva), Nāga, the earth and (goddess) Sarasvatī (should be worshipped) in the filaments.

23. After having worshipped the small drum at the centre with perfume, garlands and unguents, oblations should be made and a pitcher filled with sweet juice should be given to a brahmin.

24. Then the superintendent of the elephant, the guard of the elephant and the astrologer should be worshipped. A small drum should be given to the superintendent of the elephant and he should make it sound. It should produce auspicious and loud sounds. He should sound this while remaining on the buttocks (of the elephant).

CHAPTER TWO HUNDRED AND NINETYTWO

The greatness of cows and their welfare

Dhanvantari said :

1. A king should protect cows and brahmins. I shall describe the propitiation of cows. Cows are sacred and auspicious. The world is sustained by them.

2. Their feces and urine are the excellent destroyers of poverty. Stroking of a cow and the water from its horns would destroy multitudes of sins.

3. The urine and feces of a cow, milk, curd, clarified butter and *rocanā* (yellow pigment got from a cow) are the six constituents that are excellent and when drunk they would prevent bad dreams etc.

4. (Go) *rocanā* is capable of nullifying poison and demons. One who feeds the cow with a morsel of food would go to heaven. In whose house cows are ill-kept, that person would go to hell.

5-6a. One who gives a morsel of food to a cow belonging to another would go to heaven. One who does good to a cow would reach the world of Brahmā. One who makes a gift of a cow, one who sings her praise and one who saves her life would elevate his family. The earth becomes pure by the breath of cows. Sins get destroyed by their touch.

6b-8. The urine of a cow, the feces, milk, curd, clarified butter and the water in which *kuśa* (grass) (has been dipped) (being taken) and a night's fasting would purify even a vile person. It was practised by the gods in days of yore to destroy all inauspiciousness. If each one of the above was practised for three days, it was known as the *mahāsāntapana*. This is capable of fulfilling all the desires (of a person) and destroying all that is inauspicious.

9. It was (known as) *kṛcchrātikṛcchra*, if one lived on milk for twentyone days. The excellent men (who practised it) would become stainless, would get all the desires fulfilled and attain heaven.

10-11. One should drink hot urine, hot ghee, and hot milk, each one for three days and consume air only for the next three days. This vow known as *taptakṛcchra* would destroy all sins and confer the world of Brahmā. It is known as *śītakṛcchra* if done with cold things (as above). It was described by Brahmā. It would yield the world of Brahmā.

12-13a. One should bathe in the urine of a cow, maintain himself with milk and move with the cows eating after they had eaten. It is known as *govrata*. One would become free from the sins in a month. He would attain the world of cows and reach heaven.

13b-14a. One who mutters the *gomati vidyā* (a sacred formula) would reach the excellent world of cows. Therein he will enjoy music, dance and the company of nymphs in the celestial car.

14b-18. Cows are always fragrant. They give out the perfume of *guggulu* (fragrant resin). They are the sustainers of beings. Cows are the supreme conferers of welfare. The excellent food for gods is the clarified butter from cows. They pour out and utter purity for all the beings. They satisfy the immortals in heaven with the clarified butter purified by mystic formulas. Cows are connected with sacrificial rites such as *agnihotra* of the sages. Cows are the excellent refuge of all beings. They are supremely holy and are exceedingly auspicious. Cows are the steps leading to heaven. They are the perpetually blessed ones.

19. Obeisance to cows ! To the fortunate ones ! To the fragrant ones ! Obeisance to the daughters of Brahmā ! Obeisance to the holy ones !

20-22. One family has been made into two (such as) brahmins and cows. Γhe sacred formulas remain on one side and clarified butter on the other. The entire universe is supported by gods, brahmins, cows, holy men and chaste women. Hence they are always considered to be the fittest to be worshipped. Wherefrom (cows) would drink is known to be a sacred spot. Cows are really the Ganges and others. The greatness of cows has been told. Listen to me ! I shall now describe the treatment (of their diseases).

23. Oil mixed with rock salt and decoction of *śṛṅgavera*, *balā* and *māṃsa*, together with honey should be used for the diseases affecting the horns of cows.

24. Oil prepared with *mañjiṣṭhā*, asafoetida and rock salt or garlic alone should be used in all kinds of pain in the ears.

25. Besmearing a paste of the roots of *bilva*, *apāmārga*, *dhātakī*, *pāṭalā* and *kuṭaja* at the base of the teeth would remove the pain therein.

26. O Rāma ! Ghee heated with the ingredients used for removing tooth-ache is known to remove the disease of mouth. Rock-salt (is used) for the diseases of tongue.

27-28. *Śṛṅgavera*, the two varieties of turmeric and the three kinds of myrobalans (are useful to remedy) the stiffness of neck. The three myrobalans mixed with ghee given as a drink to cows is commended in heartache, stomachache, rheumatic complaints and pulmonary diseases. The two varieties of turmeric and *pāṭhā* may be given for dysentery.

29. *Śṛṅgavera* and *bhārgi* may be given for the diseases of the digestive organs and the pulmonary capillaries, cough and asthma.

30. *Priyaṅgu* together with salt should be given for joining the broken (bones). Oil that removes wind, when heated with *madhuyaṣṭi* (would cure) biliousness.

31. Mustard mixed with honey (would be the remedy) for (deranged) phlegm. (For the diseases) of the flesh, the same with the dust of *puṣṭaka* (would be the remedy). One should

apply oil, clarified butter and *haritāla* on wounds from which blood oozes out.

32-34. Blackgram, sesamum, wheat, cow's milk and ghee made into a ball with salt gives nourishment to the calves. It would give strength to the young bulls. Fumigation would destroy the affliction due to evil planets. Fumigation with *devadāru*, *vacā*, *māṁsi*, *guggulu*, asafoetida and mustard is beneficial for cows against pain due to evil planets. After fumigation a bell should be tied to cows.

35. If a cow is fed with *aśvagandhā* and sesamum it would increase its strength and make it yield profuse milk. For a bull that is maintained in the house, oil-cake (would be) the elixir.

36. The goddess of fortune should always be worshipped in the feces of the cows on the fifth (lunar day) for peace. (Lord) Vāsudeva (should) also (be worshipped) with perfumes etc. A different propitiatory rite will be described now.

37. (Lord) Hari (Viṣṇu) should be worshipped on the fifteenth day of the bright fortnight in (the month of) *aśvayuk* (October-November). (Lord) Hari, Rudra, Aja (Brahmā), Sun, (goddess of) Fortune and Fire-god (should be worshipped) with ghee.

38-39a. After feeding cows with curd and worshipping (them), one should circumambulate the fire. One should also arrange for a bull-fight accompanied by singing and instrumental music outside (the place). Salt should be given to cows. Brahmins (should be paid) the fees.

39b-43. In the periodical (propitiatory rite) (Lord) Viṣṇu should be worshipped at the centre of a lotus (diagram) on the ground along with (goddess) Śrī on the (occasion of Sun's transit through) Capricorn etc. The celestials should be worshipped in the filaments in the (different) directions. The Sun, the *Subhadrāja* (born as fortunate) and Bali, the Bahurūpa should be worshipped outside. The Sky, Viśvarūpā, Siddhi, Ṛddhi, Śānti, Rohiṇī (should also be worshipped). The guardian cows of the cardinal points—east etc., the Moon and Īśvara (should be worshipped) in the filaments. The guardian deities of the cardinal points (should be worshipped) in the pitchers (placed) on the petals of the lotus. Oblation should be made unto the fire with the twigs of the *kṣira* tree, mustard and unbroken rice a hundred times each. Gold and bronze should be given away to brahmins. Cows should then be worshipped and released for the sake of peace and to be endowed with milk etc.

Fire-god said :

44. Śālihotra narrated the veterinary science relating to the horses to Suśruta. Pālakāpya narrated the science relating to the elephants to Aṅgarāja.

CHAPTER TWO HUNDRED AND NINETYTHREE

Different kinds of mantras and their nomenclature

Fire-god said :

1. Listen to me ! I shall describe the science relating to the mystic formulas that would yield enjoyment and emancipation. O Brahmin ! The mystic formulas containing more than twenty letters are known to be *mālāmantra-s*.

2. The mystic formulas having more than ten letters (and less than twenty) are designated as *arvāgbija-s*. These yield results in the old age, while the *mālāmantras* in the youth.

3-5a. The formulas having more than five letters yield fruits always. The other formulas belonging to the group of *mantras* are of three kinds such as feminine, masculine and neuter. The feminine *mantras* end with (the term) Svāhā (consort of Fire). The neuter *mantras* end with (the term) obeisance. The rest are masculine. They are commended (to be used) in charms to subjugate and to drive away (evil). The feminine (*mantras*) (are used) to destroy diseases due to mean acts, while the neuter ones in other cases.

5b-7. *Mantras* (are also classified as) *āgneya* (fiery) and *saumya* (pleasing). They should be repeated at the beginning and end of the asterisms and the halves. The *āgneya mantra* is generally laid down as having the asterism at the end and the fire and the ether (in greater proportions). The rest (are said to be) *saumya*. The two (varieties of *mantras*) are commended to be used in cruel and good deeds (respectively). The *āgneya mantra* may perhaps be *saumya* by the addition of 'obeisance' at the end. *Saumya mantra* (would also) in the same way (be) *āgneya* by the addition of the syllable *phaṭ*.

8. A *mantra* would not accomplish (the result) if it is either asleep or awakened. The sleeping state (of a *mantra*) is when there is powerful (breath through the nostrils and the waking state when the breath) flows through the right (nostril).

9. By the inversion (of the letters) of an *āgneya mantra* one would get (the letters) of a *saumya mantra*. One should ascertain the waking state of both (the *mantras*) and the day for both.

10-14a. The *mantras*, whose letters are presided over by baneful asterisms and constellations, should be avoided. In order to acquire kingdom, the vowel letters which are inimical to the component letters of one's name, should be first arranged in due order. "May you go and fill the abode of the king". Thus the script is made ready. The vowels should be arranged in the different asterisms in order ending with the (asterism) Revatī. The chambers should be marked as the *siddha-s* (successful, such as the ninth, the first and the fifth chamber), the *sādhya-s* (successful in time, such as the sixth the tenth and the second chamber), the *susiddha-s* (extremely successful, such as the third, the seventh and the eleventh chamber), and the *ari* (hostile, such as the fourth, the eighth and the twelfth chamber) and the character of each *mantra* in relation to the name of the individual to whom it should be imparted, should be calculated therefrom.

14b-15. One accomplishes merely by the repetition of the *siddha* (*mantra*). The *sādhya* (*mantra*) (could accomplish) by the repetition, worship and making an oblation. The *susiddha* (*mantra*) would accomplish by mere contemplation. (The *mantra* known as) *ari* would destroy the votary. A *mantra* full of baneful letters of the alphabet is condemned by all.

16. After having been duly initiated ending with the ceremonial bathing and after having had the exposition of the *tantra* from the preceptor, one has to practise the desired *mantra* got from the preceptor.

17-18a. A person who is bold, competent, pure, devoted, bent on repetition, contemplation and the like, accomplished, who practises penance, is intelligent, knows the *tantra*, speaks the truth and is capable of restraining and blessing (the disciple) is said to be a preceptor.

18b-19. A disciple (should be) calm, restrained, clever, studied, celebate, and eating food fit for oblation. He should do service to the preceptor. He should be eager to accomplish. He (should be) instructed. He (should be) like a son, modest and capable of giving money.

20-21a. A *mantra* should be imparted by the preceptor. When it is accomplished the preceptor should repeat it a thousand times. A *mantra* that has been heard accidentally, or got by fraudulent means or by force or written on a leaf or (got) in the form of a *gāthā* (a verse) would not bear any fruit.

21b-23a. One who practises a *mantra* by means of several acts such as repetition, oblation, worship and the like, attains success by little practice. There is nothing which cannot be achieved by means of a *mantra* that has been perfectly practised. What to say about a person who has practised many *mantras*. He is really Śiva Himself.

23b-24a. A *mantra* (consisting) of a single letter bears fruit after repetition for ten lakh (a million) times. The repetition is reduced as the number of letters (in the *mantra*) is increased. In this way one has to flock together the other *mantras*.

24b-25. The *mantras* containing letters twice or thrice the *bīja mantras* should be repeated like a *mālāmantra*. A *mantra* should be repeated a hundred and eight or a thousand times if the number of their repetition has not been specified. It is known that the number of libations and anointments is in general a tenth part of the number of repetitions.

26. For one who is not able to repeat, ghee (would be the material) for libation, in all the cases, if the material has not been specified. The number of repetitions of the component (*mantras*) would be a tenth as that of the main *mantra*.

27. When the *mantras* are repeated according to their potency, the presiding deities of the *mantras* yield the desired (fruits). They get pleased with the contemplation, oblation and worship etc. of the votary.

28. The muttering of a *mantra* is ten times more meritorious than their loud repetition. Repetition with the tongue (within the mouth) is hundred times (meritorious). The mental (repetition) is known to be a thousand times (more meritorious).

29. One should begin the repetition of a *mantra* facing the east or looking downwards. All the *mantras* should begin with the *pranava* (the syllable *Oṁ*). One should restrain from conversing and eat the prescribed food.

30. One has to repeat the *mantras* remaining seated. He should look at his preceptor and the (favourite) deity alike. The places (suited for the practice) are a solitary cottage, temples and (banks of) rivers and tanks.

31-34. One who wants to gain perfection (in a *mantra*), should live on rice-gruel, cakes, milk or *haviṣya* (that is to be offered to fire) food. The votary should worship the presiding deity of the *mantra* on the lunar days and week-days such as the eighth and fourteenth days of the dark fortnight and eclipses etc. Dasra (Aśviṇī devatā), Yama (God of Death), the Fire-god, Dhātṛ (Brahmā), the Moon, Rudra, Jupiter, Diti, the serpents, the Pitṛs, Bhaga, Aryamā, the Sun, Tvaṣṭṛ, the Maruts, Indra, the Fire-god, Mitra, Indra, Nirṛti. the Water, Viśvedevas, Hṛṣikeśa (name of Viṣṇu), the Winds, the god of water (Varuṇa), Ajaikapād (one of Rudras), Ahirbudhnya (one of the Rudras), Pūṣan are the deities of (the asterisms) Aśvinī and others.

35-36a. The fire-god, Dasra (Aśvinī devatā), Umā (consort of Śiva), Nighna (Vināyaka ?), Nāga (serpent), the Moon (Candra), the Sun, the divine mothers, (goddess) Durgā, the presiding deities of the cardinal points, Kṛṣṇa, Vaivasvata (god of death), Śiva, the Moon (Śaśāṅka) and the Pitṛs are the presiding deities of the lunar days.

36b-40. Hara (Śiva), Durgā, Jupiter, Viṣṇu, Brahmā, Lakṣmī and Kubera are the presiding deities of the days of the week. I shall describe the assignment of the letters (on the different parts of the body). The letters constituting the five groups (of consonants such as *ka*, *ca*, *ṭa*, *ta* and *pa*), should be assigned on the tips of the grown up hair, eyes, the pair of ears, nose, cheeks, lips, teeth, head, mouth, arms, feet, joints, sides, back, navel and heart in order. The letters *ya* and others should be assigned on the heart. Skin, blood, flesh, fat, bone, marrow and semen are the seven essential ingredients (of the body). The regent of the letters beginning with *rasa* (essential juice) and ending with *payas* (milk) should be written.

41-42. Śrīkaṇṭha, Ananta, Sūkṣma, Trimūrti, Amareśvara (Indra), Agnīśa, Bhāvabhūti, Tithīśa, Sthāṇuka, Hara, Daṇḍīśa, Bhautika, Sadyojāta, Anugraheśvara, Akrūra and Mahāsena are the presiding deities to be worshipped.

43-46. The deities Krodhīśa, Caṇḍa, Pañcāntaka, Śiva, Rudra, Kūrma, Trinetra, Caturānana, Ajeśa, Śarmā, Someśa, Lāṅgali, Dāruka, Ardhanārīśvara, Umā, Kānta, Āṣāḍhi, Daṇḍin, Atri, Mīna, Meṣa, Lohita, Śikhī, Chagalaṇḍa, Dviraṇḍa, Mahākāla, Bālin, Bhujaṅga, Pinākī, Khaḍgīśa, Baka, Śveta, Bhṛgu, Laguḍī, Īśākṣa, Kṣaya and Saṁvarta (are also to be assigned).

47. After having written (the names of) the Rudras together with their consorts at first, then ending with obeisance, they should be assigned in order. Then the *aṅga-mantras* should be located. All the *mantras* with their constituents are capable of yielding perfection.

48-51. These *aṅga-mantras* should be completed with the hṛllekhā and vyoma and located. Then the heart and other parts of the body should be associated with the *aṅgamantras*. 'Obeisance' would be for the heart, *svāhā* (oblation) for the head, *vaṣaṭ* for the tuft, *huṁ* for the armour, *vauṣaṭ* for the eye and *phaṭ* for the weapon. Eye need not be included when the five *aṅgas* are uttered. Where there is no *aṅgamantra* (for a *mantra*), the location should be made in the self and repetition is made a million times. After having located in order the goddess Vāgīśī and the other gods mentioned, sesamum should be offered to the fire. The goddess of letters who bears the garland of letters, a pitcher, a book and a lotus would bestow the ability to compose poetry. One should do the assignment at the beginning of an act. All the *mantras* become spotless and yield perfection by (the grace of) the divine mothers even if one is not a poet.

CHAPTER TWO HUNDRED AND NINETYFOUR

The characteristics of different kinds of serpents

The Fire-god said :

1. The different species of serpents, their nature, the ten places (in the body at which a bite would be fatal), the remedial action, (the resultant) impurity and the behaviour of the (person) bitten (by the serpent) are said to be the seven characteristics.

2-3. Śeṣa, Vāsuki, Takṣa, Karkoṭaka, Abja (Padma), Mahāmbuja (Mahāpadma), Śaṅkhapāla and Kulika are the eight chief serpents. They have ten, eight, five, three, three and hundred heads in order. Every two of these serpents are said to be *brahmins*, *kṣatriyas*, *vaiśya* and *śūdras* in order.

4-8. (The serpents) born in their family (are) five hundred from whom innumerable serpents came into being. (The serpents are of three kinds such as) the *phaṇi*, *maṇḍali* and *rājila* being windy, bilious and phlegmatic respectively. The variety known as *vyantara* has these humours mixed. The serpents are known as having hoods. They bear (the signs of) cart-wheels, ploughshares, umbrellas, *svastikas* and goads. (The serpents known as) *gonasas* move slowly. They are long and bear different kinds of rings. (Those known as) *rājilas* are variegated, glossy and (can fly) across and upwards with their wings. The *vyantaras* (would have) mixed marks. (They are again classified) into four kinds as earthy, watery, fiery and windy and are divided into twentysix kinds. The *gonasas* are sixteen kinds, the *rājilas*, thirteen and the *vyantaras*, twentyone. Those which are born at an unspecified time are known as the *vyantaras*.

9-12. Their impregnation lasts for four months beginning with the three months commencing from *Āṣāḍha*. Two hundred and forty eggs are laid. The serpents swallow their young without showing any distinction such as the males, females and hermaphrodites. The eyes get opened in seven days. The outer (skin) becomes black after a month. After twelve days its faculty gets developed. The teeth appear on seeing the Sun. The teeth *karāli*, *makari*, *kālarātri* and *yamadūtikā* (grow) in twenty to thirtytwo days. There are the venomous teeth on the left and right sides.

13-14. They discard their (outer) skin after six months. They would live for one hundred and twenty years. Seven serpents (among the eight mentioned earlier) preside over the days and nights of days such as Sun-day and the like. Among them six (preside over) every week. Kulika (is the lord) of all the junctions of periods. Kulika may exercise its influence jointly with either Śaṅkha or Mahābja (Mahā-padma).

15. One *nāḍikā* (24 minutes) in between the two is the period of the Kulika. It is a malignant period in all the circumstances and especially in the serpent bite.

16-18a. The asterisms Kṛttikā, Bharaṇī, Svātī, Mūla, the three pūrvas (pūrvaphālgunī, Pūrvāṣāḍha and Pūrvabhādrapada), Aśvinī, Viśākhā, Ārdrā, Magha, Āśleṣa, Citrā, Śravaṇa, Rohiṇī, Hasta, Saturdays and Tuesdays among the days, the fifth, eighth, sixth as well as fourth, ninth and the fourteenth lunar days are malignant. The four twilight periods and malignant *yoga* (periods) as well as the (malignant) constellations are bad.

18b-20a. There would be a single or a couple or many bites (of the serpents). The bites are of four varieties—pierced, cut, apprehended and concealed. The bites in which there are three or two incisions or a single incision, pain, profuse bleeding and a bite in the leg in the night accompanied by (swelling) resembling (the shape of) a tortoise are directed by Yama (i.e. sure to be fatal).

20b-21a. A bite accompanied by burning and itching sensation (at the mouth of the bite), swelling and pain in the neck, gruelling pain and knotty (swelling) (should be known) to have the poison spread (in the body). If it is otherwise it should be taken as free from poison.

21b-25. It is inauspicious if one is bitten in a temple, an uninhabited house, an ant-hill, a garden, a hole, at a cross-road, in a cremation ground, on the bed of a river, at the confluence (of a river) with the ocean, in an island, at the meeting point of four roads, on the terrace of a building, in a flower, on the summit of a hill, at the mouth of a hole, in an old well, in a dilapidated house, on a wall and on the trees such as the *śigru, śleṣmātaka, akṣa, jambū, udumbara, veṇa* and *vaṭa* (the fig tree) as well as on a demolished compound, or at an aperture of the human body, face, heart, arm-pit, collar bone, palate, bone of the forehead, neck, head, chin, navel and feet. A messenger (who is sent to convey the news to the snake-charmer) is auspicious, if he has a flower in his hand, speaks well, is intelligent, belongs to the same sex and caste (as that of the person bitten), wears white dress, has no blemishes and is pure.

26-28. One who enters through the side door, one who carries a weapon, one who has erred, one who has a down-cast look, one who wears decoloured dress, one who has the noose etc. in his hand, one who stammers, one who holds a dry piece of wood, one who feels depressed, one who holds sesamum in his hand and clothes, one who wears a wet dress, one who wears black or red flowers on his tuft, one who presses the nipple, one who cuts the nails, one who touches the buttocks, one who scratches (the earth) with the foot (toe), one who pulls out his hair and one who cuts the grass are inauspicious messengers.

29. The sex of the person bitten should be known as male or female or hermaphrodite from he flow of the breath forcibly through the left or right or both the nostrils of the self (the snake-charmer) or the messenger.

30. One should indicate that part of the body as having been bitten which the messenger touches (when he meets the snake-charmer). It forebodes evil if the messenger moves his legs. If one has his (foot) raised without movement it indicates good.

31. If the messenger has an animal by his side (when conveying the news), it augurs good. If he is found with anything else it forebodes evil. If the animal that is present paces here and there, it forebodes bad. But (if it paces here and there) when the messenger is conveying (the message), it augurs good.

32. If the speech of a messenger is faulty at the beginning or middle, it is extremely ominous. The period that the venom would last could be known from the distinctions at the end of his speech.

33-34. The alphabets are divided into two groups—the vowels beginning with '*a*' and the groups of letters beginning with '*ka*' (*ka*, *ca*, *ṭa*, *ta* and *pa*). The group forming the vowels is known as *vasumān*. The four letters of the consonants are sacred to the Wind-god, Fire-god, Indra and Water respectively. The fifth letters belong to hermaphrodite. The vowels are sacred to Indra and water (alternatively).

35. The presence of letters sacred to Wind and Fire (gods) at the beginning of a speech of the messenger is not good. (The presence of a letter sacred to) Hari (Indra) is mediocre. (The presence of) letters (sacred) to Varuṇa (god of water) is commendable. (The presence of) hermaphrodite (letters) is extremely ominous.

36. An auspicious sentence (heard as the messenger) departs or the thundering of a cloud or the trumpeting of an elephant are auspicious. The circular movement (of birds) or crying from a fruit or tree on the left side is (also) auspicious.

37. Sounds such as music etc. would be auspicious. Such things would accomplish the result. Worthless words or words expressing a calamity, a wailing sound, a scream heard from the right (side), a sneezing (are bad omen).

38-39a. The sneezing of a courtesan, a king, a virgin, a cow, an elephant, *muraja* (a musical drum), a banner, milk, clarified butter, curd, water from the conch, umbrella, *bheri* (a kind of musical drum), fruit, the celestials, rice, gold and silver are fruitful if one comes across them on his way.

39b-40. (The sight of) an artisan holding a burning log of wood, one who is clad in dirty clothes carrying a load, one who carries an axe, a jackal, a vulture, an owl, one having the matted hair, oil, skull and cotton is to be warded off. (The sight of) ash (brings in certain) loss.

41. The malady due to poison is of seven kinds depending on the movement (of the poison) from one essential ingredient of the body to another[1]. A poisonous bite (first) reaches the forehead, then the eyes, then the face. From the face it reaches the nerves associated with speech and other essential ingredients (such as the blood etc. of the body).

1. They are the blood, flesh, fat, etc.

CHAPTER TWO HUNDRED AND NINETYFIVE

The medical treatment for a serpent bite

Fire-god said :

1-2. I shall describe to you the treatment of a (poisonous) bite by means of mystic formulas, meditation and herbs. "*Oṁ*,' Obeisance to lord Nīlakaṇṭha[1] (Śiva)". The repetition of this (*mantra*) would be an antidote for poison. Liquid cowdung with clarified butter should be drunk as a life-saving medicine. Poison is said to be of two varieties—the poison due to animals such as the serpent, rat etc. and that due to the plants such as the *śṛṅga* etc.

3-4. Lord Brahmā is represented by the soft vowels and those known as *lohita* and capable of protecting represent Lord Śiva. This (the following) is a *mantra* (bearing) the name of the bird Tārkṣya (eagle, vehicle of Viṣṇu) consisting of letters (sacred to it).

Oṁ ! burn ! A person of great intellect ! is for the heart. Garuḍaviḍāla is on the head. To Garuḍa the crest-bird of heaven is for the tuft. "O Garuḍa ! One who destroys the poison ! One who pierces ! You frighten and trample down" (is the *mantra*) for the armour. "One whose command none can dispute ! *huṁ* ! *phaṭ*" (is the *mantra*) for the weapon. "One who bears a dreadful appearance ! One who frightens all ! You frighten all ! Burn. Burn them into ashes. Oblations" (is) for the eye. (In order to worship Garuḍa with the above *mantra*) a lotus (diagram) is contemplated in the heart. The seven constituent elements (of the body are assigned therein). The vowels are arranged in the petals pointing to the eight cardinal points. The letters are located in the filaments etc. The fire (is located) near the pericarp (of the lotus). Then the snake-charmer should mentally remember it on the palm of the left hand. The letters should then be assigned on the thumb and other (fingers). Thus the constituent parts of the *mantra* of the bird are distributed.

---

1. As he has drunk the deadly poison that came out of the milky ocean as it was churned.

5-7. Then (Lord) Indra, the presiding deity of the earth, of yellow colour, is assigned in a quadrilateral of the form of a mace. The white-coloured (Lord) Varuṇa, the presiding deity of water, (is assigned) in a semi-circle like the half of a lotus. (Lord) Fire, the presiding deity of lustre, (is assigned) in a *svastika* figure (inscribed within a triangle). (Lord) Wind, (is assigned) in a circle with a dot, bearing a black garland. These are assigned respectively in the middle of the fingers beginning with the thumb in their respective places covered by golden (images of) Garuḍa.

8-10. The four letters of the *mantra* (should be contemplated) as having a good halo of similar radiance. They should be located in the formless ether, presided over by (Lord) Śiva of the form of the subtle principle of sound. The first letter (of the *mantra*) should be located on the middle fold of the little finger. The first letters of the serpents are also located as being present in their own spheres. The first letters of the earth and other elements are located on the last mark of the thumb etc. Then a wise man should locate the proximate qualities such as the subtle principles and the like on the fingers.

11-14. By the touch of this Tārkṣya (*mantra*) assigned on the hand all kinds of poisons would be destroyed. Then the letters of the *mantra* of the bird should be located in the halos in the regions of the umblicus and the joints of the body. It is excellent to have it as two fingers long. A wise man should contemplate Tārkṣa (the Eagle), who pervades the cosmic universal egg, who wears the serpent ornament known as the *candra* reflecting the blue hue of his dreadful beak and who has the great wings from the knee (to the navel) as golden coloured, from the navel (to the neck) as snow-coloured, from the neck (to the hair) as red like the saffron and from the ends of the hair as black. There would thus be a charm for a poison from the statement of a charmer who is pervaded by (the letters of) the Tārkṣya (*mantra*).

15-20a. A blow with the fist, thus charged with the Tārkṣya (*mantra*), would remove poison. Raising the hand charged with the Tārkṣya (*mantra*) and passing over (the place of bite) the five fingers, and by having a look at the person intoxicated, one would arrest the spread of the poison. One should arrest the spread of the poison by the repetition of the (following) *mantra* : "This *bhūbīja* (*mantra*), the lord of the five letters has descended from the sky. I shall arrest the excessive poison." By reversing the *bhūbīja*, the resultant *mantra*, "Flood, Flood, Yama !", well-accomplished, would remove the poison. This would raise one like a stick, by bathing him with water after repeating (this *mantra*) well. Similar result could be obtained by hearing the sound (produced) by a conch or *bherī* (war drum) after repeating (this *mantra*) properly. (This *mantra*) with the inversion of (the components of) earth and splendour would burn (the poison). This *mantra* with the inversion of (the components of) earth and wind would transfer the poison.

20b-24. The practitioner of this charm possessing the shape of the figure of Garuḍa, should practise this act inside his own house with the components of earth, fire, moon and water. The repetition of this (*mantra*) in the abodes of Garuḍa and (Lord) Varuṇa would destroy the poison. This is said to be the holy *jānudaṇḍi*. It would destroy all posions and ward off fever, diseases and untimely death by bathing and drinking (the water consecrated by its repetition) marked with the components of (the syllables) *svadhā* and *śrī*. "Oh ! Bird ! Bird ! Great bird ! Great bird ! *Vi* ! *Vi* ! Oblations ! Oh ! Bird ! Bird ! Great bird ! Great bird ! *Kṣi* ! *Kṣi* ! Oblations !" These two *mantras* of the king of birds are capable of destroying poison by chanting. (The *gāyatri mantra* of Garuḍa is) : "We contemplate the king of birds. We meditate on the lord of the birds. May that Garuḍa prompt us (our minds)". Then "Kāla and Lāṅgalī", the (*mantra*) of Nīlakaṇṭha. (blue-necked, an epithet of Śiva) bearing the insignia of tooth and stick should be assigned on the chest, neck, tuft etc. on the body in front of the fire after consecration. Hara ! Hara ! Obeisance to the heart ! To the head, for Nīlakaṇṭha, to the tuft ! Oblation to one who drank the poison *kālakūṭa*[1] ! Then the armour on the neck. (Obeisance) to the three-eyed lord wearing the hide of

1. The poison that came out from the milky ocean when it was churned.

elephants (present) in (the region of) the eye ! The faces of the Lord from the east onwards (should be then contemplated) as having (the colours of) white, yellow, red and black.

25-29. The Lord should be contemplated as offering protection and boon and holding the bow and the serpent in His hands. (Goddess) Gaurī and (Lord) Rudra (are contemplated) as His presiding deity above and on the left. After having assigned the letters of the *mantra* on foot, knee, private organ, navel, heart, neck, face, head, hands, fingers beginning with the thumb, fore-finger and folds (on the fingers) and then all of them should be assigned on the thumb. After having contemplated thus, (they) should be bound quickly with the *mudrā* (formation made with the fingers), (in the shape of) a spike. The little finger should be held by the thumb. The other three are stretched out quickly. (This is that *mudrā*.) The left hand (is used) for destroying the poison and the right hand in other acts. "Oṁ ! Obeisance to Lord Nīlakaṇṭha ! *Ciḥ* ! To the clear-necked ! *Ciḥ* ! (Obeisance) to the omniscient neck ! *Ciḥ* ! Cast down ! *Oṁ* ! Oblations ! (Obeisance) to the clear-necked, blue-necked ! To the destroyer of more than one or all poisons ! Obeisance to (Lord) Rudra-Manyu !" The poison gets destroyed by rubbing with this (*mantra*) or by repeating in the ear or by (wearing) the sandal. There is no doubt. (Lord) Blue-necked, the great lord should be worshipped by following the rule laid down for the worship of Rudra. One would destroy the poison and disease by doing worship according to the rules of Rudra (worship).

CHAPTER TWO HUNDRED AND NINETYSIX

The five constituents of the worship of Rudra

Fire-god said :

1-2. I shall describe the five constituents of the worship of Rudra. It is the most excellent that confers everything. The *śivasaṅkalpa* (resolve for Śiva) is the heart. The *Puruṣasūkta*[1] is the head. (The hymn) *adbhyaḥ sambhūta*[2] is the tuft. The hymn (called) *āśu*[3] is the armour. The *śatarudriya* (hymn)[4] is the weapon. These are the five constituents in the worship of Rudra.

3-4a. After having assigned the five constituents and contemplating Him, the Rudra hymns are repeated in order. The hymn (beginning with) *yajjāgrata*[5] is known to be repeated mentally. The sage (of that hymn) is *śivasaṅkalpa* (resolve) and the metre is said to be *triṣṭubh* (consisting of 11 syllables in a quarter).

4b-5a. (For the hymn) *sahasraśirṣā*[6] for the head the sage is Nārāyaṇa. The deity (of this hymn) is the supreme soul. The metre is known to be *triṣṭubh.*

5b-6. The sage for the hymn *adbhyaḥ sambhūta*[7] is the person going to the north. *Iriṣṭubh* is the metre for the first three hymns, *anuṣṭubh* for the next two and *triṣṭubh* for the last (hymn). The deity for this (hymn) also is the supreme soul.

7-8. Indra is the lord for the twelve hymns beginning with *āśu*[8]. *Iriṣṭubh* is said to be the metre and Pratiratha, the sage. The deities are separate for each one of the verses in the hymn of seventeen verses. The deity of the constituent part is Puruvit. The metre of the remaining deities is said to be *anuṣṭubh.*

9. Indra is the deity for (the hymn) *asau yastāmraḥ*[9]. Puruliṅga is the deity for the constituent parts. *Paṅkti* is the metre. The deities of the constituent parts are vital.

10. Parameṣṭhin is the sage for all the hymns of the Rudrādhyāya[10]. For the three hymns commencing with

1. RV. 10.90·1a.
2. TA. 3.13.1a. *Cf. adbhyaḥ sambhṛtaḥ.*
3. Could not be traced.
4. Same as Rudrādhyāya.
5. Could not be traced.
6. RV. 10.90.1a.
7. See 1 above.
8. Could not be traced.
9. VS. 16.6a; TS.4.5. 1. 2a.
10. The hymns beginning with *namaste rudra manyave:* VS. 16.1a; TS. 4.5.1.1a.

'*devānāṁ kutsasya*"[1], Prajāpati is the sage.

11. For the two (hymns beginning with) *mano*[2], Umā is the single deity and Rudra for *rudrāśca*[3]. Ekarudra is the deity for the first *anuvāka* (name of a section of the collection of hymns).

12. *Gāyatra* is the metre for the first (hymn), *anuṣṭubh* for the (next) three verses and *paṅkti* and *anuṣṭubh* for the (subsequent verses).

13. Then *jagatī* is the metre for the (next) two (verses) The Rudra (hymns) are eighty. The Hiraṇyabāhus are three. "Obeisance to Thee ! O Kirika" is one.

14. Rudra is the deity of the five hymns of the twenty mantras of the Rudrānuvāka. Bṛhatī is known to be (the metre) of the first hymn.

15. The second one is a *ṛk*. The next three are in *jagatī* (metre). The third one is a *triṣṭubh*. Then the next four are *yajur* (*mantras*) in *anuṣṭubh*. One will gain perfection by means of the *āryā* (hymns).

16-17. One would be able to destroy the poison, disease and the enemy with (the repetition of) (the *mantra*) *trailokya-mohana* (one that stupefies the three worlds). "*Iṁ, śrīṁ, hrīṁ, hrūṁ* ! Obeisance to (Lord) Viṣṇu, the stupefier of the three worlds." One could (also) destroy the poison and disease with the Nṛsiṁha (*mantra*) in the *anuṣṭubh*; "*Oṁ, haṁ, iṁ* ! I make obeisance to the fiercely brave great Viṣṇu, who is glowing and who has His faces on all sides. He is the frightening Nṛsiṁha, who is benevolent and is the destroyer of death."

18-19. This is the *mantra* of five parts that accomplishes all things. The two mantras having twelve[4] and eight[5] letters are capable of destroying poison and disease. (The goddesses) Kubjikā, Tripurā, Gaurī and Candrikā are capable of destroying poison. The *mantras* relating to them also would remove poison and make one gain good health. Similarly the *mantras* relating to Sun, (Lords) Vināyaka (the elephant-faced god) and Rudra (would give) everything always.

---

1. Could not be traced.
2. Cf. RV. 10.57.3a.
3. Could not be traced.
4. *om namo bhagavate vāsudevāya.*
5. *om namo nārāyaṇāya.*

CHAPTER TWO HUNDRED AND NINETY SEVEN

The remedial mantra that would remove poison

Fire-god said :

1-2. "*Oṁ*, obeisance to Lord Rudra! You cut down venom! (Obeisance) to the wielder of an axe of fire in his hand! Obeisance to Lord Rudra in the form of the bird (Garuḍa)! You make the bitten person get up! Shake him up! Make him converse! Rouse up the person bitten by the serpent! Make him dangle! Bind him! Release him! Oh! The Excellent Rudra! You go, strike, bend, make noise and frighten and destroy the poison with your fist! *Ṭha* ! *Ṭha* !"

The poison gets destroyed by the repetition of the *mantra* of the bird. "*Oṁ* ! Obeisance to Lord Rudra ! Destroy all kinds of poison—vegetable or animal, artificial or natural, primary or secondary ! Destroy different kinds of poison ! Destroy the venom in the bitten person ! Subdue ! Eject ! You become free from poison by the showers of darkness in the form of the clouds. Destroy ! Go forth! You neutralise the poison by ejecting it." The poison would be controlled with the repetition of this mantra. "*Oṁ*! Throw away ! *Om* Throw away ! Oblations! *Oṁ*, *hrāṁ*, *hriṁ*, *khiṁ*, *saḥ*, *ṭhaṁ*, *drauṁ*, *hriṁ*, *ṭhaḥ* !" Being accomplished by the repetition, one would be able to bind the serpents always. One could accomplish all things (by the repetition of the *mantra*) : "Obeisance to the beloved of milk-maids" having one, two, three or four letters and having the disc of Kṛṣṇa as the fifth part.

3-4a. "*Oṁ*, obeisance to Lord Rudra, the lord of ghosts ! Listen ! Make sound ! Make to rotate ! Release ! Stupefy ! Manifest ! Enter ! Golden bird ! Rudra makes known ! *Ṭha* !" This *mantra* known as the agitator of hell would destroy the poison when repeated. A person bitten by a snake should cauterize with log or stone for subduing the poison immediately after being bitten. The bitten part of the body should be cauterized with burning red lotus etc.

4b-5a. The drinking or besmearing or collyrium of the three pungent things—seeds of *śiriṣa* flower, *arka* flower and *ksirá* seeds would destroy the poison.

5b-6a. There is no doubt that the white pepper mixed with the essence of the *śiriṣa* flower would remove poison when drunk or used as sternutatory or collyrium.

6b-7. The three pungent things, *koṣātakī*, *vacā* and asafoetida mixed with the milk of *śirīṣa* and *arka* and the *meṣa* mixed with water would remove the poison when used as a sternutatory. The powder of asafoetida and all parts of *ikṣvāku* used as a sternutatory would remove the poison.

8. The expressed juice of *indrabalā*, *agnika*, *droṇa*, *tulasi*, *devikā* and *sahā* mixed with the powder of the three pungent things when eaten would remove the poison. The five parts of the *śiriṣa* eaten on the fifth (lunar day) of the dark (fortnight) would remove the poison.

CHAPTER TWO HUNDRED AND NINETYEIGHT

The treatment for the poison due to snakes such as the gonasa and others

Fire-god said :

1. O Vasiṣṭha ! Listen to me ! I shall describe to you the treatment for (the poison due to) *gonasa* and others (snakes). *Hriṁ*, *hriṁ* oblations to the stainless bird ! A charmer would remove the poison due to *maṇḍalin* (a kind of snake) by eating the betel leaf (after consecrating it with the above *mantra*).

2. Garlic, asafoetida, *kuṣṭha*, *agni*, dried ginger, pepper and long pepper (are remedies) for poison. The milk of *snuhi* and clarified butter from the cow would remove the poison due to a class of snakes called *ahi*, when it is drunk for a fortnight.

3. When one is bitten by (the snake called) *rājila*, he should drink pepper with rock-salt. Clarified butter, honey and cow-dung water (taken) with *puritaki* would remove poison.

4-6a. Thick milk and clarified butter together with pepper should be drunk with honey. Pepper, dried ginger and long pepper, the feather of a peacock, the bone of a cat and the hair of a mongoose in equal parts should be powdered after soaking with the milk of a goat. Fumigation (with the above powder) would remove all kinds of poisons. The hair (of mongoose), *nirguṇḍi*, and *kola* with same proportion of garlic burnt with the leaf of (the plant) *muni* and boiled with sour gruel (could be used for fumigation to remove poison).

6b-7. Rats are of sixteen kinds. One should drink the juice of cotton together with oil (to remove the poison due to them). The *phalini* flower will also destroy the affliction due to the rats. Eating of molasses together with *nāgara* would also remove that poison and the loss of appetite.

8-11a. There are twenty ways of treating (this poison). The group (of remedies) for removing the poison due to a spider etc. : *padmaka, pāṭali, kuṣṭha, uśira,* sandal, *nirguṇḍi, śārikā* and *śelu* should be made into a paste and applied for affliction due to the spider. The leaves of *guñjā, nirguṇḍi* and *aṅkola,* dried ginger, the two kinds of turmeric, the kernel of *karañja* made into a paste and applied (would also remedy that poison). Listen to me ! (I shall describe) the remedy that would remove the poison due to a scorpion. A paste of the mixture of *mañjiṣṭhā*, sandal, dried ginger, pepper, long pepper and the flowers of *śiriṣa* and the white water-lily used in four ways such as ointment and the like would remove (the poison due to) a scorpion.

11b-12. *Oṁ* obeisance to Lord Rudra ! *Civi* ! *Civi* ! Cut ! cut ! *Kiri* ! *kiri* ! Break ! Cut with the sword ! Pierce with the spear ! Severe with the disc ! *Oṁ hrūṁ phaṭ.* When (the herb) is given after the repetition of the (above) *mantra,* it would destroy the poison due to an ass and others (animals). The three myrobalans, *uśira, musta* water, *māṁsi, padmaka* and sandal being drunk together with goat's milk would remove the poison due to an ass and others (animals).

13. Five parts of *śirīṣa* (together with) dried ginger, pepper and long pepper would remove the venom due to the centipedes. The neck of the *śirīṣa* and its kernel would remove the poison due to a rat.

14-15. The dried ginger, pepper and long pepper together with clarified butter and made into a paste with the root of long pepper would remove the poison. (A mixture of) alkali, dried ginger, pepper and long pepper, *vacā*, asafoetida, *viḍaṅga*, rocksalt, *ambaṣṭha*, *atibala* and *kuṣṭha* would remove the venom due to all insects. A combination of *yaṣṭi*, dried ginger, pepper and long pepper, treacle and milk would remove the poison due to a dog.

16-18. *Oṁ*, obeisance to Subhadrā ! *Oṁ*, obeisance to Suprabhā ! You have been told by Brahmā that you should absorb the seed of the herbs which are taken by people without (adhering to) the instructions. After having made obeisance to them and the herbs later, the barley grains should be scattered with the fist. This *mantra* should be repeated ten times. Then obeisance should be made to that herb. (One should say) "I lift you, the one looking upwards" and take the herb.

19-21. "Obeisance to the lion among men (eminent man) ! Obeisance to the cowherd ! O Kṛṣṇa ! You yourself have admitted that one (who takes your name) will not be defeated in battle". May the medicine be successful for me ! Obeisance to Vaidūrya mother ! O Gaurī ! Protect me therein from all venoms ! O Gāndhāri ! O Cāṇḍāli ! O Mātaṅgini ! Oblations to the illusive energy of Hari ! This is the *mantra* to be used before (administering) the medicine in the case of a vegetable poison. If there is burning sensation after taking a medicine, the patient should be made to drink cold water together with the root of lotus; ghee and honey should be taken if poison persists even then.

CHAPTER TWO HUNDRED AND NINETYNINE

Recipes for the diseases of infants

Fire-god said:

1-2. I shall describe the science relating to (the diseases of) children that would destroy the evil spirits that seize children. The Pāpinī (sinister) spirit possesses the child on the day of its birth. (The child) would have trembling of the body. It would not take food and would toss about its neck. These are the reactions due to the above (spirit). It would also take away the strength of the mothers.

3-5. (An offering consisting) of fish, meat, wine, edibles, perfumes, garlands, incense and lamps (should be made to appease this spirit). The child should be besmeared with a paste of *dhātakī* (a variety of myrobalan), *lodhra*, *mañjiṣṭhā*, *tāla* and sandal. The spirit known as Bhīṣaṇī (frightful) (would seize the child) on the second night after birth. An incense made of *mahiṣākṣa* (should be offered to drive the spirit). A child possessed by this spirit would have cough with hard breathing and writhing of the body again and again. The body of the child should be besmeared with urine of goat together with black pepper, *apāmārga* and sandal. An incense made of cow's horn, tooth and hair should be offered. Offering (should be made to the spirit) as before.

6-7. The spirit Ghaṇṭālī (possesses) on the third (night after the birth). (The affected child) would cry repeatedly, yawn and make sounds. It would exhibit fear with convulsions. It would not have appetite. The child should be besmeared with a paste of *keśara* (filament of a flower), *añjana*, the tooth of a cow and tusk of an elephant together with goat's milk. An incense consisting of *nakharāji* and leaves of *bilva* should be offered. Offering (should be made to the spirit) as before.

8-9. The spirit (known as) Kākolī (possesses) on the fourth (night after the birth). (The child would have) convulsion, loss of appetite, frothing, and would turn to look in the different directions. An offering (to the spirit is made) with *kulmāṣa* and spirituous liquor. The body should be besmeared with (the scrapings of) the tusk of an elephant, the slough of a serpent and the urine of a horse. Fumigation should be done with (the vapours of) turmeric (and) neem leaves fanned by the hair.

10-11a. (The monstress) Haṁsādhikā (would affect the child) on the fifth (night). It is marked by yawning, breathing upwards and clenched fists. Offering (to the spirit) should be made with fish and the like. The child should be besmeared with (the scrapings) of goat's horn, *balā*, *lodhra*, *śilā* and *tāla*.

11b-12. The monstress Phaṭkārī (takes possession of the child) on the sixth (night). (The child would exhibit) fear, fainting and excessive weeping. It would not take food and have convulsions. The offering (is made to the spirit) with fish etc. (The body of the child) is besmeared with turmeric, *guggulu*, *kuṣṭhta*, (scrapings of) tusk of an elephant etc., and fumigation is done with the same materials.

13-19a. A child is afflicted by (the spirit) Muktakeśī on the seventh (night). There would be foul smell, yawning, exhaustion, excessive weeping and coughing. Fumigation should be done with tiger's nails. (The body of the child) should be besmeared with *vacā*, cow-dung and cow's urine. The spirit (known as) Śrīdaṇḍī (afflicts the child) on the eighth (night). (The afflicted child) would look in different directions, move the tongue, cough and weep. Offering is done as before with fish etc. Fumigation and besmearing is done with *hiṅgulā*, *vacā*, mustard and garlic. The frightful monstress Ūrdhvagrāhī (affects the child on the ninth day). (The affected child) would get agitated, have upward breathing and bite its clenched fist. Fumigation is done with red sandal, *kuṣṭha* etc. and the child is besmeared (with the same). Fumigation is done with the hair and nails of a monkey. The monstress Rodanī (affects the child) on the tenth day. (The affected child) would always weep, (the body) would smell sweet and turn blue. Fumigation is done with neem (to appease) the terrible monster. (The body) should be besmeared with turmeric and the juice of *sarja* (a kind of tree). Offering should be made outside (the house) with fried grains, *kulmāṣa* and barley. Fumigation and other such acts should be done in this manner until the thirteenth day (after the birth).

19b-22a. The terrible monster (known as) Pūtanā takes possession of the child that is one month old. The (afflicted child) weeps like a crow and breathes heavily. The body would have the smell of urine. The eyelids would close. Such a child should be bathed with cow's urine. Fumigation is done with the tooth of a cow. (The spirit should be appeased) by giving yellow clothes, red garland, red sandal, oil lamp, three kinds of sweet porridge, wine, sesamum and four kinds of flesh. Such an offering should be made for seven days at the foot of a *karañja* (tree) in the direction of Yama (south).

22b-23. (The female spirit) Mukuṭā (would seize the child) two months old. The body (of the child) would get cold. There would be vomitting, parching of the mouth and other things. Flowers, incense, cloth, sweet cake, cooked rice, lamps and (things) of black colour (should be offered). Camphor and fumigation (also should be shown).

24-26a. (The famale spirit) Gomukhī (possesses) in the third (month). (The afflicted child) would sleep (long), pass urine and motion (in excess) and cry. (This spirit should be appeased) by offering barley, *priyaṅgu*, meat, *kulmāṣa* (a kind of grain), vegetables, cooked rice and milk in the morning. Fumigation (should be made) with clarified butter at midday. (The child) should be bathed with (water mixed) with (the leaves of) five kinds (of trees). (The spirit) Piṅgalā would afflict (the child) in the fourth month. The body (of the child) would become chill, have putrid smell and be parched. That child would certainly die.

26b-27a. (The spirit) Lalanā (would seize the child) in the fifth (month). It would make the body weary. Blood would come out through the mouth. The stools (would be) yellow in colour. Offerings of fish and the like are made in the south (in order to appease that spirit).

27b-28a. (The spirit) Paṅkajā (would seize the child) in the sixth month. (Crying and modified) voice (are) the symptoms. Offering (to appease the spirit) is done with fish, meat, wine, cooked things, flowers and perfume and the like.

28b-29. (The monstress) Nirāhārā (would seize the child) in the seventh (month). (The child would have) fetid smell and the like and have toothache. Offering (is made) with flour-paste, wine and meat. (The name of the spirit that would seize the child) in the eighth (month) is Yamunā. There would be boils, desiccation and the like. One should not do medical treatment for that.

30. (The spirit) Kumbhakarṇī (afflicts the child) in the ninth (month). The afflicted child would have fever and would vomit and cry. Offering should be made with meat, *kulmāṣa* (a kind of grain) and wine and the like in the north-eastern (direction).

31. (The demoness) Tāpasī (seizes the child) in the tenth (month). The symptoms are : the child would refrain from (taking) food and have the eyes closed. (The monstress is

appeased) with (the tying of) a bell, (fixing) a banner and offering of wine and meat together with flour .on a level (ground).

32-33a. The demoness Rākṣasī (afflicts the child) in the eleventh (month). It would affect the eyes etc. There is no medical treatment (for that). (The spirit) Cañcalā (would seize the child) in the twelfth (month). There would be heavy breathing. (The child) would exhibit fear etc.

33b-34a. (The monstress) Yātanā (would affect the child) in the second year (after birth). (The child would have) pain and would cry. Offering is made with sesamum, meat, wine etc. As before bathing and other (practices are done).

34b-35. (The monstress) Rodanī (would seize the child) in the third (year). (The body would) tremble. (The child) would cry and pass urine (mixed) with blood. Cooked rice mixed with molasses and sesamum cake (should be offered) to the image (of the monster) made of sesamum flour. It is bathed with sesamum. Fumigation (should be done) with five varieties of leaves and the bark of *rājaphala* (a kind of fruit).

36. (The monstress) Caṭakā (would afflict the child) in the fourth (year). There would be swelling (in the body), fever and exhaustion in all the limbs. Offering (to appease is made) with fish, meat, wine, etc. Bathing and fumigation (are also done).

37-38a. (The monstress) Cañcalā (would seize the child) in the fifth year. (The child would have) fever, fear and exhaustion in the limbs. Offering (is done) with meat, cooked rice and the like. Fumigation (is made) with the horn of a ram. Bathing should be done with the water in which the leaves of the trees—*palāśa*, *udumbara*, *aśvattha*, *vaṭa* and *bilva* (have been put).

38b-39a. (The monstress) Dhāvanī (would afflict the child) in the sixth year. (The child would have) desiccation, insipidity and exhaustion in the body. Offering should be made for seven days. Fumigation and bathing with *bhṛṅgaka* is done before that.

39b-40a. (The spirit) Yamuṇā (would possess the child) in the seventh year. (The child would have) vomitting, speechlessness, fits of laughter and weeping. Offering consists of meat, sweet gruel, wine and the like. (Then there should be) bathing and fumigation.

40b-41a. (The spirit) Jātadevā (would possess the child) in the eighth year. (The child) would not take food and would cry. Offering (should be done) with *kṛśara* (sesamum and rice mixed), cakes and curd etc. Bathing and fumigation (should also be done).

41b-42a. (The monstress) Kālā (would seize the child) in the ninth year. (The child would make) sound by beating the arms, would roar and (exhibit) fear. The offering would be with sesamum mixed with rice, cakes, flours, *kulmāṣa* (a kind of grain) and sweet gruel.

42b-44. (The spirit) Kalahaṁsī (would possess the child) in the tenth year. There would be burning sensation, emaciation and fever. Offering should be made with the *paulika* cake (a kind of cake) and curd rice for five nights. Fumigation with *nimba* and besmearing with *kuṣṭha* (is done to appease the spirit). The possessive spirit Devadūtī (seizes the child) in the eleventh (year). (The child would utter) harsh words. Offering and smearing (are done) as before. (The spirit) Balikā (would possess the child) in the twelfth (year). There would be hard breathing. The offering and smearing (are) as before.

45-47. (The spirit) Vāyavī (would possess the child) in the thirteenth (year). The face and external organs would become emaciated. Offering (consists of) red-coloured cooked rice, incense, flowers etc. (The child) should be bathed with the five (kinds of) leaves. Fumigation (should be done) with *rājī*, and neem leaves. (The monstress) Yakṣiṇī (would possess the child) in the fourteenth (year). Colic, fever and burning sensation are the effects (due to this spirit). Offering (is made) with meat, eatables etc. Bathing for the appeasement (of the spirit is done) as before. (The spirit) Muṇḍikā (would possess) in the fifteenth (year). Discharge of blood is due to this (spirit). The mother (of the child) should always be attended to in such cases.

48. Vānarī (would seize the child) in the sixteenth (year). The child would fall to the ground, sleep always and have

fever (under the influence). Offering (is made) with sweet gruel etc. for three nights. Bathing etc. (are done as before).

49. Gandhavatī (would possess the child) in the seventeenth (year). The body (of the child) would tremble and the child would cry much. Offering (should be made) with *kulmāṣa* etc. Bathing, fumigation and smearing etc. (are done) as before. (The spirit) Pūtanā exercises her influence during the day and Sukumārikā during the whole year.

50. *Oṁ* ! Obeisance to all the mothers. Consume ! Consume the affliction that has got united with the child ! Attack ! Attack ! Explode ! Explode ! Agitate ! Agitate ! Seize ! Seize ! Manifest ! Manifest ! Thus Siddharūpa announces. Take away ! Take away ! Make the female or male child or the woman or man free from defect from the seizure of all the spirits. O Cāmuṇḍā ! Obeisance to the goddess ! *Hrūṁ* ! *Hrūṁ* ! *Hriṁ* ! Drive away (all) the evil spirits ! *Hrūṁ* ! Let the possessors go elsewhere by another way. (Lord) Rudra makes known (thus). This *mantra* would yield the desired result in all the cases of seizure of children by evil spirits.

51. *Oṁ* ! Obeisance to the Goddess ! O Cāmuṇḍā ! Make the male or female child free. Accept the offering ! Be victorious ! Be victorious ! Dwell ! Dwell ! This *mantra* that protects is read in all instances of offering being made.. May (the gods) Brahmā, Viṣṇu, Śiva, Skanda, Gaurī, Lakṣmī, and the Gaṇas protect and release the child from the affliction due to burning sensation.

CHAPTER THREE HUNDRED

Description of the mantras which remove the baneful influences of planets

Fire-god said :

1-2. I shall describe the *mantras* which would remove the baneful influences of planets and crush the planets. There would be five kinds of insanity due to joy, desire, fear, grief, eating food items which have contrary qualities and are not clean, and the wrath of the preceptor and gods etc. These are caused by the three defects (of deranged humours), their combined effect and external things.

3-5a. On account of the wrath of Rudra, the gods became the several planets. The planets would seize men and women at a river, ocean, tank etc., mountain, garden, bridge, confluence of a river, a deserted house, an entrance to a hole and a lonely tree in (any one of the following states) : one who has slept, a pregnant woman, a woman about to commence her menstrual period, and one who bathes naked after the menstrual period.

5b-8. Disrespect, enmity of men, obstacles, change of fortune, trangression of the codes of conduct relating to the gods and elders, fall from a mountain, tree and the like, brushing aside the hair on the head frequently (are the symptoms of evil influences of the planets). A person possessed (by planets) would weep, dance, have red eyes, be deformed, be agitated, suffer from pain and burning sensation, be affected by hunger and thirst and have headache. A person possessed by a planet that desires for a victim would request (saying) "Give ! Give !". A man possessed by a planet having excessive desire would desire for women, garlands, enjoyment and bath.

9. (The *mantras*) of the great Sudarśana (disc of lord Viṣṇu) that pervades the sky, twig-shaped nose, Pātālanārasiṁha and the like and the Caṇḍīmantras are capable of subduing the planets.

10-12a. One should worship the lord who is fond of *pṛśnī* (an aquatic plant), asafoetida, *vacā* and bunch of *śirīṣa* (flowers). (One should worship Him) who is the supreme person, who bears the noose, goad, rosary, human skull, who holds (in his hand) a club with the skull, lotus and mace, who has four faces, who is on a lotus amidst inner and outer staffs with skull in the orb of the Sun together with the Sun and others should be worshipped and water for sipping should be offered to the Sun who has risen.

12b. Venus (should be contemplated) as having the form of breath, poison, fire, a brahmin, pitcher and *hṛllekhā* (knowledge ?).

13-14. "*Bhūrbhuvaḥ svaḥ*" for Arka (Sun) and Jālinī the family mace (are used in the worship of Sun). The Moon (is contemplated as) seated on the lotus, having light red complexion, wearing red clothes, spreading radiance in the universe, lofty, holding lotuses in his two hands and having all the limbs adorned. Moreover the heart and other limbs (should be contemplated) as red, benevolent, conferring boons and holding lotuses.

15-16. Mars (should be contemplated) as resembling a multitude of lightning, wearing white clothes, beautiful and light red in complexion. Mercury (is also contemplated) in the same manner. Jupiter (is contemplated) as yellow, Venus as white, Saturn as dark, Rāhu (the ascending node) as resembling charcoal and Ketu (the descending node) as grey. They (should be contemplated as having) the left hand (placed) on the left thigh and the right hand (placed) on the right thigh and knee.

17. The first letters of their names would be their *bijas* (the mystical letter forming the essential part of the *mantra*). The two hands are purified with (the *mantra* of) the weapon. Then (the letters) should be assigned on (the fingers) beginning with the thumb, the palm, the two eyes as pervading the heart and the other (limbs).

18. One should contemplate the life force and carry out the location of the three basic letters (of the *mantra*) in the limbs. The vessel should be sprinkled with (the *mantra* of) the weapon and filled with water with the basic (*mantra*).

19. After having placed incense, flowers, unbroken rice and *dūrvā* (grass), the offering should be sanctified. One should then spinkle that (water) on oneself as well as on the materials for worship.

20. Then one should contemplate the absolute, pure, essence (that confers) supreme happiness. One should then (mentally) set up the seat etc. in the centre and in the different directions with (the *mantras* of) the heart.

21. One should (offer the worship) on the seat and in the (main) directions as well as the intermediate directions with (the *mantra* of) the heart. (One should contemplate) the heart-lotus on the seat and the eight female energies in the filaments.

22-23. One should worship (the goddesses) Dīptā, Sūkṣmā, Jayā, Bhadrikā, Vibhūti, Vimalā, Asighātavidyutā and Sarvatomukhī and the seat with the syllables *vāṁ*, *viṁ*, *vuṁ*, *vūṁ*, *veṁ*, *vaiṁ*, *voṁ*, *vauṁ* and *vaṁ* and then worship the Sun with (the syllable) *vaḥ*. Oh ! One who practises austerities ! Water for drinking and other formalities should be offered with (the *mantras* of) the heart and the six accessories after having invoked.

24. The two '*kha*' syllables, the two *daṇḍins*, the two *Caṇḍas*, the marrow together with the teeth, *māṁsadirghā* (?), *jaradvāyu* (?) etc. of the Sun that confer all the things (should be worshipped) with (the *mantra* of) the heart.

25. The heart etc. should be worshipped in the south-east, north-east, south-west and north-west, extending upto the pericarps with their respective *mantras*. The weapon with the eye (should be worshipped) in the forepart of the directions.

26. (The planets) Moon, Mercury, Jupiter and Venus should be worshipped in the directions commencing with the east. In the case of diseases caused by planets, one should do the sternutatory, unguent etc. with *pṛśni*, asafoetida, *vacā*, *cakra* (?), *śirīṣa* and garlic together with the goat's urine.

27. One *pala* each of *pāṭha*, mustard, *vacā*, *śigru*, rock-salt and dried ginger, pepper and long pepper ground well and mixed with an *āḍhaka* (a unit of measure) of goat's milk and the ghee prepared. (The use of this) would remove all (the defects due to) the planets.

28. One should drink the water mixed with the *vṛścika* (a herb), *ali*, *phali*, *kuṣṭha*, the salts and *śārṅgaka*. It would destroy epilepsy.

29-31. One should drink the decoction made with *vidāri*, *kuśa*, *kāśa* and sugarcane mixed with milk and boiled (as a remedy for the same). (Similarly) clarified butter boiled with essence of *yaṣṭika*, *droṇa* and *kūṣmāṇḍa* (would be a remedy). So also ghee of the five things got from a cow (would do good). Listen to me about the combination that would remove the fever. "*Oṁ* ! Let us know (the nature of) the deity that has the weapon to reduce (all the things) to ashes. Let us meditate on (that god having) single tusk. May fever make us meditate on that." One should lick (a paste made of) long pepper, pepper, turmeric, *rāsnā*, oil extracted from grapes and molasses.

32. One who has breathing trouble should lick *bhāṅgi* (hemp) and *yaṣṭi* with honey and clarified butter. Or else one should lick *pāṭhā*, *tiktā*, *kaṇā* and *bhāṅgī* with honey.

33. *Dhātrī*, *viśvasitā*, *kṛṣṇa*, *musta*, *kharjūra*, *māgadhi* and *pivara* (?) would destroy hiccup. The three should be licked with honey.

34. One should drink the juice of *kāmāli*, *jira*, *māṇḍūki*, turmeric and *dhātrī* (one of the myrobalan). Long pepper, pepper dried ginger, *padmaka*, the three myrobalans, *viḍaṅga*, *devadāru*, and the powdered *rāsnā* taken in equal proportions would remedy cough.

CHAPTER THREE HUNDRED AND ONE

The mode of worship of Sun

Fire-god said :

1-3. "*Śayyā* (bed), Daṇḍi, Ajeśa, Pāvaka, the four-faced" is the basic (*mantra*) that accomplishes all the desires. It is said for the sake of (gaining) power. The (*bija* (basic)) should contain long vowels. The constituents should be evenly set in the *bija* (*mantras*). Each collection of *mantras* would have five parts such as the *khāta*, *sādhu*, *viṣa*, *bindu* and *sakala*. Each one has a separate great merit. The *gaṇa* (should be worshipped as follows) : "Obeisance for the sake of victory. (Obeisance) to the one having one tusk ! To the elephant-faced ! One having big belly and hands !" These five constituents are common for all (the *mantras*). One would accomplish his desires by repeating a lakh times.

4-6. "(Obeisance) to the head of the *gaṇas* (goblins), to the leader of the *gaṇas*, to the lord of the *gaṇas*, and to the one who sports with the *gaṇas*." The image should be worshipped as before with the five constituents in the directions which are the petals. (Obeisance) to one having curved trunk, single tusk, big belly and elephant face. (Obeisance) to the dreadful one, to the lord of obstacles and to the one of grey complexion. One should worship these (gods), the lords of the worlds, in the (main) directions and the intermediary directions by (showing) the *mudrā* formed by inserting the two thumbs in between the (two) middle and index fingers of the clenched fists. One should (contemplate the god) as having four hands filled with *modakas*(ball-shaped sweets) and bearing a club, noose and goad. One should worship (the god) as holding the eatables with his tusk, as red in complexion, as holding a lotus and as surrounded by a noose and goad especially on the fourth day (of a lunar fortnight) and in general everyday.

7. (If the oblation) is done with the root of white *arka* (plant) it would confer all desires. (If it is done) with sesamum, ghee, rice, curd, honey and clarified butter one would get prosperity and power to subdue.

8. Lord Mārtaṇḍabhairava (the Sun god) (who) affects the skin, blood, breath and the vital energy, (who is) the cause of virtue, material prosperty, desires and emancipation (and who is) covered by the orb (is contemplated).

9-13a. (He should be worshipped such that) His five forms (are represented by) the short (syllables) and the limbs by the long (syllables). The Sun-god possessing a red complexion as the *sindūra* (vermilion) and having His consort on His left (is worshipped) in the north-east. Mars, Saturn, Rāhu, Ketu and others (are worshipped) in the angular points south-east etc. After having bathed as laid down, the Sun-god should be worshipped preceded by (the offer of) respectful water. At the end of the worship, a garland of flowers should be offered to the dreadful effulgent (form) in the north-east. Lighted (lamp), *rocanā* (the yellow orpiment got from the cow), saffron, water, red perfume and unbroken (rice), sprout (of the paddy), bamboo-seed, barley, *śāli* (a kind of paddy), *śyāmāka* (a kind of grain), sesamum and mustard together with *japā* flower should be offered. Then they (should be collected) in the vessels and should be held on the head. Then one should prostrate bending his knees on the ground and dedicate the offering to the Sun-god.

13b-14a. After having worshipped the planets with nine pitchers sanctified with their respective mystic syllables, one should bathe for appeasing the planets. After the repetition of the syllable sacred to Sun-god, one will get all (the things).

14b-15. The *bija mantras* together with *agni*, *doṣa* and *bindu*, that confer victory in battle, should be located from head to foot. The basic (*mantra*) is worshipped by (showing) the *mudrā*. After having performed the assignment on the different limbs, one has to imagine himself as the Sun-god.

16-18. (The Sun-god) should be contemplated as yellow-coloured in incantations practised for death as well as for stupefying the senses, as white for the sake of satisfaction, as black for achieving the destruction of the enemy and as the colour of the rain-bow for stupefaction. One who is always bent on doing ablution, repetition (of the *mantras*), contemplation, worship and oblation would become resplendent, invincible, prosperous and gain victory in the ocean etc. After having located (the *mantra* of the Sun) in the betel etc. and after repetition (of the *mantra*), one should offer *uśiraka* (the fragrant root of a plant). A person who touches with the hand in which the *bīja* (*mantra*) has been located would certainly charm (the person).

CHAPTER THREE HUNDRED AND TWO

Description of different kinds of potential mantras and herbs

Fire-god said :

1. The chief *mantra*, that is (known as) Sarasvatī (Goddess of learning), that which has the letters that have the directive at the end of the oblation (is) "For speech, deed, united to the side, white, and for the sake of the child is deemed to be the ship."

2. A person who repeats this collection of *mantra* a lakh times would become a wise man. The supreme (*mantra*) of the heart for Indra is "Atri, together with fire, *vāma*, eye and dot (*bindu*)."

3-4a. (Lord) Indra having yellow complexion and wielding the thunderbolt and lotus should be invoked and worshipped.

Ten lakh oblations of clarified butter and sesamum should be made and (the image) should be anointed with that. (By doing so) a king would recover the lost kingdom and progeny etc.

4b-6. (Lord Śiva) is known to be with the female energy Hṛllekhā and possesses *doṣa*, *agni*, *daṇḍi* and *daṇḍa*. After having propitiated (Lord)Śiva, one should repeat (the *mantra* of) the female energy on the eighth and fourteenth (lunar days). (The goddess should be contemplated) as bearing disc, noose and goad and as showing protection and conferring boons. One would gain prosperity, poetic skill and progeny by doing oblation etc. "*Oṁ*, *hrīṁ*, *oṁ* obeisance to (god of) desire, to the one beneficial to all the beings, to the one who stupefies all the beings, to the one who makes the hearts of all the beings glow. Come and take a place in my self (repeated)." *Oṁ*. One would subjugate the entire world by the repetition of this *mantra* etc.

7-9. "*Oṁ*, *hrīṁ*, Oh ! Cāmuṇḍā ! Burn(?)and cook (?) such and such a person. You bring him under my control (repeated). *Ṭha* ! *Ṭha* ! This mantra of (goddess) Cāmuṇḍā that would subjugate has been told. The genital parts should be washed with the decoction of the three myrobalans. (It) would subjugate (the partner). Similarly a wife should smear with *aśvagandhā*, barley, turmeric and comphor (with the same results). (So also) long pepper, eight grains of rice, twenty numbers of pepper, besmeared with the juice of *bṛhatī* would keep (the husband) under one's control till death. Besmearing with the root of *kaṭīra* and *trikaṭu* mixed with honey would also have similar results.

10-12a. A paste made of sandal wood, fruit, *karabha*, *māgadhī*, *madhuka* and honey besmeared would bring prosperity to the couple. The juice of *kadamba* and honey mixed with sugar and besmeared in the vagina (will also yield the same fruit). Pulverized *sahadevī*, *mahālakṣmī*, *putrajīvī* and *kṛtāñjali* thrown on the head would subjugate the world.

12b-13. One *prastha* (a measure) of the decoction of the three myrobalans, two *kuḍavas* (a measure) each of the juice of *bhṛṅga*, *hema* and *doṣā* and an equal (measure) of honey got from musk-rat boiled with ghee (and mixed with) turmeric dried in the shade, when besmeared, would delight (the couple).

14. One who drinks daily *vidāri*, *uccaṭā*, *māṣa* and pulverized sugar mixed well with milk could cohabit with a hundred women.

15-16a. A woman, who desires to have a son, should drink the roots of *aśvattha* (holy fig), bamboo, *darbha* (grass), *vaiṣṇavi*, *śri*, *dūrvā* (grass) and *aśvagandha* mixed with powdered *gulma*, *māṣa*, sesamum, *vrīhi* paddy together with milk.

16b-17a. The fibrous roots of *kaunti* and *lakṣmi*, *dhātri*, *vajra*, *lodhra* and the sprouts of *vaṭa* (banyan tree) should be drunk by a woman during her menstrual period together with clarified butter and milk for the sake of (getting) a son.

17b-18. A woman who desires to have a son should drink milk together with the root of *śrī* (*bilva*) and the shoots of banyan. Alternatively she may use the juice of *bilva*, shoots of banyan and *devī* as sternutatory or she may drink the root of *bilva* and lotus ground with milk together with the root of holy fig tree in abundance.

19. *Tarala* with milk and the fruits and the tender branches of the cotton tree, the tip of the *apāmārga* flower and fresh buffalow milk would have the same effect.

20-21. Four kinds of compounds are said (to be beneficial) for the sake of progeny by using the three kinds of herbs. Sugar, *utpala* flower, *akṣa*, *lodhra*, sandal and *sārivā* should be given with rice-water for abortion. One may alternatively lick fried rice, *yaṣṭi*, sugar and grapes together with honey and clarified butter.

22. A woman would have comfortable delivery if a paste of the fibrous roots of *aṭarūṣa*, *lāṅgalī* and *kākamāci* are besmeared separately below the navel.

23-26. One should drink (the juice of) red or white *japā* flower in the case of discharge of blood and semen. The eating of the filament, the root of *bṛhatī*, *gopī*, *yaṣṭi*, grass and *utpala* mixed with goat's milk and oil would make the hair grow. When the hairs begin to fall, this would make them firm.

A *prastha* (measure) of emblic myrobalan and the juice of *bhṛṅga* and an *āḍhaka* (measure) of oil and milk (boiled with) oil and *añjana* fruits is beneficial for hairs, eyes and head.

If *khāri* (quantity) of turmeric, the bark of *rājavṛkṣa*, root of tamarind, rock-salt and *lodhraka* are drunk it would remove quickly the swelling of the belly of the cow. "*Oṁ*, obeisance to the lord having three eyes! Subdue! Subdue! *culu* (2), *mili* (2)! Break (2)! One that regards the cattle! In the disc! *Hrūṁ phaṭ*! You protect the cattle in this village (2)! Appease (2)! (The lord) having bell-like ear, the leader of a host of army, the warrior is said to be having great strength. May that lord of the world who is capable of destroying the epidemic diseases protect me. These *mantras* in the form of a verse which are capable of protecting the cows should be located.

CHAPTER THREE HUNDRED AND THREE

The propitiation of the letters on one's limbs to ward off evil

Fire-god said :

1. It is known to be the period of *pauṣṇa* when the Moon reaches the natal asterism and the Sun occupies the seventh house. One has to examine one's breath then.

2. The throat and the lips move from their position, the nose (becomes) bent and the tongue (becomes) black. That person would live for seven days only.

3-4a. (The following is the *mantra* for warding off this evil consequence): "*taro meṣo miṣaṁ dantī naro dīrghā ghanā rasaḥ*, to *kruddholka*, *maholka*, *virolka*, *ulka* and *sahasrolka*." This is the eight-syllabled *mantra* of (Lord) Viṣṇu.

4b-7. These should be located in the folds of the eight fingers beginning with the little finger. The eight letters of (the eight) asterisms represented by the eight folds beginning with the first fold on the middle finger should be located in order on the head. The asterism (is located) on the index finger, the *lagnas* on the thumb as also with the middle finger. In the same way the letters of the asterisms etc. are located on the palm and thumb. (The letters of the *mantras* should be contemplated) —as red, white, tawny, green, golden and (the remaining) three as white. These letters having the above colours and set with their true state should be located in order at the heart, face, eyes, head, feet, palate, private organ and hands.

8. After having assigned the principal letters on the hand and body, the location of the constituent parts. The location on (the image of) the deity should be done as in the case of oneself except (that) the hand (is not involved).

9-12. The letters located in the different places such as the heart should be worshipped with incense and flowers. The virtues etc., fire etc. and unrighteousness etc. are located respectively on the body, seat and the lotus. The three orbs of the Sun, Moon and Fire pervading the filaments (of the lotus) should be located in order with their distinctions. The qualities *sattva* etc. and the female energies Vimalā, Utkarṣiṇī, Jñāna, Kriyā, Yogā, Prahvī, Satyā and Īśānānugrahā (are to be located) in the filaments therein in order. After having worshipped the yogic seat at the centre, (Lord) Hari should be invoked and worshipped.

13. The five practices of worship such as water for washing the feet, *arghya* (respectful offering), water for sipping, yellow clothes and ornament are all offered with the principal (*mantra*).

14. The images of (gods) Vāsudeva (a form of Viṣṇu) and others, namely four[1], should be worshipped in the four (principal) directions. (Goddesses) Śrī (Lakṣmī), Sarasvatī, Rati and Śānti should be worshipped in the intermediary directions.

15. The conch, disc, mace, lotus, pestle, sword, *śārṅga* (bow) and the garland of wild flowers should duly be worshipped in the principal and intermediary directions.

16. After having worshipped Tārkṣya (eagle vehicle of Lord Viṣṇu) outside in front (of the Lord), Viṣvaksena and Someśa should be worshipped outside at the centre and Indra and other attendant gods outside the enclosure. One would obtain everything by this worship.

---

1 Vāsudeva, Pradyumna, Aniruddha and Saṅkarṣaṇa.

CHAPTER THREE HUNDRED AND FOUR

The mode of worship of Śiva with the mantra of five syllables

Fire-god said :

1. "*Meṣaḥ, Saṁjñā, viṣaṁ, sājyaṁ, asti, dirghodakaṁ, rasaḥ.*" This is the *mantra* sacred to (Lord) Śiva that confers good.

2-4. After having worshipped the asterisms etc. well one would gain the status of the celestials etc. (Lord) Śiva, the embodiment of knowledge, the Supreme Brahman and the highest intellect (should be contemplated) in one's heart. Brahmā and other gods are born of His power and are only His manifestations. The letters of the *mantra* (gave rise) to the five elements, their respective *mantras* and their respective matter. Prāṇa and other (vital) winds, the five organs of sense and five organs of action, everything are (the manifestation of) Brahman, namely, the five letters. Similarly we have the embodiment of eight syllables.

5-8. The place of initiation sanctified by the *mantra* should be washed with (the five things got from a cow). The essential articles for worship (should be taken to the place) and (Lord) Śiva should be worshipped as laid down. After having practised the location of the *mantras* on the main image and the limbs, rice should be scattered. Then the porridge should be made ready and the milk boiled. Then it should be divided into three parts. One part should be dedicated (to the god), the second should be given as oblation and the third should be taken by the preceptor and the pupil. After rinsing the mouth and accomplishing the transformation, the preceptor should give the disciple a twig of the *kṣira* tree for (cleansing) the teeth after sanctifying it with (the *mantra* of) the heart. After having cleaned the teeth and washed the mouth, he should throw it on the ground.

9-11. It (indicates) good if it falls in the northern or western direction from the east and bad otherwise. The wise (preceptor) should make it dry by tying the tuft of the disciple who has come and make him lie down on the sacrificial altar on the bed of *darbha* (grass) together with himself. At dawn the pupil should meet the preceptor who has slept well and let him know (the dream he had). Then worship (should be done) with those benevolent words that accomplish the desires. One should worship in the circles such as the *bhadraka* that would confer all the perfections.

12. After having bathed, rinsing (the mouth with water) and besmearing the body with mud with the recitation of the *mantras*, one should bathe in the water-course sacred to (Lord) Śiva, preceded by (the recitation of) the *aghamarṣaṇa*[1] (hymn).

13-15. After having washed the hands the wise person should enter the place of worship. One has to sit in the *padmāsana* (crossed legs) and do the *pūraka* and *kumbhaka* (forms of breathing) with (the repetition of) the principal (*mantra*). One has to yoke one's soul twelve inches above the tuft, dry up and burn one's body and flood it with ambrosia. After having contemplated the divine body in that (body) one has to lead one's soul again (there). One will be purifying one's self by doing thus. After having located (the *mantras* on the limbs) one has to commence the worship.

16-19. The limbs (should be touched) by the preceptor with the letters of the *mantra* such as *naga* etc. (of the colours) black, white, dark-blue, red and yellow. The images of all (the gods) should be located in all the limbs beginning with the thumb and ending with the little finger. The letters of the *mantra* should be located on the feet, genital organ, heart, face and head. After having caused the principal (*mantra*) to pervade the head etc., one should locate the auxiliaries. The (four) feet of the pedestal (having) red, yellow, black and white (colours) in the angular points, the different limbs, the bodies and unrighteousness etc. in the different directions should be located with the *mantras*. (One should worship) therein the lotus, the three orbs such as the Sun and the three qualities.

20-22. (One has to worship) the nine energies such as Vāmā etc. on the petals of the lotus beginning with the east. The ninth one (should be worshipped) on the filament. The nine energies Vāmā, Jyeṣṭhā, Raudrī, Kālī, Kalavikāriṇī, Balavikāriṇī, Balapramathanī, Sarvabhūtadamanī and Manonmanī (respectively of the colours) white, red, white, yellow, dark-blue, golden, black, black and light red, of the form of glowing light should duly be remembered.

1. Designation of the hymn *ṛtam ca satyam cābhīddhāt* RV,10.190.

23-24. After having invoked (Lord) Śiva of the colour of crystal, having four arms, bearing the plough and trident, offering protection and conferring boons, having five faces and three eyes, from the lotus of the heart to the infinite yogic base the images of the five forms such as the Tatpuruṣa and other (of Lord Śiva) should be established on the petals.

25-26. Tatpuruṣa, white (in colour) (is placed) in the east. Aghora of black complexion and having eight hands (should be located in the south). Sadyojāta of yellow complexion and having four hands and four faces (should be placed) in the west. Vāmadeva of light red (colour) and of the nature of sporting with women and having four faces and four hands (should be located) in the north. Īśāna, the conferer of all things, having white complexion and five faces, (should be located) in the north-east.

27-31. After having worshipped duly the limbs, one has to worship the subtle Ananta. One should worship (Lords) Siddheśvara having a single eye, Ekarudra having three eyes, Śrīkaṇṭha wearing the peacock's tail in the directions of east etc. (One has to worship) the lords of learning, seated on the lotuses and having white, yellow, white, red, tawny, red, light red and white (colours) respectively bearing the trident, thunderbolt, arrow, bow and having four faces in the different directions such as the north-east etc. (The goddess) Umā and (Lords) Caṇḍeśa, Nandīśa, Mahākāla, Gaṇeśvara, Vṛṣa, Bhṛṅgariṭi and Skanda should be worshipped in (the directions) north etc. After having worshipped the lord, the thunder-bolt, club, sword, noose, banner, mace, trident, disc and lotus should be worshipped in (the directions) beginning with the east.

32. After consecrating the pupil he should be made to taste the five things got from a cow. After rinsing the mouth, he must be sprinkled (with water) with the *mantras* relating to the limbs upto the eyes and the eyes should be covered with (the recitation of the *mantra* of) the eye.

33. Then the pupil should be made to enter the door. Then the preceptor should purify (the pupil) seated on the *kuśa* (grass) to the south of the shed together with the seat.

34-36a. (Then the preceptor) should withdraw the primary principles (of the pupil) and duly get him absorbed in the supreme principle. Then the preceptor should regenerate the pupil by the process of (tāntric) creation. After having located (the supreme principle) in the pupil, he must be led circumambulating. After bringing him to the western door, (the preceptor) should make (the pupil) throw (the flowers) held in the folded hands. On whatever place the flowers fall that name should first be given (to the pupil).

36b-41. By the side of the sacrificial shed a pit should be dug up in such a way that it has the navel and girdle. The fire of Lord Śiva should be generated and worshipped. It should again be worshipped by the pupil. (Then the preceptor) should absorb the pupil in his own self after contemplation by means of the process of dissolution. Again regenerating him, *darbha* (grass) consecrated with the repetition of *mantras* should be placed in his hand. The principles such as the earth and others should be offered to the fire with (the repetition of the *mantras* of) the heart and others. After having offered hundred oblations for each one (of the principles), one should do oblation with the principal (*mantra*) of (the principle of) sky. After having offered the final oblation, one should offer eight oblations with (the *mantra* of) the weapon. (After having performed) the rite of atonement for the sake of purification, it should be completed with the residual offering. Then a consecrated pitcher should be worshipped well and the pupil bathed on the seat. (Then the preceptor) should instruct the pupil in the ceremonial practice and (the pupil) should pay respect to his preceptor by (offering) gold and other things. Thus the initiation into the five syllables relating to (god) Viṣṇu and others has been narrated.

CHAPTER THREE HUNDRED AND FIVE

The fiftyfive names of (Lord) Viṣṇu and their greatness

Fire-god said :

1. A person who repeats the fiftyfive names of (Lord) Viṣṇu would get the fruits of repeating the *mantras* and the

worship (with these names) at the sacred places (of pilgrimage) would have undiminishing fruits.

2. Puṇḍarīkākṣa (lotus-eyed) (should be contemplated) at Puṣkara, Gadādhara (one who wields the club) at Gayā, Rāghava (Rāma as the scion of Raghu) at Citrakūṭa and Daityasūdana (the destroyer of the demons) at Prabhāsa.

3. Similarly Jaya (the victor) (should be worshipped) at Jayantī, Jayanta (one who gains victory) at Hastināpura, Vārāha (manifestation as boar) at Vardhamāna and Cakrapāṇi (one who holds the disc) at Kāśmīra.

4. (One should contemplate) Janārdana (one that removes the difficulties of people) at Kubjāmra, Keśava at Mathurā, Hṛṣīkeśa (lord of the senses) at Kubjāmra and Jaṭādhara (one who bears the matted hair) at the place where the Ganges enters the plains.

5. (One should contemplate) Mahāyoga (one who ardently practises *Yoga*) at Śālagrāma, Hari at the Govardhana mountain, Caturbāhu (one having four arms) at Piṇḍāraka and Śaṅkhin (the holder of the conch) at Śaṅkhadvāra.

6. Vāmana (the Dwarf manifestation) (is worshipped) at Kurukṣetra, Trivikrama (the conqueror of three worlds) at (the river) Yamunā, Viśveśvara (the lord of the universe) at (the river) Śoṇā and Kapila (propounder of the Sāṅkhya philosophy) on (the banks of) the eastern ocean.

7. (One should repeat the name of) Viṣṇu (on the shore of) the great ocean at the confluence of the river Ganges with the ocean, Vanamāla (the bearer of garland of wild flowers) at Kiṣkindhā and Deva (lord) at Raivataka.

8. Mahāyoga (the great *yoga*) (is contemplated) at Kāśī, Ripuñjaya (the conqueror of enemies) at Virajā, Ajita (the unconquered) at Viśākhayūpa and Lokabhāvana (the creator of the world) at Nepāla.

9. One should know that (one has to repeat the name) Kṛṣṇa at Dvārakā, Madhusūdana (the slayer of the demon Madhu) at Mandara (mountain) and Ripuhara (the destroyer of enemies) at Lokākula and one should think of Hari at Śālagrāma.

10. (One should repeat the name) Puruṣa (the Supreme person) at Puruṣavaṭa, Jagatprabhu (the lord of the world) at

Vimala, Ananta (the endless) at the Saindhava forest and Śārṅgadhārin (the wielder of the bow) at Daṇḍaka (forest).

11. Śauri (the hero) (should be contemplated) at the whirlpool (called) Utpala, Śriyaḥpati (the consort of Lakṣmī) at (the river) Narmadā, Dāmodara (having the enlarged belly) at Raivataka and Jalaśāyin (one who reclines on the water) at Nandā.

12. It is known that (one has to repeat the name) Gopīśvara on (the shore of) the Sindhu ocean, Acyuta (unswerving) at Māhendra (hill), Devadeveśa (the lord of gods) at the Sahya mountain and Vaikuṇṭha (one who has united the earth etc.), at the Māgadha forest.

13. (One should repeat the name) Sarvapāpahara (Destroyer of all sins) at the Vindhya (mountain) and Puruṣottama (the foremost among men) in (the region of) Oḍhra. One should know the universal soul (residing) in one's heart. The recitation (of these names) confers enjoyment and emancipation.

14. (One has to contemplate) the Vaiśravaṇa (the great fig tree) at every fig tree, (Lord) Śiva (the auspicious) at every quadrangle, Rāma on every mountain and Madhusūdana (the slayer of the demon Madhu) everywhere.

15. One who contemplates the Supreme spirit on the earth and sky, the god having eagle in the banner in (the great sage) Vasiṣṭha and Vāsudeva (epithet of Kṛṣṇa) everywhere would get enjoyment and emancipation.

16-17. One would obtain all (the desires) by the repetition of these names of (Lord) Viṣṇu. The (performance of) ancestral rites, (offering) gifts, repetition (of the names of god) and (offering of waters of) libation in all these sacred places will have manifold (benefits). One would become verily the Brahman after one's death. One who reads or listens to this (will become) free from impurity and will obtain heaven.

CHAPTER THREE HUNDRED AND SIX

Description of the mantras to be repeated to ward off evil incantations etc.

Fire-god said :

1-2. Stupefaction, dissension, ruin, destruction, delusion, death and illness are known to be (due to) evil incantations. Listen to me ! I shall describe the means of getting relief from them. *Oṁ* obeisance to lord Unmattarudra (intoxicated Rudra) ! Stupefy (2) ![1] Make (him) wander (2) ! Threaten such and such a person ! Hurl him aloft (2) with anger ! *Hūṁ, phaṭ, ṭha* (2) : One should do oblation with honey with the twigs of *dhūrta* in the funeral fire after repeating (this *mantra*) three lakh times at night in a Cremation ground. (By this) the enemy would be wandering always.

3. (After having made) a black image (of the enemy) with red chalk, if it is pierced in the throat or heart with golden needles after repeating (the above *mantra*), the enemy would die.

4. One who wants to destroy (his enemy) should throw pulverized tail of the ass, funeral ash, *brahmadaṇḍi* and *markaṭi* on the house or head of the person.

5-7a. (I shall describe the method of worshipping the disc in the thousand-petalled lotus.) "Bhṛgu, ether, glowing fire, bhṛgu, fire armour, *phaṭ*" (is for the armour). One (should) thus (worship) in the thousand-petalled (lotus). "*Hūṁ, phaṭ*, to the disc (ācakrāya) oblations" is for the heart, (*hūṁ phaṭ*) to the disc (vicakrāya) for the head, (*hūṁ phaṭ*) to the disc (śikhācakra) of the tuft (for the tuft), (*hūṁ phaṭ*) to the disc (vicakra) for the eye, (*hūṁ phaṭ*) to the disc (*sañcakra*) for the weapon and (*hūṁ phaṭ*) to the glowing disc (*jvālācakra*) as before for the bow. (By worshipping) the disc in this way (with the constituent *mantras*), it would remove all the afflictions due to evil incantations and accomplish all (the desires). The letters of this (*mantra*) should be located on the head, eyes, mouth, heart, genital organ and feet.

1. The number 2 after the words indicates repetition of the respective words.

7b-9a. (One should contemplate the Sudarśana disc personified as) seated on the lotus, resembling the colour of fire, having large teeth and four hands, (holding) the conch, disc, mace, lotus, brush and goad in his hand, holding the bow, having reddish brown hair and eye and pervading the three worlds by means of the spokes (of the disc). If the navel is pierced with its fire, the diseases and (afflictions due to) the planets would get destroyed.

9b-10. One should draw two discs. They should be yellow. They should be bearing the disc. The spokes should be red and their inter-spaces black. The periphery should be white and the outer line black. The inter-space should bear the colour of silver.

11-12. After having brought a pitcher with water first, it should be placed in front and the Sudarśana (disc of Lord Viṣṇu) placed there. One should offer oblation in order to the disc on the south. Clarified butter, twigs of *apāmārga*, unbroken rice, sesamum, mustard, sweet gruel and clarified butter from the cow (are the materials that are offered). (One should do oblation) one thousand and eight times.

13-14. The remaining (part) of each one of the materials after the oblation should be put into the pitcher by one who knows the mode of performance. A ball made of these offerings should be placed in the pitcher. (By doing so) (Lord) Viṣṇu and others would enter that (pitcher). Then offering should be made in the south with the residual water with (the repetition of) the *mantra* "Obeisance to the retinue of (Lord) Viṣṇu who appease everything. May they accept. Obeisance for peace !"

15-16a. (It may also be performed differently). One may inscribe (the disc) on a plank, place a vessel filled with milk and perform oblation with the twigs of *palāśa* and *kṣīra* (trees) in the different directions engaging brahmins. These two oblations done after offering appropriate fees (to the priests) would destroy the spirits, etc.

16b-17. Evil incantations would be removed by writing on leaves soaked in cow's milk and without leaves. (One has to do oblation) with *dūrvā* (grass) for (prolonging) life, with lotus flowers for prosperity, with (twigs of) *udumbara* for progeny, with clarified butter at the cow-shed for cattle and with (the twigs) of all the trees for intellect.

18. *Oṁ, kṣauṁ* ! Obeisance to Lord Narasiṁha ! To one who has the flames as the garland, one who has effulgent teeth, one who has fiery eyes, one who is the annihilator of all the demons ! To one who destroys all the spirits ! To one who destroys all fevers ! burn (2) ! cook (2) ! protect (2) ! *hūṁ phaṭ* ! This *mantra* of Narasiṁha (the man-lion manifestation of Lord Viṣṇu) removes all sins. Its repetition would remove evil incantations, (evil influences of malignant) planets, epidemics, poisons and diseases. One could arrest the force of water and fire (by rubbing over the body) the ground marrow of a frog (after the repetition of the above *mantra*).

CHAPTER THREE HUNDRED AND SEVEN

Description of the mantras that would stupefy the three worlds

Fire-god said :

1-2. I shall describe to you the *mantra* that would stupefy the three worlds and would accomplish the four ends of human life. *Oṁ, śrīṁ, hrīṁ, hrūṁ, oṁ* obeisance ! Oh ! Foremost among men ! The prototype of foremost among men ! The abode of Lakṣmī (goddess of fortune) ! One who agitates the entire world ! One who opens the hearts of all women ! One who intoxicates the three worlds ! Burn (2), Make glow (2), Dry up (2), Kill (2), Arrest (2), Melt (2), Attract (2) the hearts of the maidens of the heaven and earth ! Oh ! The most fortunate one ! The giver of all good fortunes ! Conferer of desires ! (You) kill such and such a person (repeated) ! You pierce with the disc, mace, sword and all the weapons ! Cover (2) with the noose ! Strike with the goad (2) ! Hasten (2) ! Why do you tarry till accomplishing my desire ! *Hūṁ, phaṭ*, obeisance. *Oṁ*, foremost among men ! One who intoxicates the three worlds ! *Hūṁ, phaṭ* ! Obeisance to the heart !

Attract ! Oh ! One of great strength ! *Hūṁ, phaṭ* to the weapon! Oh ! lord of the three worlds ! You kill, pierce, and bring under my control the hearts of all men ! *Hūṁ, phaṭ* ! To the eyes ! Oh ! stupefier of the three worlds ! The lord of the sense organs ! Incomparable one ! One who attracts the hearts of all women ! (You) come (2) ! Obeisance ! The location of the auxiliary (*mantra*) pervading the limbs and eyes should also be done as described for the principal (*mantra*). After having worshipped, repeating (the *mantra*) fifty times and anointing one thousand times, (the preceptor) should prepare porridge in the divine fire and do hundred oblations in the fire in the pit.

3-4. Curd, ghee, milk, porridge, clarified butter and boiled milk (should be offered) separately. Twelve oblations (should be made) with (the repetition of) the principal (*mantra*). (Then one should offer) unbroken rice and sesamum a thousand times and barley, the three sweet things (sugar, honey and clarified butter), flower, fruit, curd and twigs a hundred times. After having offered the final oblation, (the preceptor) should make the disciple drink the porridge together with ghee.

5-6a. After having fed the brahmins, the priest should be pleased (by paying the fee). Then the *mantra* would get accomplished. After having bathed and rinsed (the mouth) as laid down, (the votary) should go to the sacrificial chamber restraining his speech. He should sit in the *padmāsana* (sitting posture with legs crossed) and dry up his body as laid down.

6b-11. The sudarśana (disc) that destroys the demons and removes the obstacles in the (different) directions should be placed at first. Then one should contemplate the principal (syllable) '*yaṁ*' that is at the centre of the navel. It is of the nature of the terrific wind. It is conceived as absolving all the sins from the body. After having contemplated the principal (syllable) *raṁ* situated in the lotus of the heart, one should burn with (its) flames spreading above, below and across in the head. Then after contemplation the body should be flooded with the ambrosia that flows out and in through the path of *suṣumnā* (one of the arteries in the body). After purifying the body thus, one should do *prāṇāyāma* (regulated breathing) three times with the *maṁtra.* Then the energy should be located in the hand, head, face, genital organ, throat, heart, belly, the (different) directions and everywhere in the body. The supreme lord (endowed) with all (good) characteristics should then be contemplated in the lotus of the heart after being invoked from the orb of the Sun through the aperture in the crown of the head with (the repetition of) the *tāra* (*mantra*) : "We know! To the stupefier of the three worlds ! May we meditate on the lord of remembrance, may (Lord) Viṣṇu lead us to reflect on that."

12. After (having done) the soul-worship, (the votary) should sprinkle (water) on the materials for worship and the pure vessel. After having done the soul-worship as laid down, the deity should be worshipped on the ground.

13-17. (Lord) Viṣṇu should be contemplated as riding the eagle and as remaining on a lotus over a seat composed of one's deeds etc. (He should be imagined as) having beautiful limbs, having attained the beauty appropriate to the youthful age, the reddish-brown eyes reeling with intoxication, lofty, agitated by love, adorned with divine flowers, dress and unguents, having a smiling face, being surrounded by many attendants of different kinds, as compassionate to the beings, beautiful, having the lustre of one thousand sons, bearing the five weapons, one who has attained the desires as known from his eyes, having two or four hands, one surrounded by divine women and one who is affectionately looking at the face of his consort. One should worship Him as bearing the disc, conch, bow, sword, mace, pestle, goad and noose commencing with invocation and ending with the request to leave.

18-19. (Goddess) Śrī (consort of Viṣṇu) (should be imagined) as seated on the left thigh and shank (of the lord) and as embracing the consort with her hand. (She should be contemplated) as having a well-built body, holding a lotus and chowrie in her hand and endowed with the Śrīvatsa (mark) and Kaustubha (gem). One should worship (Lord) Hari (Viṣṇu) as wearing a garland, yellow garment and as endowed with the disc etc. *Oṁ* ! Sudarśana ! The great lord of discs ! Dreadful for the wicked ! Cut (2) ! Tear (2) ! Devour mighty spells (2) ! Eat (2) ! Catch hold of the spirits (2) ! *Hūṁ phaṭ oṁ* oblations to one who remains in the water ! One as sharp as the sword ! Cut (2) ! Obeisance to the sword ! To the bow with the arrow *hūṁ*, *phaṭ* ! "We contemplate the union of the elements. We meditate on the four-fold principles. May that Brahman lead our mind (to meditate) on that." Oh ! Fire that destroys the world (Saṁvartaka) ! The embodiment of breath! You recoil (2) ! *Hūṁ phaṭ* oblations ! O ! Noose ! Bind (2) ! Attack (2) ! *Hūṁ phaṭ* ! One has to worship these weapons on the hands with their respective *mantras*.

20-22. One has to worship Tārkṣya (the eagle vehicle of Viṣṇu) in the pericarp (with the *mantra*) "*Oṁ* ! To the king of birds ! *Hūṁ phaṭ* !" Then the presiding deities of the limbs (should be worshipped) as laid down. The female energies (should be worshipped) at the places of Indra and others and Tārkṣya and others as holding chowries. Indra and others should be worshipped first and the energies at the end by the priest. Lakṣmī and Sarasvatī (should be contemplated) as yellow, Rati, Prīti and Jayā as white, Kīrti and Kānti as white, and Tuṣṭi and Puṣṭi as black (and worshipped) as laid down. (One should worship) upto the guardian deities of the worlds and then Lord Viṣṇu for the sake of gaining one's desired fruits.

23. After having repeated the *mantra*, one should contemplate (the lord), offer oblation and do consecration. *Oṁ*, *śrīṁ*, *krīṁ*, *hrīṁ*, *hūṁ* obeisance to Viṣṇu, the stupefier of the three worlds ! As before one would get all his desires by doing this worship.

24-26. One should please the *sammohanī* (*vidyā*) (the stupefier) daily with water and flowers. The principal part of the *Trailokyamohana* (the stupefier of the three worlds) is "Brahmā, Śakra (Indra), Śrī (Lakṣmī) and Daṇḍī." One would get long life by repeating (the *mantra*) three lakhs times and offering oblations (with the *mantra*) one lakh times with *bilva* (leaves), clarified butter, rice, fruits, perfumes and *dūrvā* (grass). (Lord Viṣṇu) being pleased with anointment, oblations and other acts with that (*vidyā*) would confer all the desired things. *Oṁ*, obeisance to Lord Varāha (Boar manifestation of Lord Viṣṇu) ! To the lord of (the three worlds) Bhūḥ, Bhuvaḥ, Svaḥ ! Grant me the suzerainty over the earth ! Oblation to the heart ! One would get long life and kingdom by repeating (the above *mantra*) ten thousand times daily together with the *pañcāṅga*[1] (five parts of the body).

CHAPTER THREE HUNDRED AND EIGHT

On the mode of worship of goddess Lakṣmi and others that confer immense benefits

Fire-god said :

1. (The *mantras*) "chest, together with fire, beautiful woman, Daṇḍī, Śrīḥ (goddess of fortune)" gives all prosperity. Obeisance ! O ! greatest fortune ! O ! great prosperity ! O ! One having a lustre as the powerful lightning ! Obeisance to the goddess of prosperity ! O ! Victorious ! O ! Mighty one ! Bind (2) ! Obeisance ! *Hūṁ* ! One having a big body ! One holding the lotus in the hand ! *Hūṁ phaṭ* ! Obeisance to Śrī ! To Śrī, *phaṭ*, obeisance to Śrī ! To Śrī, the conferer of prosperity ! Obeisance ! Oblations *śrī-phaṭ* !

2. The constituent parts of this (*mantra*) are said to be nine. One should resort to one of these. It would confer prosperity if repeated three lakh or one lakh times with rosary beads or lotus (seeds).

3-4. One would get wealth by worshipping Śrī in the temple of Śrī or Viṣṇu. One has to do oblation with rice soaked in clarified butter in the fire (kindled with) *khādira* (twigs). (By this) the king would be under one's control. One will have more and more growth and prosperity. Bathing done with mustard would destroy the (evil propensities of) planets.

5-9a. Oblations done with the *bilva* (leave) (with the repetition of) Śrī (*mantra*), would increase one's wealth. Then one has to contemplate the mansion of Indra having four doors in his heart. One should contemplate (the energy) Balākā,

1. The obeisance conveyed by the touching of the ground simultaneously with the two arms, the two knees, the head, chest and the eyes.

short and black sporting (and guarding) at the eastern entrance with the two hands held upwards holding white lotus flowers, (the energy) Vanamālinī of white (complexion) at the southern entrance with the hands held upwards holding red lotus flowers, Vibhīṣikā, the messenger of Śrī, having green (complextion), at the western entrance, with Her two hands lifted upwards holding white lotus (flower). Śāṅkarī (should be contemplated) at the northern entrance.

9b-14a. One should contemplate Vāsudeva, *Saṅkarṣaṇa*, Pradyumna and Aniruddha in the lotus petals carrying conch, disc and mace. They are of the colours of collyrium, milk, saffron and gold and wear good dress. One should contemplate the elephants such as Guggulu, Kuruṇṭaka, Damaka and Salila (having) the colour of silver, in the different directions such as south-east etc. in the petals. (These elephants should be imagined as) bearing golden pots. Śrī should be contemplated in the pericarp as having four arms, two of which are raised upwards and hold lotus. (She is also conceived as having the following characteristics): golden coloured conferring protection and boons with the right and left hands respectively, besmeared with white sandal, wearing a silvery garland and carrying the weapon. One would get all (his desires) by contemplating as above and worshiping Her together with Her attendants.

14b-15a. (The worshipper of Śrī) should not wear the *droṇa* and lotus flowers and the leaf of the *bilva* tree on the head. So also salt and embelic myrobalan are prohibited on the eighth and twelfth days (of the lunar fortnight) in order.

15b-16. Taking (only) sweet porridge one should repeat the *śrisūkta*[1] and anoint (goddess) Śrī with (the repetition of) that (hymn). One has to contemplate mentally as doing the rites beginning with the invocation and ending with the dismissal and worship Śrī. One would gain prosperity by doing oblations separately with (the twigs of) *bilva*, clarified butter, lotus and sweet porridge.

17-24. "Poison, buffalo, the destructive fire at the end of the world, Rudra, the effulgence, the two *bakas*." "*Oṁ hrīṁ* the slayer of the great buffalo-demon! *Ṭhaṁ*! *Ṭhaḥ*!" (is) the

1. Designation of the hymn hiraṇyavarṇāṁ hariṇīṁ 'RVkh. 5.87.1a.

principal *mantra* (of Durgā, a form of the consort of Śiva). "Obeisance to the lioness (that killed) the buffalo (demon). O! Enemy of the (buffalo) demon! Make (the enemy) whirl round (2)! *Hūṁ, phaṭ, ṭha ṭhaṁ*! Make the buffalo (demon) neigh (2)! *Hūṁ* slay the buffalo (2)! O! Goddess! *Hūṁ*! The slayer of the buffalo (demon)! *Phaṭ*!" This is said to be the Durgāhṛdaya (the heart of Durgā). Together with its accessories it is capable of accomplishing all the things. One should worship that goddess and the seat in the middle of the accessories thus: *Oṁ hrīṁ*! O! Durgā! Durgā! Protector! and oblations". Obeisance to Durgā! Obeisance to Varavarṇī, Āryā, Kanakaprabhā, Kṛttikā, Abhayapradā, Kanyakā and Surūpā (excellent complexion, noble, golden-coloured, offering protection, virgin and having good form respectively). These forms (of the goddess) should be worshipped on the leaves with the principal syllables in due order. (One should also worship the weapons) disc, conch, mace, sword, bow and arrow. One should worship this (goddess) Durgā, the tranquil one in the world, on the eighth day (of the lunar fortnight). This association with Durgā would increase longevity, prosperity, favour of master and victory. Oblation and sesamum with (the repetition of) the Īśāna mantra after the worship (of Durgā) would enable one to gain control. (Oblation made) with lotuses would ensure victory. One desirous of appeasement (should do oblation) with *dūrvā* (grass). One will gain strength (by performing oblation) with (the twigs of) *Palāśa*. Death, dissension etc. would be caused (by offering oblation) with the wings of the crow. This *mantra* would remove all the difficulties such as evil influences due to malignant planets, evil incantations and fear etc. "*Oṁ*! O! Durgā! Protector! Oblations!" This (*mantra*) together with the accessories of the victorious Durgā is said to be able to protect. One should contemplate the goddess as black, having three eyes, four arms, bearing the conch, disc, lotus, spike, sword and trident and as having a wrathful form. One would gain victory in battle. One (who wants to have) victory of sword etc. should worship Her. "*Oṁ* obeisance to the Goddess having a garland of flames, surrounded by flocks of female eagles move! Oblations to the protector!" One should repeat this *mantra* for (gaining victory in) battle. The combatant would conquer his enemies.

CHAPTER THREE HUNDRED AND NINE

The mode of worship of Tvaritā

Fire-god said :

1. I shall describe (to you) the constituent (*mantras*) (relating to the worship) of Tvaritā[1] that is capable of conferring enjoyment and emancipation. "*Oṁ* obeisance to the the supportive energy ! *Oṁ hrīṁ puru* (2) obeisance to great lion ! *Oṁ* obeisance to the lotus ! *Oṁ hrīṁ hrūṁ khecachekṣaḥ* ! *Strīṁ oṁ hrūṁ kṣaiṁ hrūṁ phaṭ* ! Obeisance to (goddess) Tvaritā ! *Khe ca* obeisance to the heart ! *Cache* obeisance to the head ! *Chekṣaḥ* obeisance to the tuft ! *Kṣastri* obeisance to the armour ! *Strīṁ hrūṁ* obeisance to the eye ! *Hrūṁ khe* obeisance to the weapon *phaṭ* !" "*Oṁ* ! We known the Tvaritā-vidyā. Let us meditate on the *tūrṇavidyā*. May the goddess prompt us (to meditate) on her." (This is the Gāyatrī mantra for the goddess Tvaritā.) Obeisance to the conferrer of prosperity. Obeisance to the syllable *hrūṁ* ! Obeisance to the syllable *oṁ* ! *Oṁ kheca* obeisance to the heart ! Obeisance to the one who is able to fly ! *Oṁ* obeisance to the fierce one ! *Kṣa strīm* obeisance to the armour ! Obeisance to the cutter ! Obeisance to the thrower ! Obeisance to the woman of the form of the syllable *hūṁ* ! To the one that gives safety ! To the victor ! To the conqueror! Protect ! *Oṁ* be firm by the command of (Goddess) Tvaritā *vaṣaṭ* ! This is the incantation known as Tvaritā. It is known as Totalā and Tūrṇā.

2-3a. After having touched the head, forehead, throat, heart, navel, genital organ, thighs, knees, shanks and feet (with the *mantra*) in order and thus complete the location spread over the whole body.

3b-6. The goddess has to be contemplated as having the form of daughter of the mountain, huntress, supreme, conferring boons and protection, having the peacock feather on the head, having the tender sprout as the upper garment, seated on lion throne together with an umbrella of peacock plumes, the dark-complexioned goddess wearing the garland of wild flowers, having the brahmin class of serpents as the ear ornament, the *kṣatriya* (class of serpents) as the bracelets, the *vaiśya* class of serpents as the girdle

1. The goddess conferring benefits quickly.

and *vṛṣala* (fourth class) class of serpents as the anklets. Then one should repeat that mantra ten lakh times.

7. In days of yore the lord took the form of a hunter and (the goddess) Gaurī also (took a) similar (form). One has to repeat (the *mantra* of the Goddess). One has to contemplate and worship Her for accomplishing all (the things) and for the removal of poison etc.

8-10. (Goddess Tvaritā) has to be worshipped in a lion seat (having) eight (petals). Gāyatrī, Praṇītā, *huṁkāra* etc. and Phaṭkārī are located in the petals in the east etc. in front of the Goddess with the principal *mantra* of Śrī. Their colours and weapons are as those of the guardians of the quarters. Phaṭkārī should bear the bow. Jayā and Vijayā should be worshipped as at the entrance holding golden staff. Kiṅkarā, Barbarī, Muṇḍī and Laguḍī (should be worshipped) outside them.

11-15. After having worshipped (them) thus, one has to accomplish (them) with materials. Oblation should be made in a sacrificial pit of the shape of the female organ of generation. One would gain gold (by doing oblation) with white grains, increasing prosperity with wheat, all accomplishments and the destruction of *iti*[1] with barley and sesamum, insanity of the enemy with rosary seeds, death (of the enemy) with (the twigs of) silk cotton tree, gain of wealth and grains with rose apple, satisfaction (pleasure) with blue lotuses, abundant prosperity with red lotuses, great prosperity with *kunda* (a kind of jasmine), disturbance in the city with *mallikā* (a kind of jasmine), good-will of people with white lilies, birth of a son with *aśoka* (a kind of flower), an auspicious and beautiful woman with *pāṭalā* (trumphet flower), long life with mango (flowers), fortune with sesamum, prosperity with *bilva*, wealth with *campaka* (flowers), desired (object) with *madhuka* (flowers) and omniscience with *bilva* (leaves).

16-17. One would get all things by the repetition (of the *mantra*) three lakh times or by doing oblation or contemplation or worship. After having worshipped with the *gāyatri* in a circle, (one should offer) twentyfive oblations. A person who offers three hundred oblations with leaves with the principal (*mantra*)

1. These are six: excessive rain, drought, locusts, rats, parrots and foreign invasions. See *Apte SD* p. 96.

would become initiated. After having taken the five things got from a cow, one should take porridge. (This is the procedure) always.

CHAPTER THREE HUNDRED AND TEN

The narration of the spell relating to Tvaritā

Fire-god said :

1-5. I shall describe (to you) the worship of Tvaritā by another method that would yield enjoyment and emancipation. One has to worship the Goddess in a diagram of the shape of a thunderbolt drawn with dust. One has to draw a lotus inside it. One has to contemplate the Goddess and draw quickly eight thunderbolts in the (main) directions and the intermediate directions and also draw pathway, entrance, ornamental arch and secondary decoration. (One has to worship the Goddess) as having eighteen hands and Her left shank placed on the lion. Two-fold fee should be offered at Her pedestal. (She should be worshipped) in the sacrificial pit in the form of the thunderbolt as being adored by serpents, and as holding the sword, disc, mace, spike, arrow and mace in the right hands and as conferring boons and as holding the bow, noose, arrow, bell, threatening posture of the first finger, conch, goad and thunder-bolt in the left hands and as offering protection.

6. If one worships this form, one's enemy would die, one would win a kingdom with ease, gain long life, become the ruler of a kingdom and gain perfections such as supernatural powers.

7-8b. There are the seven nether regions below, which are as destructive as the destructive fire at the end of the world. The syllable *oṁ* and others denote (the space) beginning with the heaven and ending with the primordial egg. One has to whirl round water with (the repetition of) the syllable *oṁ* (and repeat) "Totalā, Tvaritā" then. (Then) one has to whirl round water with (the repetition of) the syllable '*ta*' (and repeat) "Totalā, Tvaritā" then.

8c-18. I shall introduce the (method of writing the *mantra*). The group of vowels should be written on the ground. (The next group) would be the '*ka*' group (belonging to) the palatal class. The third (letter) is (the letter belonging to) the tongue and palate. The fourth (letter) is (the letter belonging to) the palate and the tip of the tongue. The fifth (letter) is that of the tongue and teeth. The sixth one consists of eight letters. The seventh one is of mixed group of letters. (The eighth one consists of) the *śa* group of letters (known as) sibilants. The *mantra* should be constructed then. The first (basic syllable) should begin with the sixth vowel and end with last of the letters of *ūṣma* (sibilants) together with *bindu* (the nasal sound marked by a dot). Then the second (letter) among the palatals is compounded with the eleventh vowel. Then the combination of the (letters belonging to) the tongue and palate would be the first simple (basic syllable). The second (letters) of the same (group of letters) should be compounded below. Then the first letter among the palatals should be compounded with the eleven vowels. Then the second letter among the sibilants is coupled from below. The second letter among the sibilants coupled with the sixteenth vowel should be compounded below with the first letter belonging to the union of the tongue and dental region. Then the second letter belonging to the mixed group should again be coupled below. Then the second letter among the sibilants combined with the fourth vowel and yoked with the first letter of the palatals should be coupled below. Then the last among the sibilants together with the *bindu* (the nasal sound) is coupled with the eleventh vowel. Then the letter formed by the union of the (two) lips is joined with the fifth vowel. Then the second of the palatals is joined with (the letter belonging to) the tip of the tongue. Then the first letter of the fifth group should be combined with half-vowel and thus the *mantra* is constructed. One should repeat (the above *mantra* coupling) with the syllable *Oṁ* at the beginning and obeisance at the end. One has to add 'oblation' (at the end) in acts of offering oblation in fire. (The rite of location of the above *mantra* should be done as follows): "*Oṁ, hrīm, hrūṁ, hraḥ* (let it permeate) the heart. *Hāṁ haḥ* (let it permeate) the head. *Hrīṁ*, burn, burn would be (for) the tuft. *Hulu, hulu* is for the armour, *Hrūṁ, śrīṁ, kṣūm* is said to be the *mantra* for the three eyes. *Kṣauṁ, haṁ, khauṁ, hūṁ, phaṭ* is for the weapon. The secret auxilliaries are assigned before (the above location is done).

19-26. Listen to me ! I shall describe the constituent parts of the *mantra* relating to (the worship of Goddess) Tvaritā. The first two (letters in the *mantra*) are said to be the heart. The third and fourth are said to be the head. The fifth and sixth are said to be the tuft and the seventh and eighth as the armour. The pupil (of the *mantra*) would be the eye. It has the characteristic (of containing) nine and half letters. It is known to be (the *mantra* of) Totalā (Tvaritā). Then (the worship of) Vajratuṇḍā (would be described). There are ten syllables in (Her worship). *Kha, kha, hūṁ* (obeisance to) Vajratuṇḍā, the messenger of Indra. *Khecarī* ! *Jvālinī* ! *Jvālā* ! *kha* ! *kha* are the ten syllables for Jvālinī (glowing) Śabarī (huntress) ! Bhīṣaṇī (frightening) ! *kha* ! *kha* ! grow ! are (the syllables) for Śabarī. *Che* ! Chedanī (one that cuts) ! Karālinī (terrible) ! *kha*! *kha* ! are for Karālī. Śravadravaplavanī (one who floods the ear and the liquid) ! *kha kha* (is for) the messenger Plavaṅgī for the sky. Strīkālakāra (one who creates women and time) ! Dhunanī (one who agitates) ! is for Śvāsī (the Goddess possessing the swiftness of breath). Kṣepakṣa! Kapila! Haṁsa (is for) the messenger called Kapilā. *Hrūṁ*! Tejovatī (one having lustre)! Raudrī (terrible one) and Mātaṅgī (huntress) (are for) the messenger of Rudra. *Puṭe puṭe kha kha khaḍga* (to the sword) *phaṭ* (for) Brahmadūtikā (messenger of Brahmā). Ten syllables of (the *mantra* of) Vaitālinī have to be discarded like the cloud and straw. (This is the method) for locating (the *mantras* relating) to the heart and the like. A wise man should locate (the *mantra* of) the eyes at the centre.

27-31. Beginning with the leg and ending with the head, beginning with the head and ending with the leg, and beginning with the navel, heart and neck and (ending) in the feet, knees, thighs and genital organ the location is done. The votary should contemplate the *vajramaṇḍala* above and the basic beginning syllables above and below that and then the cow of the form of a moon that showers ambrosia as entering (the brain) through the aperture in the crown of the head. The votary should locate the first basic syllable (*a*) in the head, face, neck, heart, navel, genital organ, thigh, knee, feet and (the fingers) such as the fore-finger again and again. One who visualises the body made up of the basic syllables as flanked above by the moon and the lotus below would not die. He would not suffer from diseases or fevers. One should locate the Goddess thus and worship Her repeating hundred and eight times.

32-41. I shall describe the postures such as the *Praṇītā* and the like. (The postures called) *Praṇītās* are known to be of five kinds. The two hands are interlocked and the thumbs are put over that. Then they are placed on the head, the two fore-fingers resting on the head. This is known to be the *Praṇītā*. That is then brought to the region of the heart. The twice-born know (the *Praṇītā*) to be an excellent one in which the little and middle (fingers) are turned upward and endowed with the basic syllables. When the tip of the thumb is placed beneath the middle finger and the fingers are mutually resting on the middle (part) of the fore-fingers, it is said to be the *Bhedanī*. This (*mudrā*) held in the navel region and the thumbs raised upwards is known as the great *mudrā Karāli*. The same located in the heart of the votary and the middle finger resting on the aperture on the head and raised upwards is said to be the *Vajratuṇḍa*. It should be placed on the *vajradeśa* (the part of the body known as *vajra*) and the wrist should be locked up by the two hands stretching the three fingers (of each hand); it is said to be the *Vajramudrā*. The postures such as *Daṇḍa* (club), *Khaḍga* (sword), *Cakra* (disc) and *Gadā* (mace) are known to have the (respective) shape. Three fingers (are stretched) and held upwards and (their bases) are touched by the thumb. It would be *Triśūla* (trident posture). If the middle finger is held upwards it is said to be *Śakti* (spear). Thus there are twenty-eight postures of the hand such as *Śara* (arrow), *Varada* (bestowing boon), *Cāpa* (bow), *Pāśa* (noose), *Bhāra* (weight), *Ghaṇṭā* (bell), *Śaṅkha* (conch), *Aṅkuśa* (goad), *Abhaya* (offering protection) and *Padmam* (lotus) (having the respective shape). The five *Praṇītā mudrās* such as *Grāhaṇi* (one that seizes), *Mokṣaṇi* (one that liberates), *Jvālinī* (one that sets fire to), *Amṛtā* (ambrosia), and *Abhayā* (that offers protection) should be employed in the worship and while offering oblation.

CHAPTER THREE HUNDRED AND ELEVEN

The location of the basic mantras of Tvaritā and Her worship

Fire-god said :

1-8a. I shall describe the (rite of) initiation etc. after having located in a lotus (diagram) furnished with (a diagram of) lion and thunderbolt. (The Tvaritā-*mantra* for this is): "*He he, huti*, Vajradanta (one having the tooth like the thunder-bolt)! *puru, puru, lulu,* roar, roar here! Obeisance to the lion seat!" There should be four lines running across and vertical. A wise man should draw nine squares (formed by these lines). Only the squares in the directions should be taken and those in the in between directions should be destroyed. Outside the angular points of the chambers there should be eight outer lines. The outer line should be divided into two so that the middle horn of the *vajra* occupies the middle of the outside of the outer chamber. The outer line would be curved. A wise man should divide it into two. The central chamber would have a radiant lotus having yellow petals. One should draw the thunder-bolt and sword above (the lotus) with black dust. The outer square should be adorned with the sign of a thunder-bolt. The votary should add four signs of thunder-bolt at the entrance. (If it is done so) the centre of the lotus and the left line will be on the same line. The centre as well as the petals (should be made) red. Initiated women (should be worshipped) in this circle. (By this) one would conquer the kingdoms of others and recover (the lost) kingdom quickly.

8b-12a. O! Twice-born! The image (of the Goddess) illumined by the *praṇava* (syllable *oṁ*) should be commissioned with the syllable *huṁ*. After repeating the basic syllable as if it had occupied the (regions of) the wind and sky, a person (should worship) it as the first one. One should worship it again in the pericarp. After having worshipped each one of the syllables from the beginning thus in the cyclic order, one should worship the subordinates of the *mantra* in the middle of the petals, Nirṛti in the south-east (corner), the eye at the centre, the weapons in the directions and Rakṣaṇa in the genital organ. Five offerings of oblations at the filaments on the left and right side should be worshipped with their respective *mantras*.

12b-18. The eight guardian deities of the world should be located outside the central circle. The respective names should be added to the last syllable of the *agni mantra* split by the sixth vowel and permeated by the fifteenth (letter). One should worship (the Goddess) in (the image of) the lion in the pericarp (of the lotus) with perfume and other things for prosperity. It should be surrounded by eight pitchers consecrated with (the repetition of the *mantras*) one hundred and eight times. After having repeated the (*mūla*) *mantra* eight thousand times and the subordinate *mantra* a tenth of that (number), one should offer the oblation in the fire-pit. (Then the fire) should be stirrred with the fire *mantra*. The fire should be placed with (the *mantra* of) the heart. Then the Goddess should be contemplated as remaining at the centre of the fire. Then the oblations for the *garbhādhāna*[1], *puṁsavana*[2] and *jātakarma*[3] are made. (The oblation) with (the *mantra* of) the heart (would be) one hundred (times). The fire should thus be generated at the centre of the fire-pit. The fire of the Goddess would glow with the final oblations made with the *mantra*. Then oblation should be made with the principal *mantra* a hundred times and a tenth of that with the subordinate (*mantra*). Then it should be dedicated to the Goddess. Then the disciple should be ushered in.

19-23a. After striking with (the repetition of the *mantra* of) the weapon, the secret subordinate (*mantras*) should be located in the disciple. The disciple should be bound with the subordinate (*mantras*) and then charged with the subordinate (*mantras*). Then the disciple should be made to throw a flower. He is then led to the sacrificial pit. One hundred oblations should be made with the principal *mantra* with barley, grains, sesamum and clarified butter. The first oblation (is intended for) the state of a plant, the next one for the state of reptiles (like the serpents), and (the subsequent oblations are) for the states of being a bird, animal and human beings, mortals, Brahmā, Viṣṇu and Rudra. The concluding oblation would be

1. Rite for impregnation.

2. Rite performed prior to the movement of the foetus for the sake of getting a male child.

3. Rite performed soon after the birth of a child.

at the end. The disciple would become initiated by a single oblation. (The disciple) would have the authority in this way. Listen to me! I shall hereafter describe (the way to gain) liberation.

23b-30. The votary who remains steadfast at the feet of Lord Sadāśiva (always benevolent) and on the Sumeru should offer one thousand oblations for improper and proper acts composed. That yogin will not be stained by *dharma* (righteousness) and *adharma* (unrighteousness). He could attain the supreme place of liberation from which he would not return. Just as water poured into (larger quantity of) water becomes merged as water, so also the mortal becomes one with (Lord) Śiva. Consecration should be made with the pitchers. One would gain victory, kingdom and all the things (by such a worship). One should worship Kumārī and Brāhmaṇī (obviously the divine mothers). Fees should be paid to the preceptors and others. After having worshipped, one thousand oblations should be offered everyday with sesamum or clarified butter. The propitiated Goddess would confer the desired things, abundant riches and anything else that is desired. (A person) who repeats the *mantra* a lakh times would become the master of a treasure. (A person) would get the kingdom by repeating (the *mantra*) twice (that) and become a Yakṣiṇī (a semi-divine being) by repeating thrice (that). (A person) would get the position of Brahmā (by the repetition) four times (that number) and then gain the place of Viṣṇu. (A person who repeats it) six times (that number) would gain great powers. (The person who repeats it) one lakh times would get rid of his sin. The repetition ten times would purify the body. (The repetition) a hundred times (would confer) the fruits of bathing in the sacred water.

31-36. (Goddess) Śīgrā (Tvaritā) should be worshipped on a cloth or in an image or on the altar. It is said that hundred, thousand or ten thousand are the counts for the repetition (of the *mantra*) or oblation (with that). After having repeated thus as laid down one should offer oblation one lakh (times) with the fat and flesh of a buffalo or goat or the body of a man. After having done the oblation with sesamum, barley, fried paddy, paddy, wheat, mango, *śriphala* (*bilva*) together with clarified butter, one should practise austerities. Equipping himself with sword, bow, arrow and the like at midnight, (the votary) should dress himself with a single (piece of) cloth of varied colours or red or yellow or black or blue. He should worship the Goddess with the same (materials). Then the wise man should set out in the southern direction and offer the victim at the entrance with (the repetition of) the *dūtimantrà*. (It should be done) at the entrances or a single tree or in the cremation ground. If it is done so a king would enjoy all pleasures and the entire earth.